Waitangi and Indigenous Rights:
Revolution, Law and Legitimation

WAITANGI AND INDIGENOUS RIGHTS: REVOLUTION, LAW AND LEGITIMATION

F. M. (Jock) BROOKFIELD

Foreword by the Hon. Justice
David Baragwanath

AUCKLAND UNIVERSITY PRESS

For Brenda

First published 1999
Auckland University Press
University of Auckland
Private Bag 92019
Auckland
New Zealand

© F.M. Brookfield 1999

This book is copyright. Apart from fair dealing for the purpose of private study, research, criticism or review, as permitted under the Copyright Act, no part may be reproduced by any process without the prior permission of the publisher.

The publishers gratefully
acknowledge the assistance of

ISBN 1 86940 184 0

Typeset by Chris O'Brien
Printed by Publishing Press Ltd, Auckland

CONTENTS

Acknowledgments	6
Foreword by the Hon. Justice David Baragwanath	7

PART I

Introduction	11
Chapter 1 Courts, Constitutions and Revolutions	13
Revolution: definitions	13
The non-revolutionary coup d'état	15
Kelsen and the revolution: change in the basic norm	17
The courts and revolutionary change	18
Courts as upholders of the constitution	18
The state under threat: emergency measures under the necessity principle	20
The court and the usurper: (i) the de facto doctrine	20
The court and the usurper: (ii) full legal recognition?	22
A supra-constitutional jurisdiction?	23
Revolutions, coups, and the ordinary citizen: when does allegiance shift?	28
The supra-constitutional jurisdiction in retrospect: merits, difficulties, limits	31
Legality and legitimacy: separate concepts	34
Prescription and the squatter's title: private law analogies: international law	34
Chapter 2 Legitimacy and Revolution	38
Durability, morality and justice in the legal order	38
Walker's case: durability of the revolutionary order	38
Justice in the post-revolutionary order: questions of sufficient legitimation	42
Losers in the revolution: their expectations of justice	44
Partial recognition of pre-revolutionary rights	
(i): Rome, Islam and Spain	47
Partial recognition of pre-revolutionary rights	
(ii): modern Western imperialism	48
Aboriginal title	51
Aboriginal treaty rights	54

Chapter 3 Revolutionary Ideology and Colonization 57
Revolutionary conquests of Western imperialism: problems of legitimacy 57
Prescription (durability) v ideological opposition 63
Christendom and Islam 64
1066 (England), 1169 (Ireland) and all that 66
English/British imperialism: ideology 69
Ideology of Western imperialism and its legacies 70
Gramsci, wars of position and of manoeuvre, and the passive revolution 74
The right to self-determination and the right to rebel; and indigenous people 75
'Indigenous peoples: a relevant concept?' 77

PART 2

Chapter 4 Aotearoa New Zealand: the Constitutional Background 85
Maori legal and constitutional orders 86
The United Kingdom Constitution 90
Preliminaries to colonization 96
An attempted revolution? The Declaration of Confederation and Independence 96
The Treaty of Waitangi 98
What was (purportedly) ceded and what was reserved? 100
Kawanatanga: a subordinate power? 102
Did kawanatanga extend to Maori? 103
The non-signatories 105
The Tribunal and kawanatanga: summary comment 106

Chapter 5 Revolutions and Counter-Revolutions 1840–1986 108
The 1840 revolution 108
Rules of the 1840 revolution 110
Maori as British subjects 110
Maori autonomy 114
Section 71 of the New Zealand Constitution Act 116
The division of the Crown: another revolution? 119
The revolution and the land: the Legislature and common law Maori title 128
Land under water as customary land 133

Chapter 6 Legitimation of the 1840 Revolution; and the Special Case of the Chathams 136
Walker, Kelsey and the 1840 revolution 136
The ideologies of colonization 139
To Christianize and civilize 140
'Use or lose' 141
A legitimated consequence of the revolution: the end of Maori slavery 141
'General principles of humanity', transcultural principles, and legitimation 143
Two violent societies 144
Pakeha rule of law: end of Maori feuding: greater protection of the individual? 145
Kelsey and the colonial courts 148
Partial recognition of rangatiratanga 150
Legislative recognition of 'principles' of the Treaty of Waitangi 151
The courts, the Treaty and its principles 152
The courts and legitimation of the revolution 157
Revolutions on the Chathams: 1835–36; 1842: legitimation? 158

Chapter 7 Conclusion: Controversial Present and (Quietly?) Revolutionary Future 163
A quiet revolution and a qualified Maori autonomy? 169
Entrenchment: the machinery of the revolution 174
The radical alternatives and overt revolution 177
Conclusion 181

Abbreviations 185

Notes 187

Select Bibliography 224

Table of Cases 236

Table of Legislation 241

Index 246

Acknowledgments

My warm thanks go to Elizabeth Caffin, of Auckland University Press, for her patience and help and to Simon Cauchi for his meticulous editing. They go also to the Hon. Justice David Baragwanath for his support and for the generous Foreword. I have benefited from conversations with Judith Binney, Keith Sorrenson and Andrew Sharp.

The book has been written in the period of indefinite (preferably long) academic leave known as retirement. I am grateful to the University of Auckland and its Law Faculty for accommodating me and to the University librarians, especially of the Davis Law Library, for their help throughout.

I owe a long standing debt of gratitude to Tony Honoré, under whose guidance the ideas on the nature and problems of de facto government, developed here in a New Zealand context, first took shape many years ago.

My greatest debt, as always, is to my wife, Brenda.

F. M. Brookfield
September 1999

FOREWORD

This is a timely book. Its themes are today's big issues — how New Zealand's legal system should be constituted at a time of change to past certainties, of rapid globalization, of possible constitutional change, of local search for security and for identity. While they deeply concern Maori, Allen Curnow has expressed the uncertainty of other New Zealanders, including those of European descent:

> Not I, some child, born in a marvellous year,
> Will learn the trick of standing upright here.

Jock Brookfield offers a path to resolution, the product of a lifetime's reflection, research and experience.

Informed participation in debate is essential to New Zealanders' effective performance of their role of citizen and the ability thereby to influence events. Otherwise, decisions will be made by default, without proper consideration and balancing of the competing values and priorities that are the stuff of a complex society. That way lies the repetition of past error and its grief, which is not yet behind us.

This substantial and readable work offers New Zealanders an alternative to such a course. By providing the wealth of Professor Brookfield's own scholarship and that of other thinkers, including those with whose views he joins issue, it will contribute mightily to an understanding of our constitutional heritage, the issues and the options, at a time when pressures for change are increasing.

He is a master of his evocative theme. As an Oxford doctor and the doyen of New Zealand public lawyers, he identifies and offers penetrating observations upon the key issues of political and legal philosophy; as a member of a long-established New Zealand family, he does so with passion. His doctoral thesis concerned the legitimacy of state succession following revolution; his inaugural lecture as Professor of Public Law at the University of Auckland tackled the expulsion of Maori from their traditional fisheries within the theme of the legitimacy of the presence of Pakeha in New Zealand and St Augustine's dictum

Set aside justice then, and what are kingdoms but fair thievish purchases? Because what are thieves' purchases but little kingdoms?

That lecture was cited in and of profound importance to the series of judicial decisions and negotiations that restored substantial fisheries resources to Maori. Professor Brookfield also took a leading part in the preparation of the Tainui argument in their momentous Court of Appeal case in 1989. He has advised the Waitangi Tribunal.

But he is no zealot, as appears from the careful balance of his argument. Professor Brookfield is not one to engage in generalities that have not been thought through. He does not, for example, support the separatism of dual legal systems within New Zealand, supporting his point with the practical illustration of joint offending by New Zealanders of Maori and Pakeha descent. Rather he examines the practical realities through a principled lens: 'justice does require constitutionally secure protection for the minority within the nation state', and, while rejecting overseas solutions that could not work in New Zealand, boldly offers his own proposals for change.

This work offers a major contribution to our future. I commend it wholeheartedly.

David Baragwanath
Judge of the High Court of New Zealand, President of the Law Commission

PART I

INTRODUCTION

Rightly or wrongly, new circumstances now apply and a number of conflicting private interests, honestly obtained, must be weighed in the balance. It is out of keeping with the spirit of the Treaty [of Waitangi] . . . that the resolution of one injustice should be seen to create another.[1]

In those words the Waitangi Tribunal[2] has explained an aspect of its statutory task. In inquiring into and making recommendations concerning wrongs done by the Crown to Maori, the Tribunal must allow for rights that have arisen under the succession of constitutional arrangements that followed the British Crown's formal assumption of power over the indigenous Maori of Aotearoa New Zealand in 1840. The wrongs into which the Tribunal inquires do of course relate specifically to the Treaty of Waitangi entered into in that year; but they may be classed generally with wrongs done whenever one people seizes power over the territory of another.

The new rights to be allowed for are those arising under legal systems (or, synonymously, legal orders) which, imposed by revolutionary seizers of power, become at least partly legitimated over time. This book is in large part a study of the process by which legitimation or partial legitimation takes place, including the role of courts in that process and in the constitutional challenges to the legal order of which they are part when issues of the government's legality or legitimacy arise. In the New Zealand context radical Maori protesters often challenge the jurisdiction of the New Zealand Courts and the legality of the government; and, in much more extreme situations in other countries, courts have been required to decide whether a government and constitution established by revolution (the ultimate and most drastic form of political protest) have become lawful.

The concept of revolution as a means of basic constitutional change, both in the overt overthrow of a government and constitution and also as a technique for giving effect to and securing a settlement of constitutional differences (the 'quiet revolution'), is used throughout the book.

Part I provides legal (including jurisprudential) and historical background and a consideration of the legitimacy of legal systems or orders established by revolution, especially in the case of the revolutionary conquests of Western expansion and colonization.

Waitangi and Indigenous Rights: Revolution, Law and Legitimation

In Part II the focus is on revolutions and attempted revolutions in New Zealand constitutional history. The Crown's assertion of power over New Zealand is treated as revolutionary in that it took from the chiefs who signed the Treaty of Waitangi more than they ceded and took from the non-signatories (who had ceded nothing). Chapter 5 goes on to consider the colonialist revolution, by which as the *British* Crown, it asserted its power, and also the counter-revolutions of Maori resistance and the (revolutionary) splitting that has resulted in the *New Zealand* Crown as a separate constitutional entity in an independent nation state.

Chapter 6 deals with the partial legitimation of the colonialist revolution and the present constitutional order. Chapter 6 also deals with the special case of the successive revolutions, Maori and then British, on the Chatham Islands and its significance in Maori–Pakeha controversies.

The book concludes by discussing present-day Treaty issues and controversies as a whole. So far as the issues are constitutional, the final chapter argues for their settlement in new constitutional arrangements to be established by a quiet revolution, preferably in a New Zealand republic. The chapter also deals with overtly and unquietly revolutionary alternatives (proposed by some) and their constitutional implications.

Chapter I: COURTS, CONSTITUTIONS AND REVOLUTIONS

Revolution: definitions

For the purposes of a constitutional theorist (though one with practical concerns as well), a revolution may be widely defined as the overthrow and replacement of any kind of legal order, or other constitutional change to it — whether or not brought about by violence (internally or externally directed) — which takes place contrary to any limitation or rule of change belonging to that legal order.

The situations we shall be considering will clarify the definition but for the moment there may be some advantage in relating it to Charles Tilly's recent analysis of the concept of revolution and showing how the treatment of revolutions in the pages that follow, undertaken from a specifically constitutional viewpoint, will differ from his.

Tilly defines a revolution as 'a forcible transfer of power over a state in the course of which at least two distinct blocs of contenders make incompatible claims to control the state, and some significant portion of the population subject to the state's jurisdiction acquiesces in the claims of each bloc'.[1]

There are in Tilly's analysis two components to a revolution, of which the first is the 'revolutionary situation', in which three proximate causes converge to create 'multiple sovereignty': the appearance of contenders for the exclusive control of 'the state, or some segment of it', the commitment by a 'significant segment of the citizenry' to the claims of those contenders, and incapacity or unwillingness of the rulers to suppress (by, it seems, normal operation of the law) those contenders or the commitment to their claims.[2] The revolutionary situation may lead to the second component, the 'revolutionary outcome', in which there is durable transfer of state power from those who held it previously, before the revolutionary situation arose, to new rulers.[3]

The revolution as Tilly defines it, complete in its two components of revolutionary situation and revolutionary outcome, rarely occurs, because in many cases the old rulers overcome their challengers, or the struggle, in the form of a civil war, leads to a permanent division of the disputed polity, or the revolutionary outcome is so gradual or so instantaneous that actual 'multiple sovereignty' never appears.[4] Further, revolutionary outcomes may be produced from some non-revolutionary situations, notably where a transfer of power in an existing state results from conquest by another 'very different' state.[5]

Where a revolution within Tilly's definition does occur, it may take the form of a great revolution such as the French of 1789 and the Russian of 1917, where the struggle is massive and its outcome is the transformation of the state and of social life.[6] A smaller revolution without great social effects may be within the definition, but the mere coup d'état, and what Tilly calls the 'top-down social transformation', may not be.[7] Tilly applies his definition to the developed states of the Europe of the last five centuries that were the subject of his special study, but it may of course be applied to modern states generally.

Now compare with Tilly's the constitutional theorist's definition I put forward as mine. The great revolutions do of course come within my definition, for they necessarily include the overthrow by illegal means, and the replacement, of the constitutional and legal order.[8] A smaller revolution, even if it appears as a mere coup d'état and does not have great social effects, comes within the definition if it includes constitutional change effected illegally but not if (as discussed below) it is a coup accommodated within the particular legal order. Social transformation and even the most radical constitutional change, however far-reaching and even though preceded by revolutionary violence or the threat of it, are not within the definition if they are achieved within the existing legal rules for constitutional change in the polity concerned. However, the definition is wider than Tilly's, in applying generally to constitutional changes unauthorized by those rules, whether or not they are the outcome of a 'revolutionary situation' and even though the change is gradual. In particular (but not necessarily exhaustively) the definition applies —

(i) where the constitutional change is brought about through conquest of the polity or territory concerned (whether or not by a 'very different' state or polity);[9]

(ii) whether the legal order overthrown or otherwise changed is the developed one of a modern state or the customary one of a tribal polity (such as a hapu in Aotearoa), in which government may be rudimentary and members of the polity live under customary rules, without the courts and legislature that characterize the developed state;[10]

(iii) where the revolutionary struggle leads to the permanent division, between the contenders, of the disputed polity;[11]

(iv) where the constitutional change, even if preceded by revolutionary violence, is the peaceable and formal means of making a complete or partial constitutional new beginning, or has that effect (the 'quiet revolution');[12]

(v) where the constitutional change is an enlargement of the legal power of a branch of the government (for example, of the legislature), achieved successfully in breach of an existing constitutional rule or limitation.[13]

Under this definition the British Crown's assumption of sovereignty over the polities of Maori iwi and hapu was revolutionary at least to the extent that it went beyond what was ceded by the Treaty of Waitangi, in the case of non-signatories to the Treaty as a conquest by Queen Victoria's very different polity and in the case of signatories either as that or as a revolutionary enlargement of power.[14] The present-day reassertion of tino rangatiratanga in forms that would either dominate the state or at least divide it into dual Maori and Pakeha polities is likely to be achieved only by a further revolution.[15] But, to adopt Tilly's terms, the revolutionary situation has not (or not yet) arisen: the New Zealand state is still containing Maori dissent by the normal operation of the law. At least so far, there is no more than the 'passive revolution', which is not a revolution at all in Tilly's definition or in mine, by which, in the Gramscian terminology of some radical controversialists, the present 'colonial' state in part maintains its hegemony through the work of the Waitangi Tribunal, by the settlement of some Maori claims, and through the degree of recognition the Courts have given to such claims and to the Treaty.[16] Finally, one may note that a 'quiet revolution' would be the likely means of establishing a settlement between Maori and Pakeha in which the Treaty or its principles would be secured in a new, written constitution.[17]

The non-revolutionary coup d'état

In some circumstances a coup d'état may not constitute a revolution within my definition, if the coup does not alter the constitutional structure[18] and if the particular legal system in which it occurs accommodates it automatically without any need for validation. This appears to have been the case in England, where historically all the functions of government — executive, legislative and judicial — have inhered in the monarch. The monarch's being deposed and replaced by a rival claimant, who seizes power in all three areas but leaves the constitutional structure unchanged, constitutes a coup *within* the monarchy. English constitutional history records a number of monarchs, termed 'de facto' by those who denied their legal title to rule, whose acts of government have not only been valid during the periods of their rule but have also been generally treated as valid when the 'lawful' monarch is restored.[19] That included the legislation of their parliaments. Thus the English legal system has, with effects for New Zealand and other territories of the former British Empire,[20] accommodated illegal change within the monarchy itself, so that it is the monarch for the time being, whatever his or her title to the Crown, who has provided constitutional and lawful government and, most importantly, whose title to rule could not be questioned in the courts by judges who necessarily were exercising his or her judicial power.[21]

But the English legal system has not accommodated republican change. The republics of 1649 to 1660 were revolutionary in their replacement of the monarchy and the structure of government. By contrast, the assumption of power by William of Orange and Mary in 1688–89, often termed the 'Glorious Revolution', was in itself merely a coup d'état within the monarchy, essentially no different from the coups d'état by which Henry IV, Richard III and Henry VII respectively seized the Crown.[22] The point is illustrated by the different fates of the republican legislation of 1649–60 and the legislation of the parliaments of the de facto monarchs: the former did not survive the restoration of the monarchy, whereas the latter has always been treated as generally valid.[23]

All that has some present-day relevance, if largely to establish contrasts, in later discussion of the effects or likely effects of revolutions or coups d'état on the past and present legal systems of Aotearoa New Zealand. One should add that, generally in tribal polities, the customary legal order of the polity must have accommodated any change in chiefly leadership that took place violently or simply as an effective assertion of power, as something in the nature of a mere coup d'état, rather than a revolution, for the actual *structure* of tribal authority is unaltered.[24] One may compare those modern states where, whatever a written constitution may formally provide, there is no general principle of legality accepted as applicable to changes in the leadership, which occur by frequent coups, except perhaps one which gives immediate effect to the political reality of the change.[25] In those cases the coup d'état may become virtually an institutionalized method of governmental change.

But generally, in modern developed states, where a principle of legality does apply effectively to regulate changes in the leadership and may be invoked by those contesting the legality of a particular such change, the coup d'état carried out in successful defiance of that principle is a revolution, even though it leaves the structure of the constitution unaltered and the perpetrators of the coup simply take over the offices and powers of the ousted regime.[26] (If the change is to be legally validated, it must be validated under the supra-constitutional jurisdiction which some modern courts have claimed — about which more later.) To that general rule a coup within the British (and possibly the New Zealand) monarchy, of the type discussed above would constitute an exception, if the legal position is the same as it has been historically in England.[27]

Kelsen and the revolution: change in the basic norm

All this may be related to the Austrian jurist Hans Kelsen's theory of the hierarchy of norms — a theory which helps in considering the constitutional nature of a revolution and the role of the courts therein, which has been applied by some courts,[28] and which has had some part in New Zealand constitutional discourse on Treaty of Waitangi matters.[29] In Kelsen's theory, the jurist or legal scientist, observing a purportedly legal order of norms which is 'by and large effective', presupposes (by an act of cognition) the *grundnorm* or basic norm upon which the order is founded and which is the reason for its validity.[30] This presupposition is that 'One ought to behave according to the actually established and effective constitution'.[31] When a revolution (as distinct from a coup d'état accommodated within the legal order) occurs and a new constitution is established in place of the old, there is a new legal order, a new basic norm being presupposed.[32] (Much of the content of the new legal order may be the same as that of the old, but the reason for validity has changed and is provided now by the new basic norm.) For present purposes I emphasize the importance of efficacy: it is in Kelsen's 'pure theory of law' the sine qua non of the existence of a valid legal order. Further, Kelsen's theory is apolitical and amoral. Revolutionary change is legally validated by its general effectiveness without regard to the moral or ideological values of the successful revolutionaries.

Identifying the basic norm of the English or the New Zealand legal order is a complex matter, involving in each case a statement of the supremacy of Parliament (that is, of the Crown in Parliament, in the exact phrase) as well as of the present monarchical base of the constitution and of the authority of the common law. In the case of the United Kingdom, the basic norm is created in part by custom and in part by the revolution effected by the establishment of the Union of the kingdoms of England and Scotland in 1706–07.[33] In the case of the tribal polities, such as those of hapu in Aotearoa, the basic norm again must be customary, for that is generally the nature of tribal legal orders.[34] We consider later the revolutionary processes by which, successively, the paramount force of the British imperial Crown was asserted over the tribal organization of Maori and the tribal basic norms replaced,[35] and the imperial Crown divided (so that the Crown in right of New Zealand assumed the obligations incurred by the unitary Crown under the Treaty of Waitangi). This was part of the revolutionary means by which the New Zealand legal order acquired a basic norm of its own, independent of that of the United Kingdom.[36]

Identifying the basic norm of a particular legal order is relatively easy where there is a written constitution rather than one established or existing in whole or in part by custom. Thus in Fiji, before the illegal seizures of power in May and September 1987, one could identify the basic norm by reference to the monarchical constitution of 1970 left in place by the United Kingdom.[37] Those seizures of power, that to some may have appeared mere coups d'état, were revolutionary in ending that constitution by illegal means and (in the final outcome) replacing it by a republican constitution and so establishing a new basic norm in place of the old.

The courts and revolutionary change

What part have courts to play in these processes of revolution and of coup d'état? The question is an important one and will be especially so when we come to consider it in the context of the Maori challenge, potentially revolutionary as it is, to the present New Zealand constitutional and legal order.[38] But there are some preliminary observations to be made.

Courts as upholders of the constitution

First, the courts are always the courts of the constitution under which they are established. Their authority can always be traced back to the basic norm of the legal order. The lower courts usually have no secure constitutional place: typically, as in New Zealand, they are created by the legislature and may be abolished by it. The superior court of a country is likely to be established by the written constitution (if there is one) to which the basic norm relates, and to be protected by that constitution from abolition by the legislature. If, as in New Zealand, there is no such written constitution, the superior court may have a less constitutionally secure position. Thus the High Court of New Zealand is at present provided for by legislation, the Judicature Act 1908, enacted by the then General Assembly under power conferred by the United Kingdom Parliament, at a time when the basic norm for New Zealand was the same as that for the United Kingdom. On one view the High Court and the prerogative power of the Crown to establish its equivalent could simply be abolished by an Act of the Parliament (whose power, we may suppose, now rests upon a separate New Zealand basic norm). But it may be that, short of a revolution, this could not be done: that is, the judicial branch of government cannot lawfully be abolished by the legislature.[39]

However, it is clear that as long as the courts (of whatever level and in whatever jurisdiction) exist, they will uphold the legal order of which they are part, at least unless and until they are required to determine whether a revolution has succeeded and the new revolutionary order has become lawful. They may find within the legal order of which they are part rules or principles under which rights of dissent, or the special property or other rights of an indigenous people, must be recognized and upheld, or citizens protected from unlawful action by the executive government or (where the legislature has limited powers) from unconstitutional legislation. All that is as much part of upholding the legal order as is recognizing and giving effect to the lawful powers of the legislative or executive branches of government under the constitution of which the courts are the judicial branch.

But the person who, pleading before any of those courts, for any reason denies its jurisdiction, ought not to be surprised or dismayed at the court's inevitable rejection of the plea; for, if the revolution comes and is successful, a like plea by a person denying the jurisdiction of a court established by the revolution will just as inevitably incur a like rejection. This may be seen as the general rule. (To the reason for it I return later.)[40]

Nevertheless, questions of legitimacy rather than legality may still have to be answered in respect of any legal order which is by and large effective. Here one illustration must suffice, from the Irish troubles of the early 1920s, both to show the general rule just mentioned and how its application may leave questions of legitimacy still to be considered: the case of *R (Childers) v Adjutant-General of the Provisional Forces*.[41] Erskine Childers was an officer in the Irish Republican Army and hence, as an Irish revolutionary, was opposed to the Treaty settlement in 1922 that led to the establishment of the Irish Free State and its provisional government. He rejected the authority of the tribunal set up by the military forces of the provisional government to try him under martial law for the illegal possession of arms. But he was subjected to the jurisdiction of the tribunal nevertheless; as would be someone in like position if the IRA had succeeded in its armed struggle and, under the revolutionary government established by it (say a provisional government in Northern Ireland), military tribunals were set up for the like purpose. But all that of course leaves the questions of the legitimacy of the IRA's revolutionary struggle unanswered — however one may think they should be answered.

The state under threat: emergency measures under the necessity principle

The courts, then, are under a duty to uphold the legal order of which they are part. But in doing so they may sometimes recognize as valid emergency action taken by the executive government or its armed forces which would be unlawful in normal circumstances but which is justified in times of extreme crisis by the principle of necessity. The exercise of martial law, when there is a state of war within the country (of which there were a number of instances in New Zealand in the 19th century),[42] is an example of such action. For the duration of the war the ordinary civil and criminal law is suspended, the jurisdiction of the ordinary courts is ousted, and the enforcement of order in the hands of the armed forces and of military tribunals outside judicial control. Thus in *Childers'* case, in the revolutionary war then raging in Ireland against the Free State provisional government, the regular court of the Anglo-Irish legal order would not intervene in the martial law proceedings of the military tribunal. Though there are some doubts about the limits applicable to martial law, its exercise is a well-recognized form of emergency action which the Crown and its armed forces may lawfully take.[43]

The court's duty to uphold the legal order is qualified by other manifestations of the necessity principle, one of which , as recognized by the courts in some modern cases under written constitutions, has allowed temporary and strictly limited deviations from the constitution for the express purpose of safeguarding it or for preserving the rule of law.[44]

The court and the usurper: (i) the de facto doctrine

Under a well-established common law doctrine the courts may, within certain limits, treat as valid official acts done by a person who, though holding public office unlawfully (for example, under a legally defective appointment), does so with colour of right. Such an officer is, of course, whether or not knowingly, a usurper, but appears to hold office lawfully. The reason for treating his or her official acts as valid is reasonably clear: one cannot be expected to deal with a public officer, who apparently holds office lawfully, otherwise than on the basis that appearances correspond to reality.[45] What I have just described may be called the narrower version of the de facto doctrine. It does not apply in a revolutionary situation, in which persons who succeed in seizing public office are not only usurpers but necessarily lack any colour of right, their rebellion being deemed notorious under the existing, that is the pre-revolutionary, legal and constitutional order.

What though if revolutionary usurpers are so successful that they form a de facto government that is at least for a time in effective control of the territory concerned? Here the public have no practical alternative during the period of effective control to obeying the usurpers. Further, the lawful government may be assumed to prefer that the usurpers should be obeyed rather than the state fall into anarchy. That is a sufficient rationale for the wider version of the de facto doctrine. Under this the courts of the pre-revolutionary order recognize as valid the day-to-day acts of government of the revolutionary regime and of public officers appointed by it, but not acts advancing or entrenching the revolution. This form of the doctrine rests on the authority of civilian writers (Hugo Grotius[46] and others); and on American post-Civil War cases, such as *Texas v White* (1869)[47] and *Baldy v Hunter* (1898)[48] in the United States Supreme Court, in which it was necessary for the Court to consider the validity of acts of government of the secessionist states. More recent cases show its application or acceptance by courts, or by individual judges, in or on appeal from Southern Rhodesia (as a rebel British colony),[49] and in Pakistan[50] and in Grenada.[51]

The Southern Rhodesian instance was the case of *Madzimbamuto v Lardner-Burke*,[52] which followed the Smith government's Unilateral Declaration of Independence of 1965. Here the Courts (including the Privy Council on appeal) had to consider the present matter, not (as in the American and other cases referred to) in retrospect after the revolutionary regime had been overthrown, but while the revolutionaries were in control of the executive and legislative branches of the government of the country. But that difference does not seem to be significant. Pending the revolution's complete and clearly established success (if that occurs), limited recognition of the revolutionaries' day-to-day acts of government, by the pre-revolutionary courts if they are still functioning, is not inconsistent with the duty of those courts to uphold the constitution of which they are part. Put in Kelsen's terms, the basic norm of the Southern Rhodesian legal order had not (yet) changed. The pre-revolutionary order remained by and large effective as long as its courts still sat as such, so that they could apply the wider form of the common law de facto doctrine (belonging to that order) to give limited recognition to the usurpers' acts.

The court and the usurper: (ii) full legal recognition?

In Southern Rhodesia the revolutionary Smith regime claimed from the country's High Court, surviving from the pre-revolutionary constitution, much more than the limited recognition of acts of day-to-day government allowable under the de facto doctrine. It claimed, and ultimately obtained, full legal recognition for itself and its (comparatively short-lived, as it turned out) revolutionary constitution.[53] The same kind of question has arisen in other cases where the pre-revolutionary courts were not swept away in the rebellion and were called on, in Tilly's situation of 'multiple sovereignty',[54] to decide whether the pre-revolutionary government remained the lawful government or had been replaced by its revolutionary competitor — in short, to decide whether or not the revolution had succeeded, in law. I come to such cases shortly.

First, though, I mention, without considering fully, that kind of question as it might arise in the very unlikely event of a coup within the monarchy.[55] That the existing judges went out of office was, in the common law of the Constitution, part of the coup d'état that deposed a monarch. The deposition constituted a demise of the Crown as if it were the actual death of the monarch (which, in some notorious instances, followed violently soon after, anyway); the demise of the Crown ended the tenure of the judges as of all other holders of public office under the Crown. There had to be a new appointment or a re-appointment in each case, the appointee taking oaths of office and of allegiance that necessarily entailed full legal recognition of the new monarch whose judicial power the appointee would be exercising. This mass going out of office, obviously inconvenient when a monarch actually dies, has, in most jurisdictions where the Queen is Head of State, been abrogated by legislation providing that the demise of the Crown does not affect the holding of public office.

The effect of demise of the Crown legislation on a coup within the monarchy is, at least in relation to judges, uncertain and depends on its exact terms. (Drafters are unlikely to have contemplated the difficulty.) It may simply make them judges exercising the judicial power of the new monarch, as if he or she had appointed them at common law; or it may put them in the supra-constitutional position about to be considered, in which they could be required to decide questions of title to the Crown (which at common law they could not do). The latter may be the position in New Zealand under section 5 of the Constitution Act 1986,[56] which is in different terms from its predecessor. If so, a coup d'état within the monarchy could not be legally accommodated in New Zealand and would as necessarily be a revolution as would a republican seizure of power.

No definite answer need be given here to what might seem to be an obscure and (in the worst sense of the word) academic question. Nevertheless, and although this work is not intended to be a practical guide for an intending revolutionary, a coup within the monarchy may be the way for him or her to proceed, with perhaps a slightly better chance (since the effect of section 5 of the Constitution Act is uncertain) of being accommodated within the law fairly swiftly than would attend a republican seizure of power.

A supra-constitutional jurisdiction?

Where a court is called upon to decide whether a new revolutionary regime has become lawful, has it the jurisdiction to do so? There are two possible views.

First, there is the older constitutionalist view that a court created under the pre-revolutionary constitution has no jurisdiction to recognize a revolutionary regime as lawful but is bound to the constitution which created it (even though it may give limited recognition to the regime's day-to-day acts of government under the de facto doctrine). Similarly, if created by a new revolutionary constitution, it has no jurisdiction to do otherwise than recognize its creator. This view is supported by the judgments of the United States Supreme Court in *Luther v Borden* (1849),[57] dealing with the Dorr rebellion in Rhode Island, and in dissenting judgments in *Madzimbamuto v Lardner-Burke* of Fieldsend A.J.A. in the Appellate Division of the High Court[58] and of Lord Pearce in the Privy Council.[59] The essence of this view is that the rule that judges cannot inquire into the validity of the constitution under which they hold office, clearly applicable in circumstances that are not revolutionary, applies also in circumstances that are. They are precluded from recognizing a new revolutionary regime as lawful, even if it is firmly and certainly established. They must maintain this non-recognition as long as the revolutionaries permit the court to function or until the judges themselves resign or are driven from office. Similarly the revolutionaries are assured of full recognition by a court which *they* set up and which indeed may be a means of securing the revolution and claiming the allegiance of citizens.

The view has good theoretical or jurisprudential support. In Kelsen's terms, the basic norm of the legal order may be destroyed by revolution. But the courts of that order, their jurisdiction being necessarily founded ultimately on the basic norm, cannot adjudicate upon the revolutionary change in the other (that is, the executive and legislative) branches of government by holding the new regime to be lawful. If the revolutionaries want full legal recognition (as distinct from the limited recognition of their day-to-day acts of government allowed by the de facto doctrine), they must complete the usurpation by appointing a new judiciary bound by their oaths of office to uphold the new revolutionary order. Of course, individual judges from the pre-revolutionary order may be willing to accept (or continue in) office under the new, but that is quite a different matter from their adjudicating upon the revolutionary change.

A certain Judge Magrath in the United States Federal Court in Charleston, South Carolina, made the point dramatically in 1860, when that state seceded from the Union. He stepped down from the bench, declaring the 'Temple of Justice closed'. A few months later, the Confederacy having been formed, he re-opened the 'Temple' as the Confederate District Court for South Carolina.[60] Clearly, he did not claim a supra-constitutional jurisdiction to give legal recognition to the new (short-lived) Confederate legal order. Rather the (pre-revolutionary) Federal Court had ceased to exist and the (revolutionary) Confederate Court took its place.

But, secondly, there is a newer view, more difficult to explain theoretically, which has found favour with the courts of a number of countries and has the powerful support of the majority judgment of the Privy Council in *Madzimbamuto v Lardner-Burke*.[61] This view is that courts, including those created by a written constitution, are authorized and required to decide when and if a revolutionary regime has become lawful. Lord Reid, delivering the opinion of the majority in that case, referred to

> the position ... where a court sitting in a particular territory has to determine the status of a new regime which has usurped power and acquired control of that territory. It must decide. ... It is an historical fact that in many countries — and indeed in many countries which are or have been under British sovereignty — there are now regimes which are universally recognised as lawful but which derive their origins from revolutions or coups d'état. The law must take account of that fact. So there may be a question how or at what stage the new regime became lawful.[62]

That is a question which a municipal court (that is, a court of the country in which the revolution occurred) 'must decide'. It is assumed that the court does have a supra-constitutional jurisdiction, exercisable in the extreme revolutionary circumstances visualized. In the context of *Madzimbamuto's* case, the Southern Rhodesian rebellion against the United Kingdom, the Privy Council had in mind a court set up under the pre-revolutionary constitution, which in fact survives the revolution in the other (executive and legislative) branches of government.

There have been other instances, notably in Uganda,[63] Pakistan,[64] Grenada,[65] Lesotho[66] and Bophuthatswana,[67] where a court has assumed a supra-constitutional jurisdiction to decide whether or not a revolutionary regime has become lawful, and has not regarded the issue as conclusively determined by the constitutional source of the court's jurisdiction. But we are left with two questions: first, how one is to explain the basis for the supra-constitutional jurisdiction and, secondly, what the principles are upon which that supra-constitutional jurisdiction should be exercised.

The first question is not an easy one and no full discussion is attempted here. Judges in Pakistan, Uganda and Southern Rhodesia thought to find the explanation in Kelsen's theory of revolutionary change in the basic norm, in effect seeing the theory as one which judges, qua judges, can apply.[68] But this seems to be a mistake. For Kelsen it is not the judge but the jurist or legal scientist who presupposes the basic norm and who, when a new legal order replaces it by becoming by and large effective in its stead, will presuppose the basic norm of the new order.[69] A person who is a judge may assume and function in that other role; but it appears that he or she, *as judge*, may function only within the legal order founded on the basic norm and cannot step outside that order to determine whether by a revolution a new legal order has replaced it. As we have seen, that in essence is the older constitutionalist view of the United States Supreme Court in *Luther v Borden*. Seemingly, the supra-constitutional jurisdiction which a court necessarily claims if, as the Privy Council says it 'must', it accepts the role of deciding whether the revolution has succeeded, is based 'on some principle of law independent of any particular system [which] authorises a judge, simply by virtue of his [or her] office, and irrespective of the source of ... jurisdiction, to recognise the revolutionary regime'.[70] Judges in Pakistan, for example, have, explained their jurisdiction in terms of their Islamic faith, seeing themselves as judges holding office in a legal order whose basic norm is the sovereignty of Allah.[71] That explanation may be generalized (in a demythologized form, for the secularist) to mean that, in any particular legal order in which the judiciary is separated from the other branches of government, there may be behind Kelsen's 'basic' norm a norm or principle more basic still upon which the judges' supra-constitutional jurisdiction is founded.

Secondly, what principle or principles must the court apply in exercising the supra-constitutional jurisdiction? We may accept that the matter can be dealt with judicially, by the application of relevant principle and apart from a judge's personal politics. The Privy Council in *Madzimbamuto v Lardner-Burke* certainly thought so.

There is no doubt that one of the principles — it may be the only principle — is that of by-and-large effectiveness. The revolution must be practically successful. If that is the only principle, then of course the test based on it is in effect in accordance with Kelsen's theory of revolutionary change; except that, because a judge applies the test in adjudicating upon the change, the basic norm is not after all basic. In doubting the reasoning but accepting the results of Pakistan and Ugandan cases where Kelsen was purportedly applied, the Privy Council in *Madzimbamuto* appears to have accepted the effectiveness test but without needing to define it further.[72]

As adopted and explained in some later cases decided in the courts of Lesotho and some other southern African jurisdictions, this test and the court's power to apply it may be stated thus:

> A court may hold a revolutionary government to be lawful, and its acts from the time it seized power to be validated, where the court is satisfied that (a) the government is firmly established, there being no other government in opposition to it and no real danger that it will be ousted from power; and (b) the government's administration is effective, in that by and large the people have acquiesced in and are behaving in conformity with its mandates.[73]

Explaining the test further in light of the cases, one may add that the obedience of the people should be over a sufficiently long period of time to show that they at least acquiesce in government by the revolutionary regime.[74] It follows that the regime's ratification by proper elections may earlier bring it legal recognition by the court.[75] Alternatively, the revolution may be so obviously successful that full recognition by the courts may occur even without elections or the elapse of a long period of acquiescence on the part of the people.[76] As to the position of a judge called on to decide the matter, whether he or she was appointed under the old legal order or the new is seen as irrelevant in the making of the decision, in a situation which is anomalous but in which a judge, again to quote the Privy Council, 'must decide'.[77]

That last sentence also states the view of some judges in Pakistan and in Grenada called on to make that kind of decision, for whom however the principle of effectiveness, or success and effectiveness, has not by itself provided an adequate test. In Pakistan, in *Bhutto v Chief of Army Staff* (1977),[78] the majority of the Supreme Court rejected the doctrine that 'effectualness of the new [revolutionary regime] provides its own legality', on the ground that it excluded 'all considerations of morality and justice from the concept of law and legality'; and they criticized 'Kelsen's theory' accordingly. Then, more specifically, in the Court of Appeal of Grenada in *Mitchell v Director of Public Prosecutions* (1985)[79] Haynes P. held that, for a revolutionary government to achieve legal status, not only must the criteria (a) and (b) of the test of success and effectiveness be satisfied but also (c) the 'conformity and obedience' of the people must be 'due to popular acceptance and support and . . . not [be] mere tacit submission to coercion or fear of force; and (d) it must not appear that the regime was oppressive and undemocratic'.[80]

At first sight the extra conditions of the legality of revolutionary change, raised in the *Bhutto* and *Mitchell* cases, might appear to give some support and encouragement to any who question the legality of a regime which does indeed effectively govern but which is based at least in part on the violent seizure of power and which they (perhaps as radical Maori critics of the present New Zealand Constitution) see as oppressive.

But there has been strong criticism that Haynes P.'s extra conditions cannot be 'reconciled with the facts of history'. The criticism is made by Ackermann J.A., delivering the judgment of the Lesotho Court of Appeal in *Makenete v Lekhanya* (1992).[81] Comments made by the Chief Justice of Lesotho on those conditions in *Mokotso v HM King Moshoeshoe II* (1988), in dealing with an earlier revolution in that country, were quoted with approval and clarify the reliance on the facts of history:

> It may well be that, to use Professor Kelsen's words, 'the individuals whose behaviour the new order regulates actually behave, by and large, in conformity with the new order', because the new regime is popular and because it is not oppressive or undemocratic. But that . . . is not the test. Throughout the course of history, there have been regimes, indeed dynasties, holding sway for many years, indeed centuries, whose rule could not be said by any manner of means to be popular and could even be described as oppressive: but

who is there to say that a new legal order was not created with their coming and going?[82]

In effect Haynes P.'s extra conditions and the Pakistan Court's reference in *Bhutto's* case to 'considerations of morality and justice' are matters going to the legitimacy of a regime rather than its legality, so far as those two things must be treated as separate. In some contexts the terms may be synonymous. Probably in most they are not: any given regime may be unquestionably legal but it and the legal order of which it is part may still at least in some measure be deficient in legitimacy. It is also possible that a revolutionary regime may be so morally objectionable that a court would invoke moral considerations to refuse it recognition. But that would be a most exceptional case.

Secondly, it is unlikely that either Haynes P. or the Pakistan Court would deny that, as a Queensland judge explained in a 1979 case,[83] some moral deficiencies of what purports to be a legal order may be affected by the passage of time, by durability. For example, where the basic norm of such an order is established by an illegal and unjust seizure of power, time will necessarily at least in part remedy the defect whether it is seen as one of legality or legitimacy.

Revolutions, coups, and the ordinary citizen: when does allegiance shift?

Ralph Dahrendorf, surveying the Eastern European revolutions of 1989, applied what he described as 'one classical index of revolutions: yesterday's high treason became today's official creed, and vice versa'.[84] At what stage then in a revolution or a (non-revolutionary) coup d'état does allegiance pass to the new regime, so that the subject or citizen may be liable for treason to it?

If a coup were to take place within the monarchy, an answer possibly still relevant to New Zealand is provided by Henry VII's Treason Act of 1495[85] — a statute no longer in force in New Zealand but which may nevertheless have been declaratory of a common law principle that perhaps remains part of New Zealand law while the monarchy lasts. On the majority view of that statute (which I share),[86] the subject's allegiance shifted to the new monarch, even as against the ousted one, as soon as the former completed the coup by assuming all the powers of government and thus according protection to the subject. (The statute made it clear that anyone whose allegiance thus shifted would not be liable for treason against the deposed monarch if and when he or she regained the Crown.)

In the treason trials of leading republicans that followed the restoration of Charles II in 1660, the Act of 1495 was held not to apply to the defendants, since there had been no monarch (Cromwell having refused the Crown) to whom allegiance could shift from Charles II as his father's successor.[87] In effect, the statute was held to apply to coups within the monarchy only, and not to republican revolutions. In considering the statute recently, after the revolutionary Unilateral Declaration of Independence of the Smith government in what was then Southern Rhodesia, the Privy Council remarked in *Madzimbamuto v Lardner-Burke* that 'it cannot be held to enact a general rule that a usurping government in control must be regarded as a lawful government'.[88] That must be correct, but there can be no doubt that the statute applied and perhaps still applies to coups *within* the monarchy.

The Act of 1495 has an antique aspect today. It remained in force in New Zealand until its repeal by the Crimes Act 1961. Before then a provision at first sight somewhat similar had appeared in the codification of New Zealand criminal law, initially in section 72 of the Criminal Code Act 1893. The substance of that section is now contained in section 64 of the Crimes Act 1961, under which:

> Every one is protected from criminal responsibility for any act done in obedience to the laws for the time being made and enforced by those in possession *de facto* of the sovereign power in and over the place where the act is done.

In *Kokoliades v Kennedy* (1911)[89] a Quebec judge dealing with a provision in the Canadian Criminal Code, substantially the same as section 64, described it as declaratory of a principle of the common law. It is not clear that that is so. The relevant common law principle appears rather to be a more limited one of which 11 Henry VII, c. 1 was declaratory, the New Zealand and Canadian provisions being intended to partly extend the principle so declared to a non-monarchical usurpation. At any rate, section 64 and its Canadian equivalent[90] (the latter being now section 15 of the Criminal Code), excuse all obedience to a usurper, whether monarchical or republican, from the sanctions of the criminal law. In effect, both sections provide for the position in any area, temporarily outside the control of the lawful government, in which a revolutionary legal system has been established and persons in the area obey the revolutionary laws. (By way of recent example, in *R v Jones and Pamajewon* (1993)[91] an Indian Nation in its claim to self-government initially supported its case by claiming (unsuccessfully, on the evidence presented) to be in de facto possession of the sovereign power over its reserve.)[92]

But by contrast with the principle declared in the Act of 1495 in relation to coups within the monarchy, the provisions we are discussing merely *excuse* obedience to the usurper's laws; without in any way recognizing or allowing that allegiance actually *shifts* so as to become legally due to a usurper during the period of usurpation, to the exclusion of the ousted ruler.

Of course a republican revolutionary regime, seizing power, will certainly claim, from those who as subjects or citizens had owed allegiance to the pre-revolutionary regime (whether monarchical or republican), the like allegiance in return for protection now afforded. It is likely that there have been many instances where the claim has been made and enforced in courts constituted by the revolutionaries, whether or not the outcome of the revolutionary struggle was beyond reasonable doubt under any test of success and effectiveness such as that formulated in the modern cases discussed above.

Indeed, a wide range of cases arising from the England of the mid-17th century republican Interregnum, from the Pennsylvania of the revolutionary War of Independence against Great Britain, and from the Fiji revolutions of 1987, show how enforcement of the laws against treason or the less serious matter of sedition may be an important means by which a revolutionary regime secures itself and ensures its own effectiveness, through courts that see themselves simply as courts of the new revolutionary order of which they are part and not as having any supra-constitutional jurisdiction.

So we have several important trials for treason against the English republican governments of 1649-60 recorded in volume 5 of *State Trials*, most of them before the High Courts of Justice set up by Parliament, in which the objections of royalist defendants to the Court's jurisdiction were (not surprisingly) always summarily disallowed.[93] Three centuries later, prosecutions for seditious speech or actions (though apparently all ultimately abandoned) were promptly brought before the Courts under the new, revolutionary Fiji legal order, against dissident Rotuman chiefs in 1988;[94] and, in 1990, against some university teachers for burning the new Fiji constitution.[95]

Coming in between the English and the Fiji cases, one reported from Pennsylvania is especially significant in showing when allegiance becomes due to a new, revolutionary, government. In the case of *Respublica v Chapman* (1781)[96] the Supreme Court of Pennsylvania, set up under the state's revolutionary constitution adopted in September 1776, had to try Samuel Chapman for treason against the new government in withdrawing from the state territory and joining the enemy, at a time when the revolutionary war had still to be won. Two aspects of the case concern us. In the Court's opinion allegiance became due to the new government when the legislature under the revolutionary constitution was convened and the executive was appointed and a government able to protect the citizen and execute the laws thus existed;[97] but every citizen dissenting from the establishment of the new government had the 'unrestrainable' right to depart, within a reasonable time, to another country. '[N]one are subjects of the adopted government, who have not freely assented to it.'[98]

The supra-constitutional jurisdiction in retrospect: merits, difficulties, limits

We have seen the willingness of modern courts in some countries to assume a supra-constitutional jurisdiction in revolutionary cases and the Privy Council's apparent recognition that the jurisdiction exists in certain extreme situations. Nevertheless, the older constitutionalist view, which would deny that the jurisdiction exists and would allow the judge to function only within the constitution (pre-revolutionary or, for that matter, revolutionary) under which he or she has been appointed, may still find favour with some judges. That view has the merit that it discourages any easy assumption by revolutionaries that their success may bring the respectability of recognition in a case before the pre-revolutionary judiciary (if the only test is that of success and effectiveness). Where the view is adopted, the revolutionaries have no alternative but to complete the revolution by replacing the judiciary. And of course the nature of the revolution may be such that they wish to do that anyway.

Exercise of the supra-constitutional jurisdiction, on the other hand, may, in 'bridg[ing] the gap between the old legal order and the new',[99] be a means of maintaining the stability of society at a time of general revolutionary upheaval. But, where the court was created under the pre-revolutionary constitution and it refuses recognition to a revolutionary regime claiming power, on the ground that the test of success and effectiveness is not yet complied with, the consequence may be that the regime will if it can simply complete or supplement the revolution by replacing the judiciary. (The consequence may be the more likely if, in effect following Haynes P. in *Mitchell v DPP* and in terms of the dicta of the Pakistan Court in *Bhutto's* case, judges seek to impose additional tests based on 'considerations of morality and

· 31 ·

justice'.)[100] In other words, whether a judge holds that he or she has no supra-constitutional jurisdiction or, accepting that he or she has, holds that the relevant test has not been satisfied, the practical consequence may be the same.

On balance, the better view is that the supra-constitutional jurisdiction exists, whatever difficulties some may find in explaining its theoretical basis. The fact that courts, including the Privy Council, have recognized or purported to exercise it in a number of cases is a strong reason for accepting its existence, on the well-established principle that judges of the superior courts are necessarily the judges of the limits of their own jurisdiction.[101] Another strong reason is that in at least one class of revolution, where radical constitutional change is carried through without violence (but possibly controversially) to effect a constitutional new beginning — for example, replacing a monarchy with a republic — it is inconceivable that judges would decline jurisdiction to decide whether the change should be validated.[102] That they would think it their duty, adapting Judge Magrath's course, to resign from the court of the monarch, or to declare it closed, before accepting office as judges in a new republican court, is scarcely likely.

Furthermore, there are rare occasions where basic constitutional change, simply through a revolutionary accumulation of, so to speak, 'facts of constitutional life' (including facts of power), has been judicially recognized or otherwise has undoubtedly taken legal effect. A most important example to be considered, significant for Waitangi issues, is the division of the once unitary imperial Crown, so that the Queen in right of New Zealand has become a separate legal and constitutional entity from the Queen in right of the United Kingdom.[103] If the supra-constitutional jurisdiction exists for this kind of revolution, there would appear no reason why it should not exist for other kinds.

On balance, I think it is also the better view that, although a court may always seek to make whatever conditions it thinks appropriate before validating a particular revolutionary change, ultimately it must be the principle of success and effectiveness which will provide the decisive and perhaps only test. Even if that is not so, the test is still an essential one. Before a court can be asked to apply it (and any further tests, if thought to be applicable), the revolutionary regime must be making a substantial claim to control of the state. In Charles Tilly's term there must be a situation of 'multiple sovereignty',[104] but one in which the revolutionary contenders for power have achieved sufficient actual control for them to constitute in fact a competing government. Where that is not the case, let alone where the would-be revolutionaries have not yet organized or set up any sort of competing regime, the general rule of normal times applies: the court will simply and without question uphold the legal order of which it is part and the constitution under which it is established.[105]

It may be helpful to refer again to *Childers'* case.[106] The court that refused his *habeas corpus* application (which if successful would have saved him from the death sentence imposed by the military tribunal trying him under martial law) was the Anglo-Irish Court which, following the establishment of the provisional government of the Irish Free State under a United Kingdom Act of Parliament, carried on until the Free State set up its own courts. Erskine Childers, as an IRA captain, recognized no 'authority or Government in Ireland other than the Irish Republican Government'[107] — which was of course a revolutionary body in relation both to the provisional government and the United Kingdom government. Childers did not in fact ask the Court to recognize the Irish Republican Government as lawful, to the exclusion of both those other governments. But even if he had and the Court were to accept that it had the supra-constitutional jurisdiction to give such recognition, it could not be claimed for the 'Irish Republican Government' that the test of success and effectiveness of the much later cases could be satisfied, whatever the moral merits of the IRA's revolutionary struggle might have been.

So also in the many present-day New Zealand cases, happily none as grim as that of Erskine Childers, where defendants (or legal commentators) make assertions of tino rangatiratanga that are inconsistent with the present legal and constitutional order and which could only be given effect by revolutionary change.[108] It is enough to say here that the arguments in support, often couched in terms of morality and justice, are really based on an alternative legal order which is not 'by and large effective' and are put forward where there is no revolutionary government making a substantial claim to control of the state. That a court might in such circumstances, unusually, think fit to deal with objections to the legality or legitimacy of the legal order and constitution of which it is part and which are under attack,[109] should not be allowed to obscure the point. The court need not do so. And it must decide the case in accordance with the principles and rules of that legal order.

To the inquiry sometimes made as to *why* it *must* so decide, the answer can only lie in the nature of a legal order that is sufficiently developed to have courts. The legal order may be overthrown by a revolution which replaces it with a new one and which destroys or negates many of the rights which existed under the old order. But in the new one, the position of courts functioning independently of the other branches of government will in general be the same as that of any such courts in the pre-revolutionary order or in any legal order. That is, subject to the constitution under which they sit and to valid legislation, it will be the function of the courts of the new order to apply the legal principles that they discern to be part of it. Now those principles may include principles that recognize some rights in effect carried over from a previous order (such as aboriginal rights carried over from the pre-revolutionary tribal legal order). But the most the contender for such rights can do is to argue that they are part of the newly imposed, *present* order. A legal challenge to the legality or legitimacy of a present legal order, in terms of the legal order which it effectively replaced, or a legal order visualized for the future, cannot be entertained in the courts of the existing order except in those extraordinary circumstances of revolution that have characterized most of the cases considered in this chapter.

Legality and legitimacy: separate concepts

Revolutionary 'legality' has been the theme of this chapter, rather than revolutionary 'legitimacy'. In the reports of some of the cases the two words are used synonymously. But there is a distinction here. I think one must accept that the test of success and effectiveness, necessarily a limited test, is generally sufficient for revolutionary legality. Success and effectiveness will, it is likely, also provide a minimal measure of legitimacy, in that some justice according to law will be done.[110] But 'considerations of morality and justice' may still deny full legitimacy to a regime that is judicially recognized as legal because it passes that limited but sufficient test.

Then it remains possible that, in some extreme circumstances in a particular legal order, considerations of morality and justice may provide a basis for a legal challenge to the validity of particular laws of an oppressive regime, whether the regime is long established or is the creation of a more or less recent revolution that satisfies the test of success and effectiveness.[111] But in relation to the *status* of a regime of the latter sort, and the order of which it is part, the considerations of morality and justice generally go to its legitimacy rather than its legality.

Prescription and the squatter's title: private law analogies: international law

The durability of the legal order is one of those considerations of morality and justice and indeed the main one to be considered in detail in the next chapter.

It will be seen as an instance of the principle of prescription, which, in the words of Professor Andrew Sharp writing in the Maori–Pakeha context, 'can make a wrong right after a lapse of time'.[112] It is likely that, as he says, all cultures accept the principle. The principle operates both in morals and in law.

Typically, when prescription operates *within* a developed legal system (as distinct from a moral system), it does so under precise rules: a person who wrongfully takes possession of land acquires or may acquire good title to it after the expiry of a certain period of time, such as 12 years.[113] Prescription has limited application in New Zealand (in contrast with, for example, England), since registered titles are generally protected against it except (to put the matter briefly) where the registered proprietor has in effect abandoned the land.[114] Nevertheless the operation of the general principle provides at first sight a useful analogy with the successful revolutionary seizure of power. This analogy was drawn by Judge President Quénet, one of the Southern Rhodesian judges in *Madzimbamuto v Lardner-Burke*,[115] who, in his dissenting judgment holding that the revolutionary UDI government had become lawful after less than three years in power, admitted the difficulty of deciding whether 'a sufficient period of what I shall call "adverse user" by . . . [that] government' had elapsed.[116] Part of the relevant passage he quoted from James Bryce's discussion of 'Sovereignty *de facto*' and 'Sovereignty *de jure*' runs as follows:

> . . . just as Possession in all or nearly all modern legal systems turns itself sooner or later through Prescription into Ownership . . . so *de facto* power, if it can maintain itself long enough, will end by being *de jure*. Mankind, partly from the instinct of submission, partly because their moral sense is disquieted by the notion of power resting simply on force, are prone to find some reason for treating a *de facto* ruler as legitimate.[117]

But as we have seen, the test of revolutionary success and effectiveness, as it has developed, does not necessarily require the lapse of a long period of time before a court may recognize the revolutionary government as lawful. Certainly it is likely that *some* time will have to elapse before it can be concluded that a revolutionary government in de facto control of a territory is both effective and firmly established with no real danger of being ousted, as that test requires. But serious deficiencies in legitimacy may remain which prescription — durability — is likely to remedy ultimately at least in part, for the reasons stated by Bryce. But it will be prescription operating extra-legally, in morality rather than in law.

One other private law analogy needs to be mentioned. In the common law which New Zealand has inherited from England merely to take possession of land however briefly and wrongly is to acquire a title to it ('squatter's title') which is good against anyone except a person with a prior (and thus better) title.[118] A squatter's title is of course precarious unless and until perfected by prescription (and the resulting extinction of the prior title). Even so, no matter how recently the squatter took possession, his or her title is recognized and respected by the law as against someone with a later claim — for example, a second squatter who dispossesses the first (and who in his or her turn will have a better title than the next dispossessor).[119]

Deference in private law to the actual possessor of land, qualified though it be, is a reminder that violent seizure of land has historically been a source of legal title both in tribal societies[120] and as an aspect of the early law of conquest that developed into the traditional doctrine of international law.[121] Thus, in the conquests that occurred in the early Middle Ages in the colonialist expansion of the military aristocracy of Western Europe — for example, in the Norman invasions of England and of Italy, and also in the Crusades — those participating appear in some cases to have acquired ownership of the lands they individually seized independently (so some claimed) of any grant by the acknowledged leader, such as Duke William in the case of England.[122] He of course by the conquest became king of the whole country.[123] There is an analogy here between the seizure of land and the seizure of power, as Judge President Quénet noted.[124] In matters of government, it is the successful revolutionary seizure of power (whether by conquest or internal revolution) which gives a legal status to the new regime and creates the legal order of which it is part (even if some issues of legitimacy have yet to be resolved).

The right of conquest recognized in traditional international law came to an end after the First World War;[125] but there have been conquests since (as in the case of East Timor, if present moves to its independence were ultimately to fail),[126] which, though illegal in international law, may still be validated in time under the doctrine of prescription as recognized in that system.[127] In the meantime, such conquests no doubt effect the same revolution in the legal order of the conquered territory as a conquest in exercise, or purported exercise, of the traditional right. The title of most nations to much of the lands they possess has ultimately been derived from conquest at one time or another, and hence from revolution. In the cases of particular conquests, courts of the conquering nation necessarily give effect to the acts of state by which the conquered territory has been annexed, at least once the fact of conquest is proved before them.[128] The courts of the conquered territory, if they continue and are not displaced by new courts set up by the conqueror, simply do so with the conqueror's authority and not in circumstances where they are likely to claim any jurisdiction to determine the validity of the conquest.

Obviously if and as long as a conquest is not recognized in international law, the revolution that results from it must remain at least in that respect unlegitimated. But also in the case of conquests under the traditional right and other seizures of territory, that have generally been recognized in international law, serious questions of legitimacy have been raised; especially where the conquest or seizure occurred in the course of colonization by a Western imperialist state.[129]

Chapter 2: LEGITIMACY AND REVOLUTION

Durability, morality and justice in the legal order

In the last chapter I suggested that the Pakistan Supreme Court's reference in *Bhutto v Chief of the Army Staff* to 'considerations of morality and justice' as a necessary part of any test for determining whether a revolutionary regime had become lawful, and the more specific tests stated by the President of the Grenada Court of Appeal in *Mitchell v Director of Public Prosecutions* to the same effect, generally related to the legitimacy, rather than the legality, of a particular regime and the order of which it is part.[1] On this view, the role of considerations of morality and justice is to supplement legality with the 'chrism of authority', so that those who govern have a moral as well as legal title to do so and in general those who are governed acknowledge their continuing obligation to obey.[2] Usually the legality created by a successful revolutionary seizure of power will, irrespective of the morality of the seizure itself, soon be supplemented by a minimal measure of legitimacy ('the minimal legitimacy of a working legal order') insofar as the revolutionary regime carries out day to day government in fulfilment of the moral responsibility automatically attaching to the seizure of power.[3]

Whether a legal order established by revolution (internal revolution, conquest, or other effective assertion of power) not only satisfies the test of revolutionary success and effectiveness but is also legitimate, in the sense that considerations of the morality and justice of the revolutionary takeover are satisfied, is not a question which a court of that legal order can be required to determine.

Walker's case: durability of the revolutionary order

However, there is an important case from Queensland, *R v Walker* (1988),[4] where the question of legitimacy was considered nevertheless; and that moreover in circumstances that did not require the Court to decide between a pre-revolutionary government and a revolutionary competitor making a substantial claim to control of the state. Prosecuted for minor property damage, Denis Walker, an Aboriginal of the Nunukel people of Stradbroke Island, argued in the Court of Criminal Appeal that he was subject only to the laws of his people, who had not consented to the imposition of British rule, and that he was not subject to Queensland law. In rejecting this argument McPherson J. recognized as revolutionary the imperial assumption of power in Australia that began with the founding of New South Wales in 1788 and which led to the establishment of the Queensland legal order. Quoting the English writer, Sir William Wade, the Judge referred to the courts' obedience to the laws they apply as 'simply a matter of political fact'.[5] He cited Kelsen: 'A legal order is regarded as valid if its norms are by and large effective'.[6] Since there was no other legal order realistically competing with that of Queensland, the Court (one may comment) was clearly justified in disposing of the question of effectiveness as a matter of political fact. That would have sufficed; but McPherson J. at least tentatively accepted the reminder of R. W. M. Dias that (in the Judge's words but with emphasis added):

> [E]lements of durability and morality enter, *or ought to enter*, into the question of the efficacy of the legal order and the processes followed by courts in deciding whether or not to recognise a new legal order. On this view what is sometime called 'legitimacy' as well as efficacy has a place in the processes of recognition.
>
> If notions of the foregoing kind are invoked, it may be said that the Nunukel legal system was at some unspecified time after 1788 overthrown by a revolution which introduced a new legal order for Stradbroke Island. The appellant obviously contests the legitimacy of that event, but the efficacy and durability of the regime, which displaced it and which now prevails, is not open to question.[7]

In speaking of durability as legitimating a revolutionary seizure of power, McPherson J. is invoking the principle of prescription, mentioned in chapter 1 in our discussion of private law analogies.[8] There, quoting Professor Andrew Sharp, we noted that that principle, accepted by all cultures, 'can make a wrong right after a lapse of time' — or, I would add, at least make it morally irrelevant.[9] Sharp has also remarked in the Maori–Pakeha context, but as a general observation, that 'no origin [of sovereign power] is innocent'.[10] In support of that he quoted Hobbes's contemporary Anthony Ascham, writing in 17th-century revolutionary England:

> As for the point of *Right*, it is a thing always doubtful, and would be for ever disputable in all Kingdoms if those Governors who are in possession should

freely permit all men to examine their Titles *ab origine*, and those large pretended rights which they exercise over the people.[11]

Add to that the even more definite observation of David Hume:

> It is certain, that if we remount to the first origin of every nation, we shall find that there is scarce any race of kings, or form of a commonwealth, that is not primarily founded on usurpation and rebellion, and whose title is not at first worse than doubtful and uncertain.[12]

In a celebrated passage which I shall be referring to more fully shortly, St Augustine likened states to 'fair thievish purchases' — to large-scale robberies.[13] His dictum may be taken to apply to all titles to rule, if, as Ascham and Hume suggest, we were to pursue them to their origins. But the principle of prescription applies. Hence H. T. Dickinson writes, in summarizing David Hume's view, that 'the legitimacy of any government depends not on its origins but on *prescription*' — in Hume's own words, on 'long possession'.[14]

This prescriptive legitimacy must be taken as a moral enhancement of a legality already resting upon the possession and effective exercise of government and of the minimal legitimacy attaching to that exercise. In McPherson J.'s judgment, the tentativeness of the emphasized alternative, 'or ought to enter', in the passage quoted above takes one back to the discussion of tests of revolutionary legality in the last chapter. Considered as a whole and in context, the passage cannot be taken to suggest that Queensland judges sitting sometime in the 19th century, much closer in time to the revolutionary establishment of the colonial legal order, before giving effect to that order ought (at least if the matter had been raised) to have satisfied themselves that the political fact of its effectiveness had been adequately supplemented by durability — in other words, that there had been enough time for the order to acquire a legitimacy going beyond the minimal legitimacy of the working legal order. (In accepting office the judges must indeed be taken to have assumed there was indeed a *sufficient* legitimacy.) But McPherson J. did in effect accept that he should explain why the Court, sitting in 1988, was morally as well as legally required to enforce Queensland law against Walker. From that one may infer that the durability of the legal order is indeed a form of prescription, but operating in morality rather than directly in law.

In the Judge's exposition, durability has in the eyes of an objective observer (which was the role he in effect assumed) a legitimating effect upon a revolutionary seizure of power and the legal order based upon it where legitimacy may have been at least in some degree lacking. This will be so whether the seizure of power takes place by conquest (including, as was the case in Australia, an effective assertion of power that amounts to conquest) or by internal revolution. Of course for those who thus seize power, whether for ideological reasons or in assertion of a legal right or simply for personal, tribal or national aggrandizement, legitimation is immediate. But for the losers or other dissenters, who did not share the ideology of the victors or admit their legal claim, or for any other reason did not support them, time at least partly legitimates the revolution and the revolutionary legal order. Dissenters come either to accept, or at least to acquiesce in, the legal order, so that (whatever their actual intention) they must be taken to consent to it by such actions as taking part in elections under it, and thus objectively enhancing its legitimacy.[15] They may of course have no practical alternative but to acquiesce; and some of them may see the legal order as sufficiently deficient in legitimacy for them to withdraw consent and attempt a further or counter revolution when the time is opportune.[16] If they are successful, the process of legitimation may then be repeated: the revolution and the legal order based upon it will be legitimate and justified ideologically in the eyes of the revolutionaries and may otherwise be generally legitimated by durability, by the passage of time.

One must not forget that for our purposes a revolution may be merely the peaceable means of making a new constitutional beginning, where the links with the old constitution are broken extra-legally by agreement of the citizenry shown in a referendum or a constitutional convention.[17] Here the revolution obviously acquires a degree of immediate and general legitimation that may be lacking where the revolution is a violent one. Nevertheless, to adapt part of David Beetham's discussion of an historical approach to explain the origins of legitimacy in a particular political system:

> Even if we... argue that constitutional rules which are collectively agreed... must carry much greater legitimacy than those... imposed... by conquest or [violent revolution], this is not decisive for the legitimacy of a political system for all subsequent time; and the less is it so, the longer the time that has elapsed since the moment of institution. Rules of power that are imposed may over time achieve acceptance....[18]

Justice in the post-revolutionary legal order: questions of sufficient legitimation

A deficiency in legitimacy may then have little to do with the actual means whereby the revolutionaries acquired the power upon which the legal order was originally based. Nevertheless the rules imposed by force of the revolution may not all come to be accepted, as distinct from acquiesced in. There may be injustice in the constitutional structure of the legal order established by the revolution; and, quite apart from that, there may be illegality, injustice or oppression perpetrated or permitted by the government under that order. Those on the losing side in the revolution may be unjustly treated if under the new legal order they are not afforded the protection for their rights and interests which they might reasonably have expected (or even have been promised as part of a revolutionary settlement, perhaps by a treaty such as the Treaty of Waitangi). Or it may be that the constitution includes insufficient provision for the democratic participation of citizens in the governance of the country;[19] or for the protection of their acknowledged rights and liberties. Or the constitution may permit, and the government may indulge in, the oppression of citizens. Or the government may govern illegally in failing to comply with the rules to which it is subject or which protect the constitutional rights of the citizen. Or it may govern unjustly or incompetently, in failing to provide 'physical security and ... the conditions necessary to material welfare', in a way that satisfies 'the general interest', as distinct from 'merely particular or sectional interests'.[20]

So far as injustices like these involve breaches of the law, the legal order may through the courts provide remedies which check the illegalities of the government (though the remedies may be ineffective against a regime determined to act illegally and despotically). Otherwise they come under the general head of 'considerations of morality and justice', to which the Pakistan Supreme Court referred in *Bhutto v Chief of the Army Staff*.[21] To repeat my own view, they are not (as was judicially stated in that case) generally part of the test of whether a revolutionary regime has become lawful, but they are nevertheless relevant to the separate matter of its legitimacy, as explained in *R v Walker*.[22] Such considerations of illegality, injustice or oppression are thus relevant to the *continuing* legitimacy of any legal order (however the order may have been established) and of the government exercising power under it.

Injustice in a legal order is necessarily a deficiency in legitimacy. If perceived as serious enough by enough citizens and if not remedied by constitutional and legal means, it may prompt the revolutionary overthrow of the regime responsible and of the legal order to which it belongs (and begin the process of the legitimation of a new revolutionary regime and legal order).

Here it is the *perception* of injustice, strongly held, that may be all-important. Anthony Fletcher and Diarmaid MacCullough quote the 'useful generalization' of Yves-Marie Bercé, that '[t]he trigger of revolt is not destitution, but injustice — and not objective injustice, but the conviction of it'.[23] For our purposes, a revolt or rebellion is an internal revolution accompanied by violence or the threat of it. Opinions may differ widely about whether the injustice claimed to exist is real, and sufficient in the circumstances to warrant the taking of revolutionary action; but it is enough in fact to trigger such action that the revolutionaries are convinced that it is.

This book is not a study of the nature of justice. I hold the view that the existence and the doing of justice or injustice in any political system and legal order are matters that can be objectively assessed, however much people may disagree about the correct assessment.[24] But a successful revolutionary seizure of power, especially if fortified by the passage of time, may affect the assessment, to the extent that it leads one to recognize that not only the legal rights of some persons but also the moral entitlements underlying those rights have been modified or destroyed; and correspondingly that new such rights and entitlements have been created for others. This occurs in a process by which any revolution, whatever the ideology of the revolutionaries and whatever real or perceived injustice motivating them, may, with the legal order based on it, achieve at least in time a sufficient legitimacy. That is, a sufficient legitimacy so that even persons who have not supported the revolution, or who have continuing doubts about the political system which it imposed, may properly accept public office in that system. If the matter is looked at, subjectively, from the viewpoint of the revolutionaries, the access of legitimacy is of course immediate and likely to be complete; assessed objectively at that point or when the minimal legitimacy of a working legal order is attained, it may still be sufficient at least for the purpose just mentioned. But durability, the moral factor identified by McPherson J. in *Walker's* case, may gradually supply at least in part any initial lack of a sufficient objective legitimacy.[25]

Durability is however only one of the relevant factors, where what is in question is the justice of the institutions and structure of the legal order (quite apart from the justice of its origins) and of the government's exercise of power under it. A. Passerin d'Entrèves, discussing the relationship between legality and legitimacy, mentions the distinction drawn by medieval writers and still alive in the 16th and 17th centuries between two kinds of tyranny, *ex parte exercitii* and *ex defectu tituli* — tyranny in the actual exercise of power and the tyranny ascribed to a ruler by reason of his or her defective title.[26] Durability, supplementing the legality afforded by success and effectiveness and any minimal legitimacy attaching to it, may not only remove any original flaw in the revolutionary title to rule but also legitimate (accord moral confirmation to) rights acquired under the revolutionary legal order (for example, Pakeha settlers' land rights in New Zealand). But the durability of any legal order cannot legitimate actual tyranny in the exercise of power.

That is clear enough in straightforward situations of oppression. But difficult questions may arise. Consider the case where legal rights, established under a revolutionary legal order and with it legitimated by the passage of time, conflict with rights which the losers in the revolution, alleging one of the instances of deficient legitimacy enumerated at the beginning of this section, claim should be recognized despite their defeat. The doing of justice in these circumstances (for example, between Maori and Pakeha) is usually a matter of contention.

Losers in the revolution: their expectations of justice

Necessarily the contention can be solved only by attempting justice either within the revolutionary legal order or within a legal order established by a further or counter revolution in which there is a different balancing of conflicting claims and interests.

To recapitulate and to carry the matter a little further. In the eyes of the winners, a legal order established by the revolution will be necessarily legitimate not only as to the new regime's revolutionary title to rule but also as to the institutions set up in the constitution of the new order. Objectively, and even for losers, the revolutionary title may be sufficiently legitimated over time. Indeed, in any objective assessment of legitimacy and to paraphrase David Beetham, the more time goes by the less significant the revolutionary origin of the regime's title to rule may become.[27] But, in other respects, at least for many of the losers, the legitimacy of the new order may remain deficient. That may be so to the extent that the new institutions and the regime in exercising power fail to fulfil the expectations of justice which the losers entertain despite their defeat. To be objectively valid, generally those expectations must take sufficient account of the success and effectiveness of the revolution and the existence of rights and expectations that have been created under the legal order based on it. If they do not and instead the losers seek, say, the full restoration of pre-revolutionary rights, then no solution is likely to be open to them other than a counter-revolution establishing a new legal order.

Whether or not the losers' expectations of justice are objectively valid may be irrelevant to what actually happens, since the trigger of revolt or revolution is not objective injustice but the conviction of it.[28] Further, the force or forcefulness, with which the expectations are urged or with which the government's response to them is made, whether or not on either side it falls short of actual violence, may affect the outcome of the expectations; so that any settlement reached is objectively unjust to the extent that it is either less generous than it should be to the losers or too generous to them (so that others suffer injustice). But the settlement in the end must be enacted into law in the legal order in which it occurs and may become accepted in time, even by those previously dissatisfied, as the closest approximation to justice that is practicable.

That true or perfect justice can never be done does not necessarily mean that justice is merely a subjective value. Kelsen thought it was and he excluded it from his positivist Pure Theory of Law mentioned in the first chapter (so incurring the Pakistan judicial criticism that we have noted).[29] In doing so he has quoted without approval St Augustine's dictum in *The City of God* (referred to above): 'Set justice aside then, and what are kingdoms but fair thievish purchases? Because what are thieves' purchases but little kingdoms?'[30] Augustine illustrated this with the story of Alexander the Great and the captured pirate. Alexander demanded to know from the captive what he was thinking of, that he should molest the sea: 'The same as you when you molest the world! Since I do this with a little ship I am called a pirate. You do it with a great fleet and are called an emperor.'[31]

It seems that most scholars take Augustine to mean, not that justice is the necessary foundation of the state as distinct from a mere robbers' band, but that all states and empires are but the creations of large-scale robbery, in which true justice, realized only in the City of God, is absent.[32] Nevertheless it does not seem that Augustine rejected the possibility of the doing, within the State, of a degree of imperfect, human justice.[33] His dictum and the story draw attention to the revolutionary element of violence and lawlessness likely to be found in the origins of the legal orders of most (or indeed, if one goes far enough back, probably all) states and other polities. It is this origin which is, together with the legal order based upon it, given at least some moral validity by the passage of time, by durability operating as a form of prescription and sufficiently legitimating the revolution or conquest. But the institutions of government so established and the exercise of power under them have still to comply with often disputable standards of justice in a particular state or polity, which continually apply since governance is a continuing matter, and which may continually change as the community's conceptions of justice change. The degree of such compliance with the standards as they are or were at any given time is one question; the degree of compliance with the standards as they should be or should have been is another. Those questions obviously relate to the legitimacy, at any given time, of the legal order established by the revolution.

These are general considerations but I relate them especially to the revolution (internal or by conquest), whereby those who lost the struggle are left with expectations of justice which are imperfectly realized in the new legal order and which, though affected by the passage of time, have not been completely extinguished. So the discussion will have some bearing on the revolutions of conquest and colonization — including the revolution begun by the British Crown in Aotearoa New Zealand in 1840, to be considered, with its constitutional aftermath and the Maori response and opposition, in later chapters.

Again, considering revolutions more generally, one should not overlook that a primary purpose of many a one, especially if carried forward with great ideological force or (as in many conquests) to gain great power or wealth, is to destroy, completely and beyond any possibility of restoration, both the pre-revolutionary legal and social order and the powers and privileges of those who have benefited under it. In such cases the legitimacy of the revolution and the new order based upon it must depend much on the ideological triumph of the revolutionaries in winning massive support. Where that is lacking or is insufficient, the new order established by force may at least partly be legitimated over time, if only because what has been done cannot be undone and so many of the losers simply no longer exist. In such extreme cases it may be unlikely that any hopes or expectations the surviving losers may have of justice as they see it will be much fulfilled in the revolutionary legal order.[34]

But it is the less extreme cases that concern us: those where the aims of the revolution are limited and the new legal order established by it incorporates, either automatically or by legislation, some of the substance or structure of the pre-revolutionary order. Where that happens, the losers may find some of their expectations of justice fulfilled, even if imperfectly. The new order may be legitimated more speedily and to a greater degree, because the losers may more readily accept its authority, as distinct from simply being compelled to obey it.

The phenomenon is especially interesting for our purposes where it occurs in revolutions wholly or partly achieved by the conquest (including assertions of power in the nature of conquest) of one state or polity over territory of another. The historical instances abound. A few only are considered here, briefly. They may be significant for illustrating the partial legitimation of new, revolutionary legal orders, occurring even where the victor may have been motivated largely by the convenience of exercising indirect rule.

Partial recognition of pre-revolutionary rights: (i) Rome, Islam and Spain

To take the Roman Empire first.[35] Roman citizens were subject wherever they were to the law peculiar to them, the *ius civile*.[36] By contrast, the subject peoples retained in general their native law and their own courts and often a measure of autonomy subject to the overriding Roman *imperium*.[37] In the criminal law protecting the safety of the Empire the Roman judicial system had jurisdiction over them.[38] These separate regimes within the imperial legal system were thus dependent on personal status (whether one was a Roman citizen or not) or on the nature of the charge. They are illustrated in the New Testament accounts of the respective trials of Jesus and of St Paul.[39]

In the Arab conquests that began in the 8th century the practice was similar, in the dealings of the Islamic conquerors with tolerated unbelievers, known as *dhimmis,* 'the people of the pact'. These consisted especially of Christians and Jews, as monotheists whose scriptures were in part recognized by Islam but whose religions had, it was thought, been superseded by the new faith. The legal position of the *dhimmis* was fixed by pacts with the Muslim authorities, which, although subjecting the *dhimmis* to payment of a poll tax and to certain other serious restrictions and disabilities, to some extent secured their freedom and autonomy both in religious and other matters.[40] (Muslim law governed them in matters of public order and the security of the Islamic state.)[41]

The principle operating in such matters is, in the term Robert Bartlett uses, that of the 'personality of the law'. He writes of it in the context of the conquests and colonization in the frontier zones of Latin Europe of the Early and High Middle Ages: here too there were separate legal regimes (no doubt always within limits that protected the state) for different groups such as Jews, Muslims and different ethnic groups of Christians.[42]

In one of those zones, the Iberian peninsula, there were in the course of the Christian Reconquest instances of this sort of legal pluralism, where Muslim communities submitted to their new rulers on terms which allowed the former a large degree of jural autonomy. Generally the practice was, Bartlett writes, 'one way of trying to reconcile the conquered to their lot'.[43] In our terms, it was an attempt to supplement the legitimacy claimed by the victors with a degree of acceptance by the conquered.

Spain is of special interest in this connexion because it shows the principle of personality of law operating under Islamic and then (as the Reconquest proceeded) under Christian rule. After the Reconquest was completed by the fall of Granada in 1492, the relative tolerance ended. Jews and Muslims who refused to be baptized were expelled, and Christian law alone became applicable to those who stayed.[44]

It seems that not too much should be made of the relatively benign aspects of conquest as expressed in the principle. In the European frontier context Robert Bartlett shows that ethnic groups not strong enough or important enough to be accorded jural autonomy did not benefit from it, and in any case the subject groups suffered serious disabilities.[45] One may add that in the Iberian peninsula the relatively tolerant Islamic rule over Christians, offset as it was by the disabilities of second-class citizenship imposed upon them, did not achieve a sufficient legitimacy to withstand the ideologically inspired force of the Reconquest. And in many cases those of the conquered who exercised over their fellows the degree of autonomy that the conquerors permitted have no doubt been seen simply as collaborators.

Partial recognition of pre-revolutionary rights: (ii) modern Western imperialism

The year 1492 marked not only the completion of the Reconquest of Spain but also Columbus's arrival in America, leading to the imperialist expansion of the West. It necessarily led also to the contacts of the legal systems of the imperialist states with the legal systems in force in the respective territories acquired by conquest, cession or settlement. The principle of allowing different legal regimes for different groups living in the same territory can be shown operating here (with attendant practical difficulties, at least in criminal matters) as a means of partly legitimating the rule of the imperialist state.[46]

The question has to be considered generally and then, more specifically, in connexion with the colonies of the British Crown.

Generally the legal systems of indigenous people survived the establishment of Western imperialist government in degrees that varied widely among the subject territories. It appears that mostly the legal systems established by the main imperialist states in their respective colonies incorporated some of the substance of the pre-existing law (if only in respect of property rights), so that it survived and continued largely as personal law of the individuals affected. For some this was Islamic law; for others it was customary tribal law. For convenience both types (and sometimes they were virtually merged anyway)[47] may be referred to as indigenous or aboriginal law;[48] though Islamic law, itself spread by conquest or colonization, was doubtfully that.

Especially in respect of property rights, incorporation could take place automatically, without need of legislation, when the new colonial (and, for our purposes, revolutionary) legal system was established, if an existing common law rule of that system had that effect. Otherwise legislation might be needed, to define the respects in which the substance of indigenous law was incorporated and survived in the new order or system. Indigenous rules that, from a Western ethical or cultural viewpoint, were repugnant to justice or morality would not be incorporated.[49] In all cases, of course, surviving indigenous law remained subject to valid legislation of the new order and, if there were settlers in the colony, it generally coexisted with the law applicable to them.

Of the British colonies, we have to consider in particular those that began as territories which the Crown acquired directly from the indigenous inhabitants, either by a treaty of cession or by annexation on conquest or (in the 'settled colonies') on settlement by British subjects with or without a measure of consent by the indigenous people.[50]

In the settled colonies (for example, the Australian colonies, and, somewhat controversially, New Zealand),[51] the British settlers establishing the colony brought the English common law with them so far as applicable to their circumstances, under what was itself a common law rule. That is, the introduction of the common law was automatic, on the Crown's acquisition of sovereignty.[52]

In colonies and territories not classified as settled but where there were British settlers, the English common law generally had to be introduced by the Crown, either by Order-in-Council or by legislation of the imperial

Parliament. In both types of colony (settled and not so classified) the common law, together with imperial and local legislation, constituted the general law of the colony.

As to the degree to which indigenous law survived for those who had been subject to it, the rule is now certain that, however the Crown acquired sovereignty over a territory, the property rights of the indigenous inhabitants survived automatically (that is, without any need for formal recognition) into the legal system established by the Crown, except where property was expressly confiscated by act of state before, or simultaneously with, the acquisition of sovereignty.[53] But the degree of automatic incorporation of indigenous law was not always certain. In principle (in somewhat Eurocentric terms), where the 'scale of social organization' of the tribal polities was such that 'their usages and conceptions of rights and duties' could be reconciled with the institutions and legal ideas of 'civilized society',[54] the indigenous legal system might have been expected to survive generally, subject to the 'justice and morality' exception mentioned above (and perhaps with a measure of self-government). But the position was not always clear. Thus, in the settled colonies it was very doubtful whether the customary criminal law of the indigenous people survived the Crown's acquisition of sovereignty; and even if it did survive, it was likely to be extinguished by criminal statutes enacted as part of the general law.[55] On the other hand, in matters of family law (for example, questions of the validity of customary marriages or adoptions), the customary law was generally held or assumed to survive in all colonies (though there were some contrary decisions).[56]

In the United States (to treat them here as the successors of North American colonies of the Crown) the Indian Nations have long had the status of 'domestic dependent nations', a status carried forward from the British Crown's practice of treating with them as sovereign nations in order to avoid trouble and conflict (and despite their being within the areas claimed by it on grounds of 'discovery' or cession from another power).[57] The status has carried with it, subject to the plenary power of Congress, inherent rights of self-government with a consequent survival of separate (but subordinate) legal systems for the Indian Nations.[58] There was early Canadian authority to support a similar common law continuation of limited rights of Indian self-government, to be explained on the same historical basis.[59] But it appears that the Canadian recognition of such rights under the protective provisions of section 35(1) of the Constitution Act 1982 is to apply only to any specific rights of self-government or self-regulation that can be upheld under the general tests for establishing aboriginal rights, rather than to any general right based on the concept of domestic dependent nation status.[60] As to Australia, the High Court has held that the Aboriginal people do not have that status, on the ground that the relationship between them and the settlers has been different from the corresponding relationship in North America.[61] Whether the concept might have been applicable in New Zealand is a matter we shall return to later.[62]

To whatever extent indigenous law was automatically incorporated, it was part of the common law, but probably in the special sense of being, in Professor Brian Slattery's words, 'part of a body of fundamental constitutional law that was logically prior to the introduction of English common law' as a whole;[63] or, as the Supreme Court of Canada described it in tentatively approving that view, it 'was arguably a necessary incident of British sovereignty'.[64]

In the case of many colonies (not classified as settled) with large indigenous populations, the survival of pre-existing legal systems of indigenous law, customary or Islamic, was usually provided for by British legislation. It was used — perhaps much as the Romans and later conquerors used it — as a convenient means of indirect rule of the indigenous people. The main limitations imposed were that customary law was not enforced where it was held to be 'repugnant to justice or morality' (or some similar formula) and that the colonial regime had or could assert, at least ultimately, a monopoly of force.

The resulting dualism or pluralism, where the general law and the customary law of an indigenous people from a pre-colonial legal system coexisted, is said to have caused many difficulties.[65] It appears that in the African colonies the difficulties were remedied in part by legislation and judicial practice having the effect of making African customary law applicable territorially, rather than personally according to the individual's tribe.[66] As to customary criminal law, K. Roberts-Wray, writing in 1966, noted a general tendency for it to be eliminated except where it was reduced to statutory form.[67] The difficulty and likely unfairness of administering dual or plural systems of criminal law — where, for example, several persons involved in the same incident of criminal activity are subject to different systems — is obvious.[68]

That kind of difficulty does not arise in the case of the doctrine of aboriginal property rights, entailing as it does the legal protection of such rights.

Aboriginal title

Basic to the doctrine of aboriginal title is the proposition that, upon the Crown's acquisition of sovereignty by whatever means, the property rights of the indigenous people (as of other inhabitants) were preserved, except where at the time the Crown acquired sovereignty it simultaneously seized property by act of state or where it had already done so.[69] Thus, in relation to the ownership or use of land and rights such as fishing and hunting rights (not necessarily specific to particular land), the doctrine of aboriginal title recognized by the Courts incorporated as part of the common law much of the substance of pre-existing, indigenous customary law.

The 16th-century Spanish theologian Francisco de Vitoria argued persuasively, against opposing views, that the Indians in the conquered territories, having given no just cause for war, had rights of ownership which the invading Spaniards could not lawfully interfere with.[70]

This is part of the general conclusion he reached after examining the legality (which in his thought is really the same as legitimacy) of the Spanish conquests in America.[71] Vitoria denied to the Spanish Crown any right simply to expropriate the property of the Indians. (That much of the actual practice of the Spanish colonists was inconsistent with Vitoria's doctrine is for our present purposes irrelevant.)

For Vitoria the basis for the Indians' right to their property lay in natural law.[72] It may be possible to discern ultimately a similar basis for the common law doctrine of aboriginal title. The immediate origins of the latter, however, appear to lie in British colonial practice, as it developed from about the middle of the 18th century at the latest,[73] displacing the contrary view (held by some writers in the previous century) that the Indian communal use of the land could be lawfully disregarded by the English colonists.[74] The doctrine received legal recognition in George III's proclamation of 1763 (on the British conquest of New France);[75] and by the United States Supreme Court early in the following century, notably in judgments of Chief Justice Marshall that accepted the colonial origin of the doctrine.[76] Consistently with the United States cases, the doctrine was recognized by New Zealand Courts in 1847 and 1872 but fell into judicial disfavour shortly thereafter, to stay there until it was re-established firmly in a line of decisions beginning in 1986.[77] There were some similar sharp differences of opinion among Canadian judges, again until acceptance and development of the doctrine by the Supreme Court of Canada in and since the 1970s.[78] The doctrine was recognized by the Privy Council in a number of cases over the years[79] and by the High Court of Australia in and since 1992.[80] Until comparatively recently it was not completely clear that the doctrine operated automatically upon the acquisition of British sovereignty — that it was not dependent on express recognition by the Crown (as courts had held or indicated in some cases).[81] The doctrine has been compared with the common law recognition of local communal rights of a customary nature, which still applies in parts of England.[82]

The common law doctrine was less generous than that of Vitoria in that it was qualified by another doctrine, that of act of state, which generally governed — and to a large extent still governs — the Crown in its dealings with persons who do not owe it allegiance. By an act of state the Crown could, when acquiring sovereignty over a territory, simultaneously seize property of the inhabitants. The seizure, like the acquisition of sovereignty itself, might be wrongful — illegitimate in our sense; but that was a matter for the conscience of the Crown and not for a court. The act of acquiring sovereignty and the simultaneous seizure of property were both acts of state, into the propriety of which the courts would not inquire.[83]

At first sight the act of state doctrine might seem morally outrageous. (But one has to remember that it evolved when conquest and seizure was a usual method of acquiring territory. One would not have expected courts to try to assume jurisdiction to oversee the process.) There are however limitations to it, which are not our concern here except for one of great importance: in general the Crown could not — cannot — plead act of state in its dealings with persons who owe it allegiance and are thus under its protection. Thus, having acquired sovereignty over a territory, and in doing so having left intact the property rights of the inhabitants, the Crown could not in the future seize any of their property by an act of state; for they were now its subjects, owing it allegiance.[84]

It is true that, in colonies where the English common law applied, the radical or paramount title to all land became formally vested in the Crown upon the acquisition of sovereignty, in accordance with the basic feudal structure of English land law (so that settlers could obtain land only by Crown grant).[85] But in accordance with the common law doctrine, the land remained burdened with the aboriginal title until that was lawfully extinguished. There is some difference of opinion as to what means have constituted lawful extinguishment. Purchase from the holders of that title by the Crown (as the only purchaser the doctrine permits), or valid legislation (imperial or colonial) that expressly extinguishes the title, are lawful means.[86] Either means cleared the land of the aboriginal title so that the Crown could properly grant it. But what is unclear is whether the Crown, by a grant made under the royal prerogative that simply ignored the rights held under the aboriginal title, could validly extinguish those rights to the extent that the grant was inconsistent with them. The High Court of Australia has held that the Crown could do that.[87] But there are cases to support the contrary view that the Crown had no such prerogative and that, without an Act of Parliament clearly authorising it to do so, it could not extinguish aboriginal rights in land by a unilateral act (such as a Crown grant).[88] That view is consistent with the limitation on the act of state doctrine described above.

I have been describing the doctrine of aboriginal title and some of the uncertainty that attaches to it in general terms only; more will need to be said specifically in the New Zealand context.[89] Generally the doctrine does not depend on any treaty or agreement made with the indigenous people whose rights are in question.

Aboriginal treaty rights

Nevertheless in many cases aboriginal title has been the subject of a treaty which may purport to preserve or to provide for aboriginal rights, including some (such as a right to limited autonomy) that go beyond matters of the ownership or use of land or other proprietary rights. Such treaties were among the many entered into by the British Crown in North America with the Indian Nations from early in the 18th century. In Canada the legal status of the treaties was at one time unclear. They are not treaties in international law; they have been described as 'unique' and 'sui generis'.[90]

'[E]xisting aboriginal and treaty rights' are now 'recognized and affirmed' by section 35(1) of the Constitution Act 1982.[91] In the United States, consistently with the 'domestic dependent nation' status of the Indian Nations, the Federal government continued the Crown's practice of making such treaties, until the Appropriations Act of 1871 ended the practice.[92] The treaties have legal effect under Article VI of the United States Constitution, subject to Congress's plenary power over Indian affairs.[93]

In the 19th century, the process of colonization was carried out worldwide with a liberal use of treaties, not only by the United Kingdom but by other imperialist powers, often with small tribal polities. It appears that in the earlier part of that century the treaties were regarded as valid in international law.[94] Under later developments treaty-making capacity was denied to 'Native Chiefs and Peoples', but this is irrelevant in the case of treaties like the Treaty of Waitangi which, made in 1840, was valid by the principles prevailing at the time.[95] But even if all such treaties were regarded as international, as the Treaty of Waitangi finally was in 1941 by the Privy Council in *Te Heuheu Tukino v Aotea District Maori Land Board*,[96] they were still subject to the general rule applied in that case that treaty provisions form no part of municipal (or domestic) law, except so far as incorporated or given effect in an Act of Parliament. Thus, by contrast with the doctrine of aboriginal title, the specific provisions of any treaty with the indigenous people did not become part of the common law of a territory except so far as imperial or colonial legislation gave effect to them. (And anyway, as we have seen, even aboriginal title under the common law doctrine could be extinguished by legislation, if (as is thought) not by mere exercise of the royal prerogative.)

To a considerable extent this vulnerability of aboriginal treaty rights has been removed in Canada, where they share with other aboriginal rights protection under section 35(1) of the Canadian Constitution. Difficulties remain, both in determining the rights for the purpose of that section[97] and also as to the extent of the legislative power to infringe upon them.[98]

It is well established — and this applies generally to treaties between the Crown and aboriginal peoples — that such a treaty is to be interpreted *contra proferentem*, against the Crown as the party who prepared and put the treaty forward. And the treaty must be liberally construed and doubtful expressions resolved in favour of the indigenous parties.[99]

The partial recognition of indigenous law and custom, so far as it effects the reconciliation we have been considering and despite its attendant difficulties, may well have helped to legitimate Western colonial rule to some degree, and in varying degrees, as with imperial rule in previous colonizations. The motive of 'reconcil[ing] the conquered to their lot', that we noted in Robert Bartlett's account of the colonizations in the frontier zones of Europe would have been present in modern Western colonizations;[100] although (as no doubt in those earlier cases also) often with a rather different and more positive emphasis, on securing the goodwill and cooperation of the colonized as allies and to protect the colony.[101] But there was a continuing deficiency in the legitimacy of colonial rule of the United Kingdom and other Western states that was not sufficiently remedied over time to counter the movements, violently revolutionary in some cases, which have led to the independence of now almost all of the former colonial territories; or, in the case of the Republic of South Africa, the replacement of a European with a multiracial government in what had been one of the self-governing British Dominions. In the case of the other former Dominions, where the Queen remains Head of State of each independent realm, the deficiency was carried over from the days of their onetime colonial status, to be at least partly remedied (especially in Canada, with the substantial protection the Constitution provides for indigenous rights) in each case. But again in each of those cases the extent of the deficiency and the means of making it good remain controversial.

Chapter 3: REVOLUTIONARY IDEOLOGY AND COLONIZATION

Revolutionary conquests of Western imperialism: problems of legitimacy

The triumph of revolutionaries in any particular revolution may in whole or in part be an ideological one.[1] Desire for power or wealth may no doubt provide strong motivation also and in some cases (often those classed as coups d'état but which may be revolutions in our terms)[2] the principal motivation. Whatever the ideology or motivation of the victors, for those who are the losers in the struggle the passage of time and the durability of the new order may induce a sufficient acceptance, and thus prescriptively legitimate the new order. But perceptions of injustice on the part of the losers, despite any partial recognition of their pre-revolutionary rights in the new order and often strengthened by ideological considerations, may lead in turn to a further revolution, perceived if it occurs soon enough as counter to the first.

Revolutions by conquest, where the conqueror has proceeded to colonize the territory of the defeated, have not always been ideologically impelled, even in part. The world lives with the effects of innumerable conquests of one polity over another, and it would be fruitless to inquire if there was any ideological cause or motivation for many of them or which ones have been legitimated by their success and durability. Some, like William of Normandy's conquest of England, have been successful assertions of what was thought to be a legal right to rule, made at a time when the relevant law (if any) was uncertain. Others were motivated by desire for revenge for some perceived wrong, as often in tribal warfare. Many were motivated by desire for wealth or land; which in the case of modern colonization by the imperialist West was given a purported ideological justification on the Lockean grounds that lands regarded as unoccupied or insufficiently used could rightly be expropriated.[3] But the West claimed other less self-serving ideological justification as well, to be discussed below.

Traditional international law was no doubt realistic in recognizing a right to conquest in general without reference to the justness of the conqueror's cause. But, as we have seen, international law no longer recognizes the right of conquest. That causes no problem for the analyses in this book: the Indonesian conquest of East Timor was illegal in modern international law and the more certainly is illegitimate — contrary to morality (though it might be validated ultimately by prescription).[4] But the questions now raised over the legitimacy (and in some instances the legality) of conquests under the traditional right and of similar seizures of territory are difficult ones. So far as I know, such questions have been raised almost solely where the conquest or seizure has occurred in the course of colonization by a Western imperialist state. (One exception, the complaint of the Moriori of the Chatham Islands that relates to the Maori invasion and conquest of 1835–36, before the Waitangi Tribunal, will need to be considered later.)[5]

Although traditional international law, as it developed, did not qualify the right of conquest with the requirement that the conqueror's cause be just, a long-established doctrine of the Just War dealt not only with *how* war could be justly waged, once it was undertaken (*ius in bello;* which did become regulated in international law) but also with the *causes* for which a war might justly be waged (*ius ad bellum*).[6] The latter branch of the doctrine of the just war is of course reflected now in modern international law; apparently it was, until the right of conquest ceased to exist, part of international morality only. But it is clear that some at least of those theorists who expounded it did so in the belief that they were expounding the law, at a time when it was thought that under the ideal, non-positivist natural law (*ius naturale*) both war and slavery were unlawful but that both were allowable, subject to restrictions, under the law established by the actual practice of nations (*ius gentium*).[7] And in Western Christendom, except insofar as the successive Popes claimed jurisdiction to pronounce in such matters, the only sources for the relevant restrictions were custom and the writings of the theorists.

Did the doctrine of the Just War apply to the dealings of the imperialist Christian states of Western Europe with the indigenous peoples of the Americas? That those peoples were not Christians and were in certain respects 'barbarous' and that it was the duty of Christians to spread the Gospel, if necessary by force of conquest, were urged by some 16th century writers, such as Juan Gines de Sepulveda, in justification of the Spanish conquests and seizure of territories.[8] Notably opposed to that view, on a differing interpretation of natural law, were, among others, Bartolomé de Las Casas and Francisco de Vitoria.[9]

I take Vitoria first. In his lectures entitled *De Indis* (On the American Indians) delivered in 1539, he specifically rejected the various grounds upon which justification was claimed for the Spanish conquests, but allowed, hypothetically, that Spaniards had the right to travel in the territories in question (so long as they did no harm to the Indian inhabitants) and to preach the Gospel to them. If the Indians obstructed the exercise of those rights, the Spaniards could lawfully make war on them to the extent necessary to enforce the rights.[10] Vitoria maintained that the Indians possessed true dominion (*dominium*) over their territories and possessions, a view significant for matters of government as well as property. Anthony Pagden and Jeremy Lawrance remark that Vitoria 'left his king [Ferdinand] with only a slender claim to jurisdiction . . . in America, but no property rights whatsoever'.[11]

Vitoria's general conclusion that religious difference in itself afforded no just cause to make war and seize territory by conquest was supported by the later 17th-century publicists Gentili[12] and Grotius.[13] Noting this, Sharon Korman comments that 'such progressive doctrines must be seen as protest against the practice of the times and not as a reflection of it.'[14] Nevertheless there was some official concern on the part of Spain that its dealings with the Indians should be legally and morally justified, concern shown in legislation passed (but repeatedly circumvented) to protect them from gross abuses inflicted by the colonists. The official Spanish concern in these matters was in part prompted by the work of Bartolomé de Las Casas, who, in part from his own colonial experience, wrote and argued against the forcible conversion and the enslavement of the Indians and the atrocities and abuses committed by his fellow Spaniards against them.[15]

The efforts of the Spanish Crown to protect the Indians that had come under its rule and the Spanish theorists' treatment of the whole matter of the conquests as one in which disputable moral and legal issues arose appear to have been largely unmatched by their contemporaries in 16th and 17th century colonization, the English, Dutch and French; though the practice of at least the English changed for the better by the 18th century.[16] As to the earlier period, where the title of Spain and that of Portugal to their respective colonial territories rested in part on an arguable interpretation of the papal bulls of 1493 and partly on discovery and taking of possession, the titles of the English, Dutch and French rested largely on the latter considerations and on the authority claimed by Christian rulers as a matter of divine grace.[17]

Christian ideology provided (through the obligation to spread the Gospel) a justification for colonizing the newly 'discovered' territories. Because of the then territorial nature of Christendom, 'Christian mission . . . was inconceivable except as colonialism . . .';[18] so that 'to evangelize was to colonize' and vice versa.[19] Closely related to the duty to spread the Christian Gospel was the duty to civilize, and these, together with the moral right to appropriate under-used land, provided the fuller ideology that inspired and sustained the developing imperialism and creation of empires on into the 19th century. (To say this is of course not to overlook or discount the grosser motivations that lay behind these conquests, as behind many others.)

The above discussion points to the two grounds upon which the modern objections of indigenous peoples to post-colonialist legal orders and institutions of government (such as those of New Zealand, Australia and Canada) are based: it is objected both that the ideology of the mission to Christianize and civilize provided no sufficient justification for the imperialist colonizing enterprises and also that some of the methods of colonization and of maintaining power (for example, in the committing of atrocities) were immoral. And those objections have been applied to Western imperialism and colonization generally, whether or not the colonized people were indigenous in any strict sense.[20] Accordingly, much of what follows should be considered in that wider context.

To put the matter in terms of the West's own doctrine of the Just War,[21] there was no just cause for the West's colonial wars and it often waged the wars by unjust or immoral methods. The matter of the atrocities or alleged atrocities of those wars is still important because, as is much emphasized (for example) in Frantz Fanon's bitterly anti-colonialist writings,[22] it necessarily adds to the continuing sense of deep grievance. But in any final assessment of that aspect of grievance, the atrocities of both sides have to be considered, since the doctrine requires even those unjustly attacked or subjected to wage their war of resistance or (counter) revolution by just methods. (This has been recognized by the South African Truth and Reconciliation Commission where the atrocities of both the state and the African National Congress in the revolutionary war against *apartheid* have been the subject of its report.)

Even if the imperialist Western states, including the post-colonial states, had waged their wars by just methods and without committing atrocities, the ideological or other justification for initiating and carrying on those wars would still be in question, as would the consequences of those wars in the seizures of lands and the setting up of constitutions and legal orders. I turn to that question, and the difficulties to which it leads, in a wider consideration of the legitimation of revolutions by conquest.

Writing about some imperialist poetry of Britain and America, the Oxford Professor of Poetry James Fenton has remarked that imperialism (and he is dealing with that of Western Europe) 'may be described as an immense intrusion into other people's business'.[23] The description may be accepted. But it seems to apply to conquests in general (or at least to those resulting from an unprovoked attack), and not only those carried out by the Western imperialist states. Certainly it should apply to those which, like the latter, are conquests by people of one culture over people of another.

We have then to inquire whether the revolutionary conquests by the imperialist states are in a unique class; and, if so, why?

There is a tendency for the Western conquests that followed Colombus's 'discovery' of America in 1492 to be placed in a class of their own. As Professor Bernard Lewis has written:

> Those who are familiar with modern thought will know that in this expansion of western Europe there was a special quality of moral delinquency, absent from such earlier, relatively innocent expansions as those of the Mongols, the Huns, the Ottomans, the Arabs, the Aztecs — even from the concurrent expansion of the Muscovites....[24]

Similarly, though apparently without the irony, Bill M. Donovan writes of Las Casas' *The Devastation of the Indies*:

> For the modern reader, . . . [the book] raises the profound question whether something intrinsically immoral in the West's ethos has underlain all Western/non-Western relations from the earliest voyages of discovery.[25]

A few pages before, Donovan had in effect indicated the kinds of matters that might need to be considered before one could attempt to answer that question:

> There can be no doubt that the cruelties . . . [Las Casas] denounced occurred on a large scale. . . . Nonetheless his one-dimensional portrayals of evil Spaniards and moral natives render any detached discussion of Spain's colonial experience difficult. Las Casas, and many of his modern supporters, oversimplify the cultural differences among native tribes. It is hard to feel sympathetic for Aztecs who were arguably as ruthlessly brutal conquerors as were the Spanish.[26]

And Donovan had contrasted the warlike and aggressive Aztecs with the 'peaceable Arawaks' who had been attacked without offering the Spaniards 'even the flimsiest pretext for just war'.[27]

For immediate purposes it is not so much the brutality of both the Spaniards and the Aztecs that concerns us as the fact that the latter as well as the former waged wars of conquest on peoples of other cultures. If the Spanish conquests of the Aztecs and for that matter, of the Incas, were, to adapt James Fenton's words, 'immense intrusions into other people's business', so also (it is likely) were the conquests that created the empires of those peoples. And, as Bernard Lewis implies in his ironic comment, there can be no reason for seeing the imperialist conquests and expansions by the peoples he mentions as any different in that respect from those of the Western imperialist states.

In many if not most instances the conquests being discussed would have been, so to speak, trans-cultural. As for conquests occurring within the same culture (for example, Maori tribal wars), the conquered polity might well experience the conquest as to some degree validated by custom and as therefore less of an 'intrusion' — less of a wrong — than if the conqueror were of another culture. But still as an intrusion and a wrong, that required to be avenged.

What though of the effect of time on these intrusions by revolutionary conquest? Enough has already been said to indicate what the answer to that should be. I suggest that, until the right of conquest recognized in traditional international law came to an end after the First World War,[28] the position was as it still is with internal revolutions, and that the principle of prescription applies. Let me state and consider it again, referring to the present problem. Within most cultures there has been a principle which objectively legitimates the wrongful but successful assertion of force, making wrong action right or at least morally irrelevant, whether it occurs by way of internal revolution within a single polity or (until recent times) in the revolutionary conquest of one polity over another. (This is quite apart from any ideological legitimacy or other justification claimed by the successful revolutionaries in either type of case.) At least in developed systems, the passage of time — prescription — has supplemented and ultimately even completed the legitimacy of the new order. There appears no reason why this principle, which clearly applies within a culture, has not applied trans-culturally to legitimate at least in part the great cultural expansions that occurred before the right of conquest was abolished.[29]

Why should the principle not be applied to what remains from the imperialist expansion of Western Europe in post-colonialist countries such as New Zealand? It appears to be the view of many critics that it should not. At first sight a possible reason might be the vastness of that expansion; but that in itself is not relevant, for the claims of a particular colonized people to freedom stand independent of the claims of any other. Another reason might be found in the brutality, and the racial and cultural arrogance, that often accompanied Western expansion; but arrogance and brutality have not been peculiar to Western conquerors. The best explanation of the critics' view seems to be simply that the principle of prescription might apply at some time in the future; but that we live too close in time to the conquests and the other successful assertions of power by which that expansion took place for them to be legitimated by it. That could be correct if complete legitimation were claimed for them, but not necessarily if partial legitimation only is claimed — that is, a partial legitimation sufficient to validate to a large extent the legal systems which have resulted from the conquests and to enable rights which have arisen under those systems to be morally as well as legally recognized. But the legitimation is incomplete insofar as the substance of some rights (of property or of governance) which were part of a particular system displaced by the conquests has not been as fully accommodated in the new system as it should have been; and that some generally acknowledged wrongs done in the course of the conquests have still to be redressed.

It will be seen that this is to steer a middle way between extremes: between the view that, in the post-colonialist countries such as New Zealand, Australia and Canada, the successful Western conquests and the ensuing prescription have already destroyed all moral (as well as legal) claims of the conquered and the view that in those countries (to adapt the words of a prominent Maori)[30] the passage of time cannot justify an imposed power or destroy the rights of those who have been subjected.

Prescription (durability) v ideological opposition

Morality as affected by history is likely in the case of any particular country to be against either of those extremes and to support the middle way. But the matter is complicated because, again in particular cases, no matter how long a period may elapse from the completion of a revolution by way of conquest, nevertheless the conquered cause, though it lie more or less dormant for long periods, may retain some cohesive (ideological or cultural) support that from time to time erupts in civil disorder or even actual rebellion. In all such cases the order imposed by the original revolution, long lasting as it is and generally maintaining its control and effectiveness, may well be thought to have a large measure of objective legitimacy; but it remains vulnerable to the threat of overthrow by a further revolution and the resulting replacement of its institutions. This further revolution will of course be ideologically and culturally justified to those who carry it out and it will also be justified by any objective injustice that may have prompted it. But then too it may require in turn to be legitimated more fully by the passage of time, by the durability of the legal order it has imposed.[31]

I turn now to some historical instances from the long struggle between Christendom and Islam and from British and Irish history, which will show how those principles, of prescription and durability on the one hand and of ideological or cultural opposition on the other, have interacted. They are instances which remain relevant to modern controversies over colonization which have survived into the post-colonial world.[32]

Christendom and Islam

To begin with, it has to be emphasized that the inclusion in the ideology of Western imperialism of a mission to spread the Christian Gospel was a response to what was thought to be a divine command. Muslims were no less certain of a divinely imposed obligation to spread their faith (in their case by *jihad*, by holy war) and no less certain of ultimate victory. Both faiths made universalist claims and had similar views of the conflict between them. Bernard Lewis writes:

> [T]he frontier between two rival, universal religions and civilizations had no geographical fixity, but would move with the tide of battle until — in the common conviction of both — it ended with a final victory of the true faith.[33]

In the first thousand years of this ideological conflict, which ended with the failure of the second Turkish siege of Vienna in 1683, Christendom was much of the time on the defence against Islamic expansion. That since then it has been the Christian or (now) post-Christian West that has been dominant in the conflict has influenced greatly the anti-imperialist ideologies of the cultures which, like those of Islam, have suffered from the expansion of the West. The conflict between Islam and the West, even before 1683 and going back to the Crusades, has for some critics become part of the history of the struggle against Western expansion and colonization.

But there is no good reason for that, unless we recognize the expansion of Islam that began in the 7th century AD as itself validated not only ideologically in the eyes of its adherents but by the durability of Islamic rule in the territories conquered and long retained (and of course, at least in some form, still retained in the territories of individual Islamic or part-Islamic states of the present day). Jerusalem, under Christian government as part of the Eastern Roman Empire, fell to Muslim forces in 638, six years after Muhammad's death. It returned to Christian government when it fell to the Crusaders in 1099, to be retaken by Islam 88 years later. The claim of the Crusaders was obviously in large part ideological, 'an attempt to recover by holy war what had been lost by holy war'.[34] It was also based on what, if one refers back to the private law analogies that we have discussed, can be described as a property claim to prior title, in that the Holy Land had been Christian land before the Muslims conquered it. (From the Christian view point the Crusade was 'an act of *decolonization!*')[35] Against that, modern Arab intellectuals and others have seen the Crusades generally as the precursors of Western colonialism.[36] But the latter view, apart from its Islamic ideological basis, must — again on the private law analogy — rest on prescription: the Islamic conquests of the 7th century were legitimated by the passage of time.[37]

Then consider the course of the similar Christian–Islamic struggle in Spain and Portugal. The kingdom of the Visigoths was defeated by the Muslim armies early in the 8th century, after their North African conquests, and most of the Iberian peninsula came under Islamic rule. But in turn the Muslims were overcome in the ideologically inspired Christian Reconquest, completed by the capture of Granada in 1492. Again there was an appeal to a prior and therefore better title: 'Al-Andalus belonged to the Christians from the beginning until they were conquered by the Arabs. . . . Now . . . they want to recover what was taken from them by force. . . .'[38]

If the Reconquest is to be seen as part of the imperialist expansion of Western Europe, that again can only be if Islamic rule in Spain is regarded, perhaps not unreasonably, as having been legitimated by the passage of time, so that the moral claim to prior title had been extinguished. If so, the Reconquest has itself needed to be legitimated in the same way. Today not even the most committed anti-colonialist is likely to deny that it has. A conquest by Islamic fundamentalists no doubt would begin the legitimating process all over again. But it is unlikely to happen.

The Arab conquest and subjugation of territories already occupied by peoples of other cultures, which were in turn later colonized by the West, was also 'an immense intrusion into other people's business';[39] unless of course one accepts the Islamic ideological justification for them. In the Algerian struggle against French imperialism, those of the 'natives' (as Frantz Fanon in his *The Wretched of the Earth* calls them) who were Arabs were not indigenous people, in the sense of being original occupants, but successors of the colonists who came with the Arab conquest of Byzantine Africa in the 7th century. That the indigenous people were the Berbers[40] could not of course in any moral sense disentitle the Arabs from joining with them to resist and finally to overthrow the French imperialists in Algeria. To adapt very loosely the private law analogies, vis-à-vis the comparatively newly arrived French the Arabs had the prior and better title.

But the position is complicated because it was conquest by the Ottoman Turks, and not Western Europeans, that effectively ended Arab hegemony in North Africa, in the 16th century. The resultant incorporation of Arabs in the empire of their co-religionists was no doubt less of an 'intrusion', and more readily legitimated in their eyes, than subsequent conquest by the West. Nevertheless it appears that the Ottoman conquest was 'a dramatic upset which the Arabo-Islamic tradition conceals even today, as if the destroyers of the past greatness of the Arabs had been, not the Turks, but the Westerners. . . .'[41] But the complication of prior conquest goes back further. Frantz Fanon, not much disposed to show the African wars of independence as anything but a clear-cut struggle of 'natives' against Western colonizers who had subjugated them, acknowledges it as one of the 'weaknesses' of the movement of African unity that '[t]he missionaries . . . [are able] to remind the masses that long before the advent of European colonialism the great African empires were disrupted by Arab invasion.'[42]

1066 (England), 1169 (Ireland) and all that

The central Western Europeans known as the Franks or Normans, who reconquered Spain and Sicily for Christendom and established the comparatively short-lived Crusader kingdoms in the Holy Land, also conquered England in 1066. Anglo-Saxon England was already part of Latin Christendom, acknowledging the authority of the Pope. The conquest by William of Normandy was thus not a religiously inspired crusade against unbelievers or heretics. It was rather the enforcement by self-help of what William, who believed himself to be the designated heir of Edward the Confessor, saw as a legal claim to the English Crown.

Merely as such it might have been the kind of coup d'état that, in terms of the present study, could have been accommodated in a continuing English constitutional order and not a revolutionary conquest.[43] And that would have been consistent with the myth of the Ancient Constitution, expounded and celebrated as history by Sir Edward Coke and other 17th century common lawyers.[44] However, the thorough imposition of the Conqueror's rule, the seizure of lands by him and his followers, and the ensuing colonization, have marked the Norman Conquest as revolutionary in nature.[45]

The legitimacy of the English constitutional and legal order that began with the Norman Conquest was long disputed by those who, invoking an idealized conception of the vanquished Anglo-Saxon England, ascribed many of the perceived injustices of successive rulers and of the order itself to the imposition of the 'Norman Yoke'. Christopher Hill has shown that the myth of the Norman Yoke persisted until well into the 18th century.[46] It is not that the injustices were necessarily mythical — there was a long history of those that were not — but that their continued association with the Conquest was; for the Norman colonists had long ago become English[47] and the ancestral origins of members of the ruling classes had become irrelevant. It was the injustices themselves that provided at least part of the ground for some of the various rebellions (including the Civil War that led to the revolutionary establishment of the English republic of 1649–1660) and potentially for the violent social revolution that never took place. It was the injustices then that made for a legal order and a governance deficient in legitimacy. (That the rule of law, despite its misuse as a weapon of class — and imperial — domination and oppression, was nevertheless a countervailing source of some legitimacy, and that the deficiency has been remedied by democratic and social reforms, are matters we shall return to later.)[48] The actual revolution in government and colonization of England carried out by the Normans must be seen as legitimated by time and by a durability that in substance only the short-lived English republic has interrupted.

The Norman conquest was carried into Wales and there also was followed by colonization.[49] The Welsh were permitted to retain their customary law in a separate polity (though it was progressively modified)[50] until the incorporation of the country in the Realm of England by statute of the English Parliament in 1536,[51] under which English common law and statute law alone became applicable. Legitimation over time must certainly have taken place, with the important qualification that the Welsh have retained a significant cultural identity which supports the measure of constitutional devolution granted by the Government of Wales Act 1998.

By contrast, the Norman Conquest did not extend to Scotland; though a measure of Norman colonization, much less extensive than in Wales, did take place, and Scotland was partly 'Normanized' but under the Scottish kings.[52] The long history of Scottish resistance to English claims to overlordship, the country's existence, at times precariously maintained, as a separate kingdom until the union of the Crowns in 1603 was followed by the union of the Parliaments in 1707, and the maintenance of a separate legal system and separately established Church — all together with a strong cultural identity combine to demonstrate Scotland's identity as a separate nation. Its status as such is now recognized in the partial autonomy — greater than that for Wales — granted by the Scotland Act 1998.

In yet a further contrast, the Anglo-Norman conquest of Ireland of 1169–70 and the ensuing colonization have been followed by centuries of ultimately unsuccessful effort to create a complete and permanent legitimacy for rule by the English, and then the British, Crown.[53] Ireland was an English colony that became a separate kingdom with its own Parliament (albeit one over which the English, then British, Parliament claimed supremacy) until the Act of Union of 1800 created the Parliament of the United Kingdom. The failure of the Crown 'to establish a legitimate authority within the dominant [Roman Catholic] political community in Ireland'[54] led to the creation of the Irish Free State in 1922 (constitutionally transformed by peaceful revolution into Eire in 1937).[55] Ulster, predominantly Protestant, remained as part of the United Kingdom. The long history of '[p]olitical ideas, myths and ideologies [that] have been used to explain, rationalize and justify'[56] the positions taken up by the various communities in Ireland from the medieval period onwards cannot be treated here; nor can the history of the Irish legal system in which pre-conquest customary law was replaced by the common law of the conquerors, remaining today as the Irish common law within the structure of the Irish republic.

Despite the historical, ideological and political complexities, Ireland affords a clear example of conquest and ensuing colonizations that in over 700 years failed to obtain a sufficient legitimacy to extinguish ideologically based counter-claims to Irish independence (except where, arguably, colonization had by the passage of time become legitimated in the Protestant North, in Ulster).

The reader may notice here a different conclusion from that tentatively suggested in respect of Islamic rule in Spain, which was that there legitimation over time did occur. It would not be useful to pursue the comparison too exactly. Perhaps in both cases there was no more than partial legitimation over time — by prescription — of Islamic rule and English then British rule, respectively. At all events, to express the matter very generally, in each case those who had established their power by revolutionary conquest were, after centuries, forced to yield to ideological opposition that had never been completely subdued. And those to whom they had to yield — the Christian peoples of the Iberian peninsula in one case and the people of what is now the Republic of Ireland in the other — could satisfy the criterion of geographical coherence and other criteria entitling them to (in modern terms) self-determination.

English/British imperialism: ideology

The English conquests of Ireland and of Wales lead one to consider more specifically the ideology that was claimed to justify and legitimate them and which developed into that of later British imperialism. At least in its ultimate form and apart from the Lockean element,[57] the ideology of English, and then British, colonization was (like that of Western colonization generally) one of Christianizing and civilizing the peoples of the territories acquired. Its beginnings may be traced back to the 12th century, to an English (Norman English) perception of Celtic societies, such as those of Ireland, Wales and parts of Scotland, as culturally different (which they were) and 'barbarous' (even though Christian).[58] This perception 'obviously functioned in part as an ideology of conquest',[59] which was claimed to justify the subjugation of Ireland and Wales.

Scots, Welsh and Irish joined with the English in the activities of British imperialism, in which however the English hegemony persisted in many matters (as in the reception of English — never Scots — law into the settled British colonies). Strong feelings of cultural superiority, which the English originally felt over their Celtic neighbours, and the mission to convert as well as to civilize, provided much of the ideology of the Empire. Linda Colley writes:

> [T]he Protestant worldview which allowed so many Britons to see themselves as a distinct and chosen people persisted . . . long after the passing of the Catholic Emancipation Act in 1829. . . . For most Victorians, the massive overseas empire which was the fruit of so much successful warfare represented final and conclusive proof of Great Britain's providential destiny. God had entrusted Britons with empire, they believed, so as to further the worldwide spread of the Gospel and as a testimony to their status as the Protestant Israel. And this complacency proved persistent. Well into the twentieth century, contact with and dominion over manifestly alien peoples nourished Britons' sense of superior difference. They could contrast their law, their treatment of women, their wealth, power, political stability and religion with societies they only imperfectly understood, but usually perceived as inferior.[60]

Ideology of Western imperialism and its legacies

That 'sense of superior difference' no doubt characterized generally the imperialist ideologies of the expansionist Western states. But it characterized also the conflicting imperialist ideology of Islam, in which the religious element is much stronger than it came to be in the case of the (now post-) Christian West, what was once territorial Christendom. We are left with the results of revolutionary conquests partly inspired or prompted by those conflicting ideologies and indeed the results of innumerable other conquests, which may or may not have been ideologically inspired, in whole or in part. Neither Christianity nor Islam, nor for that matter the expansionist ideology of the now defunct Soviet Union, would today be seen, except by some fundamentalist adherents, to justify the revolutionary conquests and seizures of territory that at the time, to those who carried them out, were ideologically justified. By contrast, an ideology of freedom or liberation may justify the overthrow by further revolution of the order imposed by an imperialist conquest; though not, I suggest, where on the principles we have discussed that order has acquired a partial but sufficient legitimacy.

And yet, when imperial rule established by revolutionary conquest is in its turn overthrown by revolutionaries, some of the institutions and principles of that rule and the legal order that it imposed may in substance survive the overthrow and become part of the order created by this further revolution. For example, the abolition of slavery has become, so to speak, a legacy of Western imperialism, to be set against the West's long involvement in the slave trade and the long history of slavery in the colonies. It is a legacy that has survived the demise of the empires of the West, simply because the old principle of natural law that slavery is wrongful has become part of the shared morality of people generally, whether at one time they were colonizers or colonized, and has become part of the international law of human rights.[61]

Another legacy of Western imperialism, a more controversial one,[62] is the rule of law in the form characteristic of Western legal orders. Something must be said about this, to show what kind of legacy it is and why in the view of some it has been a doubtful benefit.

The rule of law may exist in some form in tribal polities with undeveloped legal systems, in which arbitrary power is limited and its exercise regulated, and individuals are accorded a measure of procedural and substantive justice, under customary law.[63] Generally in such systems (though, it seems, not necessarily in all of them) there are no judges specially charged with carrying out judicial tasks: the legal system is one of 'executive law', which, Ian Hamnet writes, is 'the characteristic *legality* of chieftainship';[64] in which, under customary law, administrative and judicial functions are not differentiated. But at least to the extent that chiefly power is not effectively limited by custom the rule of law is absent in such systems.[65]

We may make an immediate comparison with the Western concept. In most if not all Western states, and in states that have (so to speak) accepted the Western legacy of the rule of law, there is in some form an effective separation of powers, in which the legislative, executive (or administrative) and judicial powers are separate.[66] The separation, it seems, is essential to the rule of law in any modern developed state. (That is true especially of the separation of the judicial power.) Further, in most such states there is a basic, written constitution which sets the limits to the powers of the legislature as well as those of the executive. In New Zealand and in the United Kingdom there is no such constitution and the Parliament claims sovereign and unlimited legislative power. If that claim is allowed, in accordance with what tends to be the orthodox view,[67] then (unwritten) constitutional conventions[68] alone can regulate and control Parliament's exercise of its power; so that, for example, constitutional convention forbids it to pass an Act conferring on the Crown (as the executive) plenary powers to rule arbitrarily and by decree, to the effective exclusion of the rule of law. A constitutional convention is (in its nature) not law, and Parliament has the power simply to ignore it. But the convention just described is among the very strong ones and, if the orthodox view of the sovereignty of Parliament is correct, the rule of law depends on it in both New Zealand and the United Kingdom. Within a legal system in which the rule of law is secured by a basic written constitution or by constitutional conventions effectively limiting the legal supremacy of a 'sovereign' parliament, the law — whether created by valid legislation passed in accordance with the rules of law-making or created or declared by judicial precedent — is administered by professional judges in fair procedures, independently of the other branches of government; and a person's powers, rights or liabilities, guilt or innocence, are determined accordingly, and at least an approximation to substantive justice is achieved.

Historically there are numerous instances where, in the Western states themselves or their empires, as in other states, law has been the engine of racial or class oppression, through the passing and enforcement of formally valid but draconian legislation; or through legal manipulation by judges and their failure to give effect to the professed values of the rule of law.[69] The record might support some scepticism as to whether the rule of law is a benefit at all; and it might support the doctrinal objection of many Marxists that law is simply the instrument of the ruling classes, so that (in the words of the British historian E. P. Thompson) '... the rule of law is only another mask for the rule of a class'.[70] Thompson, whose Marxist credentials were impeccable, brilliantly demonstrated the use of law as a weapon of class domination in 17th-century England. But he concluded nevertheless that, though much of the rhetoric was humbug, the rule of law itself was not. Rather, in imposing 'inhibitions upon power', it was 'a true and important cultural achievement'.[71] He added:

> More than this, the notion of the regulation and reconciliation of conflicts through the rule of law — and the elaboration of rules and procedures which, on occasion, made some approximate approach towards the ideal — seems to me a cultural achievement of universal significance.[72]

And then, turning his attention to the rule of law in the colonies:

> Transplanted as it was to even more inequitable contexts, this law could become an instrument of imperialism. For this law has found its way to a good many parts of the globe. But even here the rules and the rhetoric have imposed some inhibitions upon the imperial power. If the rhetoric was a mask, it was a mask which Gandhi and Nehru were to borrow, at the head of a million masked supporters.[73]

A detailed study of the use of law as an instrument of British imperialism would be a vast undertaking. One can be certain that it would show throughout the colonies many instances where, often through the use of martial law or of emergency powers conferred by legislation on the colonial government, the protection given by the rule of law to the citizen was temporarily removed. Further, even in the normal application of the law of public order (for example, in regard to sedition), imperial power was asserted and maintained and far from always justly. Nevertheless, as Thompson reminds fellow Marxists, 'there is a difference between arbitrary power and the rule of law',[74] which, however imperfectly, limits such power. And in its nature the distinction applied both in Britain and in its colonies, as it applies wherever the rule of law exists.

The rule of law has become associated closely with the democratizing of government that has occurred since the 18th century (in which E. P. Thompson's study was set) and with the developed concept of human rights today enshrined in the Universal Declaration. I do not attempt to assess how far different legal systems of different cultures show the rule of law, especially when it is understood to include generally political and human rights of the individual. Often the complaint is made that the emphasis in the West on the rights of the individual and the protection the rule of law gives to them is opposed to the communal concepts of customary systems and simply a form of cultural arrogance. However, whatever the communal aspects of many forms of oppression, it is as individuals that people are killed, injured or imprisoned or subjected to the seizure of their property; and, at least to the extent that the rule of law in legal systems of a Western type efficiently protects the individual from suffering such things at the arbitrary whim of those exercising power, the imperial legacy of such a system to a colony is worth preserving.

No doubt many of the customary systems of law of the sorts displaced by imperialist revolutionary conquest, notwithstanding their strong communal emphasis, displayed sufficient characteristics of the rule of law to give individuals some protection against, for example, arbitrarily inflicted death or injury.[75] Nevertheless it is obviously most unlikely that in the developed societies of modern states the primitive communal models could provide the full protection of the modern rule of law. In short, this legacy from the colonial past is unlikely to be discarded except, of course, where and to the extent that the power of an oppressive government is sufficient to achieve that end.

Especially because in the New Zealand context there is some neo-Marxist scepticism about the role of the rule of law in Maori and Treaty matters,[76] it should be said that E. P. Thompson's praise of the rule of law has been criticized as inconsistent with Marxism, in that he 'ascribes an intrinsic value to the goal of ensuring the legality of government action'.[77] It is said, in effect, that the Marxist can be concerned for legality and liberty only where and to the extent that particular institutions and policies either 'hasten progress towards a revolution' or permit or encourage the individual's 'freedom for self-affirmation through labour'[78] that will be achieved in the Communist society. By contrast, E. P. Thompson appears realistic in his view that, in whatever kind of society, there will always be a role for the rule of law in inhibiting the exercise of arbitrary power.[79]

The historian Christopher Hill has rather less clearly than Thompson shown a revisionist Marxist view of the rule of law, in *Liberty Against The Law*, a study of law as an instrument of oppression in England, mainly in the 17th century. Remarking on the surprise Thompson had caused some of his readers 'by praising the rule of law *after capitalism's victory in England* ',[80] Dr Hill shows that changing economic conditions enabled working-class people to use the law to improve their position and that the democratization of law (especially through the extended franchise) greatly mitigated its oppressive role. (In fact E. P. Thompson's recognition of the value of the rule of law is much more general than the words I have emphasized would indicate.)

As we have seen, an essential principle of the rule of law in its Western form is that of the separation of powers. In particular, a judiciary separate from the administrative and legislative branches of government and whose independence is adequately secured is essential to the rule of law in a developed society. Support for the criticisms of E. P. Thompson's heresy could be found in the view of the neo-Marxist Antonio Gramsci that the separation of powers, which 'encapsulate[s]' the 'entire liberal ideology', has (one infers) no place in the 'essentially innovatory' conception of law that he propounds.[81] Thus there would be no place for it in a Communist state except as a matter of practical convenience in the division of tasks. Gramsci's work has been influential in the New Zealand context mentioned above. I turn now to part of his work that has been particularly so.

Gramsci, wars of position and of manoeuvre, and the passive revolution

In Gramsci's analysis of the class war there is a distinction between, on the one hand, the ideological 'war of position' waged against the ruling classes and, on the other, the 'war of manoeuvre' (or movement), the frontal attack on the power of the capitalist state itself. The war of position, successfully waged, is the means by which a revolutionary group wins hegemony and consent,[82] so that (it seems) the war of manoeuvre may become unnecessary or have a merely minor role.[83] The war of position is waged by non-violent methods, such as 'boycotts, propaganda campaigns, counter cultural education, non-violent demonstrations, and the like . . .',[84] under the cultural and moral leadership of the 'organic intellectuals' of the proletariat and its allies. (Opposing them are the 'traditional intellectuals' defending the hegemony of the capitalist state.) One infers that the legitimation of the revolutionary legal and social order depends primarily on the ideological victory in the war of position, which brings majority support for the new order.[85] A complete legal break with the past will occur, and effect will be given to the revolutionaries' 'innovatory' conception of law.

Linked with the concept of the war of position is the concept of the 'passive revolution' which the dominant regime in the capitalist state, in order to contain the unrest of the oppressed classes, itself carries out, through minimalist reforms and concessions and through drawing into its structure elements from the leadership of those classes; but which also, because the dominant regime feels itself under attack, affords opportunities for advancing the revolutionary cause in the war of position.[86]

It seems that, in the contexts of indigenous or colonized peoples where he is invoked, what Gramsci wrote is relevant to them not as such but as part of what are seen to be the oppressed classes of the imperialist or colonialist state. At all events, in both colonialist and non-colonialist situations, it is the complete economic and moral transformation of society which, on a Gramscian view, is both the process (through the ideological war of position) and the goal of the revolution; and which legitimates whatever violence (in the war of manoeuvre) is necessary to establish the new order. Shorn of reference to such a universalist and optimistic goal, the Gramscian concepts under discussion can be applied in any revolutionary situation where there are perceived oppressors and oppressed, including one which is likely to arise when the goal of transforming society fails to be achieved. For my purposes the concepts may usefully explain (at least in part) the ideology of the 'counter-hegemonic discourses' of radical controversialists in the New Zealand post-colonial context to be considered later.[87]

The right to self-determination and the right to rebel; and indigenous people

In the course of an extensive (non-Marxist) analysis of the right to rebel,[88] Professor Tony Honoré has discussed, in the light of relevant international instruments, the right of groups to self-determination and independence. His purpose is to 'sketch a paradigm of the unit in which this right inheres', and the denial of which provides a context in which the right to rebel may be exercised:

> A group which (i) consciously possesses a certain degree of separateness from its rulers or neighbours as regards language, culture, religion, ethnicity, history, topography and social mores, and in addition (ii) is geographically coherent, sufficiently numerous, economically viable and in general has the capacity to assume the responsibilities of a member of the international

community, satisfies the paradigm. Often only some of these criteria will be satisfied. Both the degree of separateness of the group and its capacity to form a viable sovereign state are to some extent matters of degree on which judgments may properly differ.[89]

(It will be apparent that not only a large number of one-time colonies of the Western imperialist states have satisfied these criteria but also, as already mentioned, the Christian territories of the Iberian peninsula and the part of Ireland that now constitutes the Irish Republic.)

Honoré does not deal with the claims of indigenous peoples as such; his criteria apply whether or not the group concerned claims to be indigenous. But the international recognition of the rights of indigenous peoples that is gradually taking place is already strengthening the claims of such peoples in relation to their respective states and is clearly relevant to the right to rebel as he has analysed it.

On that analysis, a state's denial of self-determination to an indigenous people who satisfy the criteria may give rise to a right of rebellion or, in our terms, of revolution. But the extent to which the right is recognized in international law and whether it is (as Honoré treated it) a right of complete secession are in doubt. The international right appears to have been limited to the former colonies and to cases where the fundamental rights of the residents of the unit have been seriously violated by the state from which secession is sought.[90] Apart from that, it appears that it is the success of a secession (even unsupported by any right) that may (at least ultimately) bring about the international recognition of a seceding unit as a new state.

Of course, if a particular indigenous people is 'geographically coherent' and 'sufficiently numerous', without satisfying the other criteria, it may be able to claim a limited territorial autonomy. On the other hand, if the people is not geographically coherent because the individuals constituting it are largely dispersed among the other citizens of the state, self-determination can only be given effect in some other special but very limited constitutional arrangement. Further, some other claims to indigenous rights become more difficult to meet. For example, a separate criminal justice system, which should be possible at least in a modified form where the people can claim territorial autonomy, becomes much more difficult to establish where no such claim can be made.[91] Generally the rights of an indigenous people, even when the United Nations Declaration (shortly to be referred to) is finally made, will have to be interpreted and given effect in light not only of the prescriptive effect of the passage of time but also of general human rights and perceptions of morality that have come to be shared alike by the indigenous people and those of the dominant culture.

Of the relevant international instruments applicable to indigenous peoples, S. J. Anaya regards the International Labour Organisation Convention on Indigenous and Tribal Peoples, No. 169 of 1989, as 'international law's most concrete manifestation of the growing response to indigenous peoples' demands'.[92] Convention No. 169 recognizes in its preamble

> the aspirations of [indigenous] peoples to exercise control over their own institutions, ways of life and economic development and to maintain and develop their identities, languages and religions, within the framework of the State in which they live.

Specific provisions in some areas are made accordingly. Further, the international human rights Covenants of 1966 recognize the right to self-determination of 'all peoples', but it is not certain whether an indigenous group is necessarily a 'people' for the purposes of the covenants.[93]

However, the Declaration on the Rights of Indigenous Peoples, under preparation by the United Nations Working Group on Indigenous Populations, is likely to leave no doubt on that matter.[94] The draft Declaration (1994) provides in Article 3:

> Indigenous peoples have the right of self-determination. By virtue of that right they freely determine their political status and freely pursue their economic, social and cultural development.

The Declaration, like the Universal Declaration of Human Rights, will take effect in international morality rather than international law but will obviously enhance the legitimacy of claims by indigenous peoples that may be brought within its terms. But there are likely to be difficulties of interpretation. For example, unless the point is clarified in the final Declaration, it will be uncertain in what circumstances the provision just quoted declares a right to secede.

'Indigenous peoples: a relevant concept?'[95]

One important difficulty that does remain is the scope and definition of the term 'indigenous' and its practical and moral relevance to questions of legitimacy. The difficulty is indirectly pointed to in a comment of Professor

Douglas Sanders on the recognition by the Nordic States in the 1970s that the Sami people in their north were indigenous:

> This represented the first time that a government recognised a minority as 'Indigenous' when the majority population was also Indigenous *or very old*.[96]

The words I have emphasized suggest that there may be good reason why those who have been long in occupation but may not be the truly original occupants should be treated as if they were indigenous. In fact they are often so treated, in territories which were colonized by the West. But generally, to make the point yet again, the effect of the passage of time should be one of the factors most relevant to the claims and counter-claims of peoples who have in succession become the dominant occupants of a territory, assuming a dominance over peoples who were there before them. Not only does the passage of time affect the merits of competing claims but it may make the inquiry as to who are the indigenous people of a particular territory an impossible one to undertake. Hurst Hannum writes:

> If there are few 'problems' with indigenous people in contemporary Europe, it is because most of the conquests or assimilation of the original inhabitants occurred hundreds rather than scores of years ago.[97]

The difficulties over the concept of indigenous peoples have been overcome (whether or not satisfactorily) by using it only, as in the definition appearing in a United Nations study (1986/7), in respect of distinct 'peoples having a historical continuity with pre-invasion and pre-colonial societies that developed on their territories', where 'pre-invasion' and 'pre-colonial' refer only to the activities of Western imperialist states.[98] More specifically, in the words of the Mikmaq delegation at the first session of the Working Group on Indigenous Populations:

> Those people we call indigenous are nothing more than colonized peoples who were missed by the great wave of global decolonization following the second world war, particularly where independence was granted, not to the original inhabitants of a territory, but to an intrusive and alien group newly arrived.[99]

There 'original' means 'pre-colonial' in the sense just mentioned. The quotation accurately states what has come to be the customary use of those terms in much official discourse, now that the decolonization of the Western empires, where it could feasibly be carried out by granting independence to colonized people who were not necessarily indigenous in a strict sense, has been largely completed. That the 'intrusive and alien group[s] newly arrived' include those in the Americas whose origins lie partly in colonizations of several centuries ago, as well as those in Australasia from more recent origins but organized in the firmly established polities of today, draws attention to the different ways in which the legitimating effect of success, custom and the passage of time (prescription) have applied.

To consider this is a convenient way of viewing in retrospect some of the material covered so far but also to elaborate on it a little. Where one state or tribal polity of 'indigenous' people conquered another, at any time (even very shortly) before colonization by the West, the conquest appears at least in many cases to have been legitimated by success reinforced by the passing of time. Where the conquest was by one tribal polity over another ethnically the same as the conqueror, it may be (as in Maoridom) that inter-tribal custom was also a legitimating force: the defeat is experienced as less of an 'intrusion' than conquest from outside the quasi-international society of the tribes of the same ethnicity. But (it seems) conquest from outside that society, unlegitimated by any such custom, may still be a fact which time has largely legitimated. In particular, the legitimation has been sufficient at least in some cases to enable a long-ago conquered people (who were arguably 'indigenous' in the strict sense) to unite with those who had been their conquerors (necessarily not strictly indigenous), in order to defeat a later conqueror from the imperialist West and together to establish an independent nation state. The alliance of Berbers and Arabs in the Algerian war of independence against the French is an example.

On the other hand, the vast empires of the Western imperialist states failed to become fully legitimate over time. This was in part because the colonized peoples retained their cultural identities and never fully accepted their subordinate status, and in part because the ending of the traditional right of conquest in international law brought into question the legitimacy of at least more recent imperialist conquests. But Western expansion survives insofar as the empires are now represented by one-time colonies, consisting substantially of settlers and their successors, that have become independent states either as a result of violent revolutions (in the case of the original states of the USA and the South American republics) or purportedly by formal and peaceable grant by the imperialist state (in the case of New Zealand, Australia and Canada).[100] Each of those independent states has, so to speak, inherited from the original imperialist parent (or incurred through its own expansion) deficiencies in legitimacy related to the outstanding claims of colonized or 'indigenous' peoples.

It will be apparent that in much modern controversy the concept of the indigenous people has been seen as morally significant largely if not only in relation to the peoples colonized by the Western states. Any practical or moral difficulties in distinguishing between the colonized peoples who were indigenous in the sense of being truly original occupants and those who were not have been solved by treating colonized and indigenous virtually as synonymous terms. It is antecedent occupation — antecedent to Western colonization — rather than original occupation, that has become the relevant criterion.

The principle, that antecedent occupation gives the occupants rights which may survive against those who displace them by conquest or other means, is sound in this context, as it must be generally in the conflicts between peoples whether of the same or different ethnic groups. The principle is however subject to a second, equally general, that the passage of time prescriptively validates revolutionary seizures of power (including those taking place by conquest or colonization) and may modify and ultimately extinguish the remaining rights of the conquered or colonized. But, thirdly, that principle in turn may be subject to the principle of the right to rebel where the subject people retains a strong cultural identity, and other criteria (geographical coherence, etc.) are satisfied. And even if the criteria are not sufficiently satisfied, the legal order put in place by the conquerors or colonizers may be deficient in legitimacy to the extent that the outstanding rights of the subject people, as modified but not yet extinguished by the passage of time, have not been given effect.

It will be remembered that those principles are relevant to the legitimacy of legal orders and of governments rather than to matters of legality. But the first two of them are closely analogous to the private law principles discussed at the end of chapter 1.

In all of this, the concept of indigenous people, if we confine it to a territory's original occupants, is morally relevant to the extent that their taking possession of an empty land gives legality to their presence (in the sense that their customary legal order becomes operative in the territory) but simultaneously gives full legitimacy as well. After all, there were no rights of prior occupancy requiring to be legally and morally extinguished. Yet if an indigenous people by custom recognizes principles of conquest and seizure of power — principles of revolution — in their inter-tribal relations, the moral relevance of their status as strictly indigenous people in relation to intruders from another culture cannot be great. The original occupants cannot easily deny that those principles, if customarily recognized within their own culture, may apply transculturally also. Indeed, as we shall see in connexion with Maori as conquerors and colonizers of the Chatham Islands in 1835,[101] they are likely to assume in their own intrusions into a territory where they are not the original occupants that the principles do apply transculturally; so that, quite apart from any ideological justification (say, religious or political) that might be invoked in some cases, their enterprise, if successful and if its success is secured by time, is in effect self-legitimating.

In short, principles of revolution are not culturally specific and may operate transculturally as well. Yet, in relation to any colonization achieved by conquest or some equivalent assertion of power, the problem of the rights of the previous occupants — rights attaching to their antecedent possession — remains. It does so whether or not the previous occupants claim as being indigenous in the sense of being aboriginal or include those whose possession is antecedent but based on a prior successful and long-established colonization. Again, in their common struggle for independence against the newly and insufficiently established French, both the indigenous Berbers and the Arab descendants of the 8th-century Islamic conquest and colonization had the rights of antecedent possession, and the right to rebel as Honoré has analysed it. As between Berber and Arab the question is now obviously a different one.[102] When it happened, the Islamic subjugation of the Berbers was, to use James Fenton's phrase once again, an immense intrusion into other people's business,[103] and needed the legitimating effect of time.

In the remaining chapters we shall consider aspects of the Western expansion that embraced Aotearoa New Zealand and the moral and legal questions arising from it when the revolutionary principles already discussed are applied in this more local context. The general moral questions that hang over the expansion of the West, already mentioned in the discussion of Bartolomé de Las Casas above, apply to all territories and states that began as colonies founded in that expansion, including New Zealand. The questions and what I think to be the correct answer to them are well stated by Bernard Lewis and should be borne in mind as we move on to the specifically New Zealand context:

> Why, then, did the peoples of [Western] Europe embark on this vast expansion and, by means of conquest, conversion, and colonization, attempt to create

a Eurocentric world? Was it, as some believe, because of some deep-seated, perhaps hereditary vice — some profound moral flaw? The question is unanswerable because it is wrongly posed. In setting out to conquer, subjugate, and despoil other peoples, the Europeans were merely following the example set them by their neighbors and predecessors and, indeed, conforming to the common practice of mankind. . . . The interesting questions are not why they tried, but why they succeeded and why, having succeeded, they repented of their success as of a sin. The success was unique in modern times; the repentance, in all of recorded history.[104]

Lewis goes on to discuss convincingly the reasons for the success of Western expansion through conquests and colonization. Of the reasons he gives I mention here only 'the mixture of appetite, ferocity, smugness, and sense of mission that are essential to the imperial mood and that . . . [the Western European states] shared with their various imperial predecessors'[105] (and, one might add, with their 20th century adversary, the Soviet Union). The list may be adjusted to account for conquests of another sort, where (as, for example, in tribal warfare) the conquerors may lack an ideological sense of mission but have in abundance the appetite and ferocity necessary for success. My own concern, rather different from Lewis's, has been to consider the revolutionary principles under which conquests of both sorts — two species of revolution — have been legitimated in varying degrees but in some cases remained subject, in turn, to revolutionary overthrow.

PART 2

Chapter 4: AOTEAROA NEW ZEALAND: THE CONSTITUTIONAL BACKGROUND

Dr David Williams, in a useful study of New Zealand constitutional origins,[1] initially used a Kelsenian approach to trace the *grundnorm* of the country's legal system back from the Constitution Act 1986 to the 'Glorious Revolution', in England, of 1688–89 — though he went on, patriotically, to discard it as irrelevant to 'the legitimacy of the modern nation state of New Zealand'.[2] My own view is that the seizure of the Crown by William and Mary in those years was in itself a coup d'état, accommodated in the English legal order, rather than a revolution; the *grundnorm* of the English legal system did not change.[3] But a modified Kelsenian approach and the concept of revolutionary changes in the *grundnorm* or basic norm are useful aids in constitutional analysis. Specifically in relation to the New Zealand legal order or system, I discern several revolutions. In this chapter and the next we consider especially the revolution that began in 1840 with the Crown's seizure of power in Aotearoa,[4] the counter-revolutions of Maori in their resistance to the Crown, and the revolutionary transformation of the Crown as an imperial unity into the Crown in right of New Zealand as a separate constitutional entity. That last development has combined with the formal severing of constitutional links with the United Kingdom Parliament (which took place with the enacting of the Constitution Act 1986), and the movement in fact of paramount power from London to Wellington, to create the present basic norm of the New Zealand legal order.

The proclamations of British sovereignty over New Zealand were made by Lieutenant-Governor Hobson on 21 May 1840.[5] This was the beginning of the Crown's assumption of power, at least partly by revolution, over the Aotearoa of the Maori. In this chapter we first consider the legal orders involved, with special reference to their constitutional nature: the Maori legal orders and the imperial legal order which superseded them through the Crown's assumption of power and from which sprang the legal order of the colony, and ultimately that of the present independent nation state.

Maori legal and constitutional orders

For the Maori legal orders I must rely entirely on the work of others or on inferences which I draw from such work. Undoubtedly those legal orders were customary in nature, and undeveloped (or primitive, in a non-pejorative sense) in that they lacked the organs of government — executive, legislative and judicial — that characterize developed legal orders. In terms of Justice E. T. Durie's definition of Maori 'custom law', Maori had 'law generated by social practice and acceptance as distinct from "institutional law" which is generated from the organs of a super-ordinate authority'.[6]

Earlier we considered briefly the nature of customary legal orders in relation to Kelsen's theory of the *grundnorm* or basic norm, noting the difficulty of identifying it in more than the most general way where the basic norm is created by custom and there is no written constitution to which it relates.[7] It appears correct for the provisional analysis that follows to refer to Maori legal orders (in the plural) because each hapu, as the basic political unit,[8] would have had its customary legal order and basic norm, however similar the legal orders were in content; and because the hapu clearly appear to have constituted a miniature international community of 'many small principalities',[9] in which the relations between hapu were governed by the customary rules of a miniature international legal order with its own basic norm. But any complete discussion of the matter would have to take account of the complex nature of Maori tribal organization; shown, for example, in Angela Ballara's recent study, in which the hapu of the 18th century appear not only as independent political units but in many cases as members of loosely organized communities that could be unrelated to the larger descent groups of the iwi, which at that time generally did not function as political units.[10] Then, too, the discussion would have to take account of the iwi revival that Ballara dates from the end of that century, when hapu began to find it necessary to combine in the larger descent group for effective corporate action, though without losing their separate identities as hapu.[11] No doubt a more precise legal study is necessary, but it seems to be the case that the international community of hapu included within it the loose federations of the 18th century and later the iwi as quasi-federations, which were accommodated in the miniature international legal order I have postulated.

The uncertainty and fluctuations of hapu boundaries, noted by scholars,[12] make no difficulty for the above analysis. It is sufficient for the criterion of effectiveness that the hapu's customary legal order was by and large effective[13] within an area or areas that could be approximately identified. Nor is the settling of disputes by the parties themselves, described by Justice E. T. Durie as 'usual amongst Maori',[14] a difficulty. Utu (as punishment of offences by 'an action of equal or greater weight')[15] and muru (ritualized plunder),[16] whether within a hapu or between hapu in the tribal international society, must be seen as the Maori form of the customary remedies of self-help that Kelsen, commenting on Western international law, noted as 'characteristic of primitive law'.[17]

One of the custom-created norms or rules of the international legal order of the West is that treaties must be kept: *pacta sunt servanda*.[18] Moana Jackson, arguing for Maori familiarity with the concept of treaties, has shown that the same rule applied between the tribal polities, treaty breach being a frequent cause of war between them.[19] We may see the rule as part of their miniature international legal order.

Is it appropriate to refer to the 'rules' (tikanga) of the Maori customary legal order? Except in regard to the comparatively strict processes and procedures that constituted kawa, Justice E. T. Durie appears to have doubted whether it is.[20] In a paper prepared for the Waitangi Tribunal (1994) he preferred to speak rather of 'principles' or 'values', emphasizing the flexibility of the applicable customs, of tikanga. But the 'sufficient . . . regular[ity]' he predicates of the norms of tikanga, so that they constituted 'law',[21] seems to me to permit the use of the word 'rule', as used for example in H. L. A. Hart's well-known analysis of a legal system. In Hart's terms, there clearly were in Maori society 'rules of primary obligation',[22] enforced by social pressure and (where applicable) the sanctions of the community (for example, punishment for breach of tapu). These primary rules would generally have been changeable (in Hart's phrase) 'by the slow process of growth'[23] or alternatively, as Justice Durie puts it, by the 'ability [of tikanga] to change without institutional intervention'.[24] The latter alternative would include the former; but it is perhaps intended to extend also to legal change by agreement within a tribal polity, of the sort referred to by the Privy Council in 1919 when it approved certain decisions of the [Maori] Appellate Court recognizing developments in tikanga that occurred after the 'arrival of Europeans':

> It may well be that . . . [Maori] as a race may have some internal power of self-government enabling the tribe or tribes by common consent to modify their customs. . . .[25]

Such a power, itself necessarily based on custom, would really be a means of 'institutional intervention' by (in the Privy Council's phrase) a 'quasi-legislative internal authority'. In Hart's terms, there would be a 'secondary rule', enabling swifter legal change than could be achieved by slow evolution in the individual customs constituting tikanga.[26]

What is meant is best explained by considering an aspect of the Declaration of Confederation and Independence of 1835 (discussed more fully below). Had the legislative Congress of Chiefs, of Rangatira, purportedly established by it actually functioned, and had there been no Treaty of Waitangi and no European colonization, the Declaration would certainly have been a means of introducing into the legal orders of the hapu to which the Declaration applied the Hartian 'secondary rules', that characterize a more developed legal order. Under these the customary primary rules of obligation could on the initiative of the Congress of Rangatira have been swiftly and efficiently changed and supplemented by legislation, to meet the needs of an Aotearoa uncolonized but inevitably radically affected by continuing contact with Europeans.

A similar result but one applicable throughout the whole country would have been achieved had a Maori 'King of New Zealand' emerged through one chief's defeat of his rivals. Professor Ranginui Walker has speculated about this as a possible ultimate outcome of Maori political development, had colonization not occurred.[27]

The office and authority of a rangatira was obviously of first constitutional importance in Maori legal orders. It was to some extent an hereditary office, insofar as the eldest son of a rangatira's senior wife was the preferred heir; but that rule was flexible and 'if he was incompetent or too young to exercise mana he was passed over'.[28] No doubt incompetence or any other perceived failing, or just the ambition of a powerful rival, could bring about the deposition of a rangatira by what in our terms would be a mere coup accommodated in the customary legal order, rather than a revolution.[29] A rangatira's mana was not only his honour or prestige but (especially, in some contexts) his chiefly power and authority[30] — his rangatiratanga. In certain circumstances it could be temporarily transferred or delegated.[31] Justice Durie describes the mana of a rangatira as 'identical with the mana of the people'.[32] It was exercised democratically to a large degree; though in emergencies it could be exercised as absolute power.[33] Durie quotes as 'probably accurate' Edward Shortland's portrayal of Maori society as 'a democracy, limited by a certain amount of patriarchal influence'.[34] Individuals, other than slaves, 'possessed many political freedoms'.[35]

Both Professor Sir Hugh Kawharu and Moana Jackson have written of rangatiratanga as including the 'power over life and death'.[36] But one must no doubt take the power as subject, save in emergencies, to the control of custom and, in some measure, of informal democratic procedures.

In the view of some, no part of the mana and rangatiratanga of the signatory chiefs could have been transferred and ceded to the Crown by the Treaty of Waitangi. To make such a cession would have been beyond their powers. We return to consider the that view later.[37]

If a chief was deposed by coup rather than revolution, the latter for our purposes seems to be the correct term for the constitutional effect of a conquest in Maori tribal society, as it has been among the nation states of the West (and indeed perhaps universally). The legal order of the conquered hapu is superseded by that of its conqueror in the territory affected. There was a rudimentary doctrine of the Just War in that 'the use of force for the acquisition of the territory of another' was regarded in '[t]he traditional systems of Oceania, including that of Maori' as 'improper unless backed by rights claimed by some legitimate principle or cause (take)'.[38] One may conclude that an improper inter-tribal conquest would, like the conquests of Western imperialism described by James Fenton, be 'an immense intrusion into other people's business';[39] though the less immense for occurring within Maori culture (and hence perhaps partly validated by custom) rather than from outside it. But, in any event, 'as in most societies, time could legitimate original violence'.[40] In other words, a conquest achieved by wrongful violence was legitimated over time by the principle of prescription.

Closely linked to these constitutional matters of authority and of conquest in Maori society is the matter of the complex customs, relating to land, in which conquest was one source of title but only one.[41] Under generally known rules and customs of Maori society, a hapu held its land communally, often in discontinuous territories; and also intersecting use rights, not definable by hapu, existed over specific resources or in respect of particular activities and could be held personally or by whanau. Such use rights could be gifted and were heritable from an ancestor with mana over the land.

For the limited purposes of a constitutional theorist, the above may sufficiently outline the Maori legal orders, especially in relation to the land and to tribal revolutions and coups. What then of the imperial legal order brought by the British Crown on its proclamation of sovereignty and assumption of power over Aotearoa New Zealand? We need to consider certain aspects of that order, including the legal position and power both of the Queen in whose name the Treaty of Waitangi and Hobson's proclamations of May 1840 were made and also of her imperial Parliament and the representative colonial legislature it was to create in New Zealand in 1852. What is said will be relevant too to the present New Zealand Parliament that succeeded the latter.

The United Kingdom Constitution

The constitution of the United Kingdom is an unwritten constitution (as is that of New Zealand), in the sense that there is no basic constitutional instrument defining the institutions and powers of government. It was established by custom that became law and by the union, which may have been revolutionary, of the Parliaments of England and Scotland in 1707.[42] Historically, in England, there was a unity rather than a separation of powers, with all powers — executive, legislative and judicial — inhering in the monarch. But, again by constitutional custom that became law, the powers separated; a separation reproduced in essentials in constitutions of the Westminster type like that of New Zealand.[43] (Even so a certain basic unity remains, important formally and symbolically but with some practical implications as well.)[44] The monarch has long exercised executive power on the advice and legal responsibility of ministers and judicial power through his or her judges. Parliament, exercising what came to be seen as legislative power is, in the words of one historian, 'an emanation from the Crown'.[45] The formal words of enactment of each piece of United Kingdom legislation indicate this, in declaring enactment by the Queen on the advice of the Lords and Commons 'in Parliament assembled'. Hence too the phrase 'the Queen [or the Crown] in Parliament' as the constitutionally exact designation of what is usually simply termed 'Parliament'. Despite these historically based complications there is an effective, legal separation of powers.

Queen Victoria's title to rule was based on William of Orange's coup d'état ('Glorious Revolution') of 1688–1689 and on the Act of Settlement 1700 (passed by his Parliament of England and in the relevant part still in force in New Zealand)[46] that settled the succession of the Crown. She was, in a phrase adapted from Henry VII's Treason Act of 1495, 'monarch for the time being', which in my view is in itself a legally sufficient title to rule.[47] But if that title were called in question (which could not happen in the courts of the judges exercising her judicial power), no doubt the principle of prescription would have provided a sufficient answer, in extinguishing the claims of the Stuart dynasty ousted by William of Orange's coup. Even if in accordance with my analysis we deny the description 'revolution' to that coup,[48] it is still the case that Queen Victoria's title to rule in the United Kingdom rested ultimately on an unlawful seizure of power, which may be compared with the taking of power in Aotearoa New Zealand in her name by means that were (as we shall see), at least in part, unlawful in relation to the Maori legal orders.

Maori understandably took it to be significant that it was in Queen Victoria's name that the British made the Treaty of Waitangi and purported to assume sovereignty in the proclamations of May 1840. Hence many Maori have looked to her and her successors personally for redress of wrongs. How realistic have they been in this? As already mentioned, in law the monarch could in general exercise power only on the advice of ministers who took legal responsibility for his or her actions. A powerful monarch originally had much actual freedom in choosing ministers who would carry out policies that had royal approval. But the freedom was eroded by the development of constitutional conventions of (in a different sense) responsible government, under which the prime minister (on whose advice the monarch appoints all other ministers) and the ministry must command the confidence of a majority in the House of Commons as the elected House. In that sense they are responsible to it. The monarch's choice of ministers has became limited accordingly. So also by convention the monarch must act, and only act, as advised by her ministers.[49]

Apart from some ill-defined reserve powers,[50] these modern constitutional conventions generally govern the exercise of the Crown's powers — both statutory and prerogative powers — and the relationship between the Queen or her Governor-General on one hand and her ministers on the other, in countries where she is Head of State. But in the 19th century the conventions were still being established. Queen Victoria retained a degree of personal involvement and influence in government far greater than that of her successors, including the present Queen.[51] One may suggest that in the 19th century Maori perception of Queen Victoria as personally bound to them by the Treaty of Waitangi was not entirely unrealistic. But the perception became less and less realistic as the conventions developed; and the matter was complicated also by the modern doctrine by which a plurality of Crowns displaced the Crown as an imperial unity. Thus the powers of the Crown (to use the impersonal term) have become, through the development of constitutional convention that the Queen must follow her ministers' advice, in effect powers of the ministers themselves. And they had to have the confidence of the elected House of Parliament.

Then one must consider the extent of the Crown's powers, including those of the Crown in Parliament. That the judges were the monarch's judges had not, in England, been an obstacle to their defining the prerogative powers of the Crown under the common law, to setting legal limits to what the monarch could do. They generally retain that jurisdiction today in most if not all countries where the Queen is Head of State, confining the Crown within the powers allowed it by the prerogative or conferred on it by parliamentary legislation. But it has long been accepted that the same limits did not apply to parliamentary legislation itself, to the Acts of the Crown in Parliament. Thus Henry VIII in a celebrated statement to the Lords and Commons in 1543, often quoted by the historian G. R. Elton, declared:

> ... [W]e be informed by our judges that we at no time stand so high in our estate royal as in the time of Parliament, wherein we as head and you as members are conjoined and knit together into one body politic. . . .[52]

That statement may be taken to anticipate the future doctrine of the supremacy, or sovereignty, of the Crown in Parliament, which in its extreme form allows no legal limits to that body's legislative power and no power to the Courts to review the validity of legislation.[53] The doctrine is important to this study for two reasons. First, it defines the power which the United Kingdom legislature claimed over Aotearoa New Zealand, on the assumption of sovereignty in 1840, as over other colonies and territories of the British Empire;[54] and which the New Zealand legislature itself has claimed since the constitutional changes of 1947 referred to later in this chapter. Secondly, it indicates the nature, within certain limits, of the legislative power which that legislature conferred on subordinate legislatures created by it in many of the colonies. These colonial legislatures were empowered by their United Kingdom parent to legislate for the 'peace, order and good government' (or some similar phrase) of the colony: a power which has generally been interpreted to be a plenary power equal to that of the United Kingdom Parliament itself, except for a territorial limit in respect of the particular colony and except for the standard limitation (qualifying the empowering formula) that a colonial legislature could not make enactments 'repugnant to [that is, conflicting with] the law of England'. (From 1865 that phrase became restricted to Acts of the United Kingdom Parliament extending 'by express words or necessary intendment' to the colony.)[55] Apart from those limitations, the Acts of a colonial legislature empowered by the standard phrase were, like the Acts of the imperial (i.e. United Kingdom) Parliament, beyond judicial review: the exercise of the plenary power could not be called in question in the courts on the ground that a particular piece of legislation was not in fact for the 'peace, order and good government' of the colony.[56]

Thus, except for the limits mentioned, the power of a colonial legislature under the customary formula was a supreme power. To that extent the doctrine of the supremacy or sovereignty of Parliament applied to a colonial legislature like that created by the New Zealand Constitution Act 1852, as it applied and applies to the United Kingdom Parliament; and as it applies now to the New Zealand Parliament, as a Parliament no longer subordinate to the United Kingdom body and not restricted by a written constitution. (The autonomy of the colonies, including those like New Zealand that became 'Dominions', and their ultimate transformation into independent nation states, has depended on the United Kingdom Parliament's removing applicable limits and purporting to abandon its legislative power over the polity hitherto subordinate to it.)

For our purposes the essential elements of the modern doctrine of the sovereignty of Parliament are that, to quote Professor Leslie Zines, 'any legislative act ... is law no matter how evil or horrendous its provisions';[57] and that Parliament cannot bind itself for the future, so that any Act it passes it may later repeal by the normal legislative process. The latter element creates a difficulty in the way of, for example, Parliament's purporting to restrict itself from repealing some particular piece of constitutional legislation (say, an Act giving effect to the Treaty of Waitangi). I comment on this difficulty later. In the meantime it is the first element that is our concern. As I have written elsewhere, in effect questioning the orthodox doctrine:

> The great difficulty about a Parliament claiming sovereign or plenary powers is that we know what it can do from what it has in fact successfully and effectively done in the past; but that does not mean logically that it has power to do perhaps horrendously evil things such as authorising the extraction of confessions by means of torture when it has not done this in the past.[58]

Similar considerations may have been among those that prompted Cooke J. (now Lord Cooke of Thorndon) to challenge the orthodox doctrine of the sovereignty of Parliament in several judgments in the 1980s and to suggest that there are common law rights, such as the right not to be tortured, that lie so deep that even Parliament cannot override them.[59] Since then the use of torture has been forbidden by section 9 of the New Zealand Bill of Rights Act

1990 and made criminal by the Crimes of Torture Act 1989. Both those Acts could be repealed. But could Parliament lawfully pass an Act authorizing torture? On the orthodox doctrine it could (and judges would either have to give effect to the Act or resign). But if one asks what precedent there would be for Parliament to do this, the answer is that there is none in New Zealand and apparently none in England; though in England there were at one time cruel punishments permitted by the common law (such as hanging, drawing and quartering for treason) and some (such as burning to death for heresy) imposed by statutes repealed centuries ago.[60] But these ancient precedents would not carry much weight today. One could argue strongly in favour of Cooke J.'s view that there are both basic common law rights that even Parliament cannot infringe, such as the right not to be tortured; and (to go to related matters covered by his dicta) basic constitutional foundations that it cannot destroy (except by a revolution). Thus, to develop one of his suggestions, Parliament could not abdicate its powers by transferring them to the executive (the Crown alone) and enabling it to rule by decree.[61] And in his Hamlyn Lectures (1996), he has followed up an earlier (1982) dictum doubting the power of Parliament 'to take away the rights of citizens to resort to the ordinary Courts of law for the determination of their rights'[62] with this (after allowing the clear power of Parliament to reform or reorganize the courts):

> But the total abolition of an independent judiciary is unthinkable; its existence is the basic rock of the constitution. An Act wholly replacing the independent judiciary by a congeries of administrative tribunals with members holding office at the pleasure of the government of the day can scarcely be imagined; and I believe that the courts would not uphold it.[63]

But if, as I think, agreeing with Lord Cooke and disagreeing with the orthodox view, there are common law limits on parliamentary power that would prevent it from certain extreme actions, those limits are uncertain. (In the orthodox view the admitted restraints are merely constitutional conventions, which Parliament may ignore.) As the latter instances discussed show, the limits would at least ultimately protect the separation of powers, upon which the rule of law in part depends.[64] But having regard to the orthodox doctrine held by many, the uncertainty and insecurity of the limits are such as to make a formal written constitution desirable, to define the limits clearly and the better to protect them. That is a matter to be returned to in a later chapter.[65] For the moment the point is that, even if we limit legislative power to what Parliament has successfully and effectively done in the past (without regard to the ancient precedents referred to above), that power has often been exercised in the making of draconian legislation and that comparatively recently.

The point is well shown in *Grace Bible Church v Reedman* (1984),[66] a South Australian case, where a plaintiff failed to establish that there is a basic common law right of freedom of religion, which the state Parliament[67] could not abridge by legislation requiring the non-government school the Church conducted to be registered. This infringement of the freedom might of course have been justifiable anyway, even if the right existed. However, the basis of the decision was in part the precedents provided by parliamentary statutes interfering with freedom of religion, of which in England and then in the United Kingdom there had been many. One Judge referred more widely to the 'sweeping powers' that the Parliament had 'always claimed and exercised . . . over fundamental rights of individuals. . . .'[68]

The South Australian Court decided the case before it by taking into account some of the history of the claims to supreme legislative power successfully made by the United Kingdom Parliament which originally created the Parliament of South Australia and originally empowered it in its colonial days. Similarly, when the New Zealand colonial Parliament passed the New Zealand Settlements Act 1863 for the confiscation — the raupatu — of lands held by Maori, the legality of the Act was established from the relevant historical precedents for that kind of legislation.[69]

At present, though, my concern is to emphasize generally the supreme power claimed by the United Kingdom Parliament at the time of the Treaty of Waitangi and of the assertion of British sovereignty over New Zealand that followed soon after; and to link that power constitutionally with the Crown itself. When Henry VIII was advised by his judges that he was never as legally powerful 'as in the time of Parliament', Parliament was an event, rather than the institution that it became. But even as an institution, protected by the doctrine of the separation of powers, the Parliament was still an emanation of the Crown, correctly termed the Crown (or the Queen) in Parliament. To put the matter inelegantly but accurately, Queen Victoria claiming sovereignty over New Zealand in 1840 (by a process that was in part at least to be revolutionary in relation to the iwi and hapu of Maori) brought with her the supreme legislative power of herself in Parliament, with limits either imperfectly defined or (in the orthodox doctrine) non-existent.

Preliminaries to colonization

James Cook's 'rediscovery' of New Zealand in 1769 and the invasive contact of Europeans with Maori that ensued brought about several exercises or purported exercises by the British Crown of authority in respect of the country even before 1840. So there is the New South Wales Governor Macquarie's proclamation of 1813, which referred to Maori as 'under the protection of His Majesty and entitled to all good offices of his subjects'.[70] That proclamation was not necessarily inconsistent with statutes of the imperial Parliament, of 1817, 1823 and 1828, which referred to New Zealand as outside the dominions of the Crown but nevertheless claimed for it some criminal jurisdiction in the country.[71] Then there was the appointment, perhaps of doubtful validity, of the missionary Thomas Kendall as a Justice of the Peace in the settlement of Kororareka in the Bay of Islands;[72] and the appointment, in its results of some constitutional importance, of James Busby as British Resident in 1833.[73]

An attempted revolution? The Declaration of Confederation and Independence

Busby assisted certain Ngapuhi rangatira in the setting up of the Confederation of United Tribes of New Zealand by the Declaration of Confederation and Independence of 28 October 1835, to thwart the territorial ambitions of Baron de Thierry.[74] Made by the rangatira as 'hereditary chiefs and heads of the tribes of the Northern parts of New Zealand', the document declared the 'Independence of our country' (clearly the 'Northern parts' referred to, not the whole of New Zealand) and constituted it an 'Independent State', naming it 'The United Tribes of New Zealand'. A very rudimentary constitution for it was included: '[a]ll sovereign power and authority within the territories of the United Tribes of New Zealand' was declared vested collectively in the signatories, to the exclusion of any person not authorized and empowered by them. They were to meet annually 'in Congress' for the making of laws and invited 'the Southern tribes . . . to consult the safety and welfare of our common country' and join the Confederation. They requested the protection of the 'King of England' (William IV) for their 'infant State'. Some other tribes in fact acceded to the Declaration; and, through the Colonial Office, the King's protection was granted in somewhat cautious terms.[75]

Professor Jane Kelsey may well be correct in describing the 'fictional entity' of 'United Tribes' as 'politically unsustainable, practically unworkable and *culturally inconceivable*'.[76] There is support for thinking that the first two of those epithets were applicable;[77] was the third? Kelsey contrasts the expectations of Busby (who, of course, certainly hoped a united New Zealand would ultimately result through accessions to the Declaration) with 'the different, but profound, significance' of the document for the Maori signatories: 'the English [sic] King was now honour-bound to recognise and protect their independence'.[78] Presumably she must mean the then existing independence of each hapu. It may be that further research will shed greater light on the expectations of the rangatira and on the effectiveness of the Confederation. If in fact, after all, they, or some of them, intended what Kelsey sees as the 'culturally inconceivable', purporting to break the rules of the Maori legal orders by setting up a legislature that would make laws for the territories of the Confederation, then their intention was revolutionary. A new basic norm for a developed legal order, for progressively more and more of the country as tribes acceded to the Declaration and the system in fact became 'by and large effective', would have come into existence by peaceful revolution. But it seems that the Kelsenian condition of effectiveness[79] was at most only doubtfully fulfilled during the brief constitutional life of the Confederation[80] — which apparently ended when the member chiefs became parties to the Treaty of Waitangi.

However that may be, in fact it is the revolutionary interpretation of the 1835 Declaration that has been adopted by some present-day Maori in support of claims to the tino rangatiratanga secured by article 2 of the Treaty of Waitangi. In *Re Manukau* (1993)[81] the applicants (for a declaration as to land rights) sought to invoke the Declaration, claiming that it created a sovereign state and that it was the basis for legal rights available today to iwi or hapu that were party to it. The plea failed, Temm J. holding that the Court had no power to embark on the question 'whether the Declaration created a sovereign state in New Zealand'. We may see this as a case where the Court regarded the matter as determined by the source of its jurisdiction within the present legal order.[82] But even if it had not done so and had embarked on some such inquiry, it must be very doubtful whether the existence of a functioning legal order under the Confederation would have been established.

At all events the embryonic Independent State of the United Tribes of New Zealand did not survive as some kind of autonomous entity in the colony established by the British Crown's at least partly revolutionary seizure of power that began in 1840. Among the different dates that are arguably significant, I take Hobson's two proclamations of 21 May 1840 as marking that beginning.[83]

Queen Victoria's sovereignty was proclaimed over the North Island on the ground of cession by one of the proclamations; and over the South Island and Stewart Island on the ground of discovery by the other.

The Treaty of Waitangi

The cession referred to in relation to the North Island was of course that which on one view (and in terms of the English version) was accomplished by the Treaty of Waitangi, signed by rangatira of many (but not all) North Island hapu and by those of some South Island hapu. There were over 500 signatures to the Maori version of the Treaty, some obtained at the ceremony in the Bay of Islands on 6 February 1840 and the rest when copies of the Treaty were circulated through most parts of the country. That some important rangatira, notably in the centre of the North Island, such as Te Wherowhero of Tainui and Te Heuheu of Tuwharetoa, did not sign was constitutionally significant and will have our attention shortly.

As to the terms of the Treaty, so often discussed and so controversial, I must repeat the essential points in sufficient detail for the discussion that will follow. The parties were Queen Victoria on the one hand and on the other the Rangatira of the Confederation (established by the Declaration of 1835) and also independent Rangatira not belonging to it. The preamble (in Sir Hugh Kawharu's translation of the Maori version)[84] recited the desire of the Queen to maintain the authority of the Rangatira and to make an agreement with them for the establishment of government in New Zealand for the welfare both of Maori and of the many British subjects who had come to the country.

By article 1, the signatories ceded to the Queen kawanatanga (a transliteration of 'governance') in the Maori version, sovereignty in the English version.

By article 2 tino rangatiratanga (the highest chieftainship) was reserved to the Rangatira over their villages (kainga) and treasures (taonga), in the Maori version. The English version of that article reserved to them, for as long as they wished, 'their Lands and Estates Forests Fisheries and other properties' that they might 'collectively or individually possess'. Both versions accorded to the Queen a right of preemption over the parts of the land they were willing to sell.

Under article 3 in both versions, Maori received the protection of the Queen; and also (though there seems to be some possible difficulty here with the Maori version) the status of British subjects.[85]

As to the status of the Treaty of Waitangi, views have differed. Stating what became the orthodox view, in *Wi Parata v Bishop of Wellington (*1877)[86] Chief Justice Prendergast denied the capacity of indigenous tribes to cede sovereignty and said that the Treaty, insofar as it purported to cede sovereignty, was a 'simple nullity'.[87] On the other hand, as we have seen, the Privy Council in *Te Heuheu Tukino v Aotea District Maori Land Board*[88] treated it as a valid treaty but applied against it the normal rule that provisions of international treaties do not become part of municipal or domestic law unless given effect by statute. Some modern legal writers, including Sir Kenneth Keith,[89] Dr Paul McHugh,[90] Dr Benedict Kingsbury[91] and latterly Professor Ian Brownlie,[92] have rejected the Prendergast orthodoxy. Brownlie points to the facts that 'the British regarded Waitangi as a real treaty' and that it appears in authoritative collections.[93] He adds (with implied reference to the 19th-century developments that lie behind the Prendergast view):

> Moreover, the fact that *subsequent* developments in international law doctrine denied treaty-making capacity to what were described as 'Native Chiefs and Peoples' is irrelevant. Facts have to be appreciated according to the principles of international law prevailing at the material time.[94]

These 'revisionist' views have been criticized.[95] I am a revisionist myself. But in any case, if the Treaty of Waitangi was a valid treaty in the international law of Western states, it is no longer in force as such: either the treaty itself[96] or the ultimately successful assertions of imperial power that followed it extinguished the international personality of the chiefs. The giving of effect to the reciprocal promises in the Treaty was, in Brownlie's words, 'transferred from the plane of international law to the plane of internal public law'.[97]

We turn then to the key terms of the Treaty and the controversies concerning their interpretation, bearing in mind that, as noted in regard to the treaties with the North American First Nations, the Treaty (whatever its original international standing) must be interpreted *contra proferentem*, against the Crown as the party preparing it: it must be liberally construed and doubtful expressions resolved in favour of Maori.[98] Like many of the North American treaties, Waitangi was inexpertly drawn up; but there is the particular difficulty with it, that there are material differences between the versions that make for some uncertainty. It was then perhaps inevitable that in relevant legislation effect or consideration is to be given to the 'principles of the Treaty of Waitangi' rather than the Treaty itself.[99]

What was (purportedly) ceded and what was reserved?

On the *contra proferentem* approach, the kawanatanga (or governance) ceded by article 1 in the Maori version cannot have meant the same as the sovereignty of the English, except that for the purposes of international law the Queen would be sovereign. Apart from that, what did kawanatanga signify? In particular, did it include any of the mana or rangatiratanga of the signatory chiefs? If it did, then the tino rangatiratanga purportedly reserved by article 2 was in fact a modified rangatiratanga. To adapt the words of McGechan J. in one of the *New Zealand Maori Council* broadcasting cases, the kawanatanga ceded by article 1 rests uneasily with the tino rangatiratanga reserved by article 2.[100]

Many writers have expressed views on the matter, not all of which can be referred to here. What follows is a summary and discussion of some that may be taken as representative.

First, there is the view of Professor Sir Hugh Kawharu, given in evidence before the Waitangi Tribunal and quoted thus in its Kaituna report (with apparent approval):

> [W]hat the chiefs imagined they were ceding was that part of their mana and rangatiratanga that hitherto had enabled them to make war, exact retribution, consume or enslave their vanquished enemies and generally exercise power over life and death.[101]

At first sight somewhat complementing that view, Professor Ranginui Walker writes that the chiefs understood kawanatanga to mean 'the establishment of a system of government to provide laws that would control British settlers and bring peace among warring tribes'.[102] They understood that article 2 confirmed their 'own sovereign rights' — their rangatiratanga — in return for this 'limited concession' of governance.[103] But in Walker's view governance or kawanatanga was a subordinate power: in New Zealand the Governor exercised it 'at the behest and on behalf of the chiefs'.[104]

Professor Jane Kelsey holds a similar view on that last point but suggested (in 1990) a much more limited application of kawanatanga to Maori:

> The Crown was granted the limited power of kawanatanga — in this context clearly seen by Maori as a subordinate power aimed primarily at achieving law and order amongst settlers, thereby protecting Maori rangatiratanga.[105]

But the qualifying word 'primarily' dropped out of a conference paper she gave in 1993: 'The English [sic] Queen was granted rights of kawanatanga (governorship in the sense of delegated authority)over *her* people.'[106] This Kelsey contrasted with the tino rangatiratanga reserved to Maori by article 2: 'supreme authority or independence . . . of the Hapu, collectively through the rangatira or chiefs, over their lands, villages and way of life'.[107]

In an interview published in 1995 she is reported to have expressed the same view and to be 'quite clear about what the Treaty of Waitangi means and that those who say it is ambiguous simply do not like what it says'.[108]

But she has since allowed that, though tino rangatiratanga is the 'absolute authority' of the iwi and hapu[109] and kawanatanga is 'subordinate authority',[110] 'it is a point of debate whether that was only over . . . [Queen Victoria's] own or extended to Maori'.[111]

She may of course still be as certain of her own view on the matter and of her side in the debate. If so, it is a certainty shared by other radical writers, notably Moana Jackson:

> So what Maori people did, in Article One, was grant to the Crown the right of kawanatanga over the Crown's own people, over what Maori called 'nga tangata whai muri', that is, those who came to Aotearoa after the Treaty. The Crown could then exercise its kawanatanga over all European settlers, but the authority to control and exercise power over Maori stayed where it always had been, with the iwi.[112]

Jackson's view, though its emphasis is sharper, is consistent with the conclusion reached by Dr Claudia Orange in her extensive study, that 'from the emphasis [in the Treaty] on protection, Maori might have expected that they were being offered an arrangement akin to a protectorate'.[113]

One may hope that the debate referred to by Kelsey will continue to go forward. In effect partly summarizing it as far as it has gone and stating his own conclusion, Professor Mason Durie contrasts 'all the rights and powers of Sovereignty' ceded in the English version of the Treaty with 'te Kawanatanga katoa' of the Maori.[114] He remarks that 'kawanatanga (governance) has a lesser meaning than its weighty English equivalent' and that 'its meaning to Maori would have depended on their connecting it with some aspect of their own experience' — experience which in relation to a 'central type of government was limited to the few who had ventured overseas'.[115] Nevertheless, allowing for the differences in meaning between the two versions of the Treaty 'and the debate about whether sovereignty was actually ceded or not, at the very least the Crown did obtain the right to govern'.[116] (He clearly implies that the right extended to the governing of Maori.) There was however (to adapt his words slightly) a lack of understanding on both sides: by Maori as to the wide powers the Crown would claim under the Treaty and by the Crown as to 'its obligations to construct a state which would enhance the Maori interests it guaranteed to protect'.[117]

Professor Durie's statement of the matter is of course inconsistent with the propositions that kawanatanga was merely a subordinate power and that it extended only to British subjects and not to Maori. On the first of those propositions there is a little more to be said, from reference both to the Treaty itself and also to some recent study of the meaning of the word in the light of Christian contexts where it is used and which in 1840 were familiar to many Maori.

Kawanatanga: a subordinate power?

First, if the power were merely delegated or subordinate, presumably the indefinite term for which it was granted ('for ever' in Sir Hugh Kawharu's literal translation)[118] could be ended by the chiefs. If so, in what circumstances? Could they withdraw the power at will, acting individually? To some extent the conclusions one reaches here might depend on whether the power extended to Maori or not (a question I return to below). If the power did extend to Maori and was, as Ranginui Walker thinks, merely subordinate, how could the Crown fulfil what he sees as its Treaty obligation to 'bring peace among warring tribes' — when warring chiefs could simply withdraw its power to intervene? It would seem unthinkable that the granting of kawanatanga was other than permanent if Maori were to be subject to it. But even if they were not, would the chiefs likely have thought that they could at will withdraw the Crown's power over its own people?

Secondly, studies of the meaning of kawanatanga have recently been advanced by the Revd Dr Ken Booth's examination of the use of the word in the Bible and the Anglican Book of Common Prayer, both of which were reasonably well known to many Maori through the work of the missionaries.[119] Dr Booth notes that in 1840 only the New Testament and the Book of Common Prayer were available in full in Maori, the Old Testament not becoming available until 1847. But he gives instances of the use of the word in relation to God (whose authority is in its nature not delegated or subordinate) in both the

New Testament and the Prayer Book as well as in the Old Testament, detecting no differences in use. Booth concludes from the examples he gives that '"Kawanatanga" is not about delegation, but about rule and control, whether delegated or direct' and (differing somewhat from Claudia Orange) that the power was not minimalist but extended to 'all legitimate powers associated with government'.[120]

Of course if the power extended to British subjects only, no modern controversialist would wish for ideological reasons to deny those conclusions. It is only the extension of kawanatanga to Maori, with what (from Sir Hugh Kawharu's statement of the matter) seems to result in an inevitable lessening of rangatiratanga apparently contrary to the literal terms of article 2, that difficulty arises.

Did kawanatanga extend to Maori?

It is necessary to look more closely at the view of Moana Jackson and (though held by her a little less clearly) Jane Kelsey. Jackson has made clear the basis for it. He has explained that no chief had the power to transfer the mana of his tribe,[121] some of which (I comment) would have necessarily been included in the ceding of any part of rangatiratanga amounting to 'all legitimate powers associated with government'. In legal terms such a transfer would be ultra vires — beyond the chiefs' powers — and therefore invalid, whether or not they intended to make it. It is curious to note an unexpected measure of agreement in the conclusions reached respectively by Mr Jackson and Chief Justice Prendergast. The latter thought that as a matter of international law the chiefs lacked capacity to make a treaty of cession.[122] Mr Jackson thinks that as a matter of domestic or municipal law — Maori customary law — they lacked that capacity. And no doubt he might apply to the Treaty the phrase used by Kelsey of the Independent Confederate State purportedly set up by the Declaration of 1835: any such transfer of mana would be 'culturally inconceivable'.

This radical view has certain merits. It gives full force to the apparently emphatic language of the Maori version of article 2 and eliminates any conflict between that article and article 1. In confirming the signatory chiefs in full possession of their rangatiratanga, it leaves them in that respect in the same position as the non-signatories, who certainly ceded nothing. True that it appears to conflict with article 3 of the Treaty, if the Maori version is to be interpreted as, like the English, making Maori British subjects. But to state very briefly the effect of Sir Hugh Kawharu's literal translation of the Maori version, his 'reconstruction' of that translation and his explanatory comments, article 3 may have been understood rather as protecting the tikanga (customs) of *Maori*, 'since no Maori could have had any understanding whatever of *British* tikanga (i.e., rights and duties of British subjects).' He concludes that article 3 'reinforces the guarantees in Article 2'.[123] Though without referring specifically to this interpretation, Kelsey perhaps has it or something like it in mind in stating that, under the Maori text, '[t]he laws and religions of the Hapu were to continue, and their rights were to receive the same respect as those of the English [sic]'.[124]

These are difficulties I am not competent to pursue. But, somewhat as with the Independent Confederate State, what if the chiefs who signed the Treaty or some of them did intend under article 1 to transfer to the Crown part of their mana — not the absolute sovereignty that the Crown was to claim under the English version and in fact asserted — but sufficient to provide the Crown with the 'all legitimate powers associated with government', over Maori as well as Europeans? However question-begging the word 'legitimate' is in that context, and whatever the difficulties still of reconciling articles 2 and 3, the possibility must be there that some did have that revolutionary intention (if revolutionary it was). The views of Kawharu and Mason Durie described above are certainly based on the assumption that they did have some such intention. And, faced as they were with an unprecedented confrontation with a completely alien power, it cannot be unlikely that at least some did. (Of course, on the radical view of Mr Jackson and those who agree with him, the purported grant or cession would remain invalid nevertheless.) And then there is one other possibility which, I suggest with diffidence, must also be there: that the apparently irreconcilable differences in opinion shown above may in fact mirror the differing expectations of the various chiefs. It is surely likely that, for whatever reason, they did not all understand the effect of the Treaty in the same way or intend the same thing.

Except in one respect. It is surely impossible that any of the signatories can have intended to cede to the Crown the full power which it claimed and ultimately enforced throughout the country. One must remember that the sovereignty of the Queen proclaimed on 21 May 1840 carried with it the sovereignty of herself in Parliament. The Crown in Parliament at Westminster claimed the sovereignty or supremacy (absolute power, in the orthodox view), which is similarly claimed by its historical successor the New Zealand Crown in Parliament. That power has since 1840 been exercised over the Treaty itself, often in derogation of it and with at best only such effect given to the rangatiratanga reserved by article 2 as (to speak briefly) the Parliament (imperial or New Zealand) has from time to time seen fit. To that extent the expectations of all the signatory chiefs must have been defeated.

It may be that all treaties of cession or purported cession, or agreed mergers like that between England and Scotland, are correctly described as revolutionary, whatever the observance of forms of law and the due giving of effect to them.[125] If that is right, then the launching of New Zealand as a colonial polity in 1840 would have been revolutionary even if the Treaty of Waitangi had been exactly observed (whatever the practical difficulties of deciding what exact observance required) and chiefs of all the hapu had signed it. (And in that case the revolution would have been partly legitimated by the Treaty.) But, as we have seen, the assumption of power by the Crown is revolutionary in a much more obvious and radical sense. If it is difficult to reconcile the first two articles of the Treaty with each other, it is far more difficult — indeed impossible — to reconcile with those two articles what the Crown in fact did. To the extent that the power asserted and seized by the Crown exceeded what was ceded, the seizure was a revolutionary act in relation to the customary legal systems of the hapu of the signatory chiefs.

The non-signatories

The imperial seizure of power over the hapu of the signatory chiefs is then revolutionary, if to a disputable extent because of the differing views of the effect of the Treaty. There can be no dispute, however, that the seizure of power in accordance with the proclamations of May 1840 was radically revolutionary in relation to the hapu of the non-signatory chiefs who of course had ceded nothing. That the Treaty has become, however uncertainly and falteringly, a constitutional standard, against which the conduct of the Crown towards Maori and the Maori claims to rights against the Crown are to be assessed, should not obscure this important fact about the country's colonial constitutional beginnings. The acceptance of the Treaty by more than 500 signatories might give a partial moral legitimation to the Crown's assumption of power (though of course not insofar as that assumption exceeded the terms of the Treaty) but there was no majority rule, either in law or morals, which in any way bound the non-signatories and their hapu. The surprising statement of the Waitangi Tribunal in its *Te Whanau o Waipareira Report* (1998) that '[t]he Treaty of Waitangi was signed by rangatira of hapu, on behalf of all Maori people, collectively and individually'[126] is justifiable if seen as recognition of the constitutional standard the Treaty has certainly become, in particular under the very statute establishing the Tribunal, the Treaty of Waitangi Act 1975; and which (in the Tribunal's view) would support the recognition of the claim of urban, non-tribal Maori accorded by the Report. As a statement of what happened in 1840 it can scarcely be correct.

The Tribunal and kawanatanga: summary comment

Necessarily the Tribunal has under the guidance of the courts had to reach its own understanding of the effect of the Treaty and of the Treaty 'principles' which under its statute it must apply in considering the claims of Maori without regard to whether or not claimants are of hapu signatory to the Treaty, since the statute is (for good reason) silent about any such distinction. The Tribunal, itself constituted by a legislature which depends at least historically on the seizure of power by the Crown in 1840, recognizes that under the Treaty there passed to the Crown a kawanatanga over Maori that amounts to (in Dr Ken Booth's phrase) 'all legitimate powers associated with government'. In its *Report on the Muriwhenua Fishing Claim* (1988),[127] the Tribunal noted that '[s]overeignty, in law, is not dependent on the Treaty but on the proclamations that followed the signings at Waitangi' but thought it 'nonetheless important to consider whether sovereignty was founded in consensus'. The Tribunal concluded that there was consensus: the Queen 'as guarantor and protector of the Maori interest... had perforce an overriding power'; and the chiefs, despite early 'resentment among' them 'when the Governor and his magistrates sought to bring Maori within the scope of the new laws', were trying to preserve under article 2 a form of local autonomy 'not amount[ing] to complete sovereignty but a kind of local self-government in Maori districts...';[128] which would not be inconsistent with the supremacy of the Crown.

All that partly supports the Tribunal's opinion in the *Orakei Report* that:

> In the Maori text the chiefs ceded to the Queen 'kawanatanga'. This is less than the sovereignty ceded in the English text, and means the authority to make laws for the good order and security of the country but subject to the protection of Maori interests. The cession of sovereignty however is implicit from surrounding circumstances.[129]

The 'surrounding circumstances' should be limited to those 'exist[ing] at the time of [the Treaty's] execution',[130] which must have included the early resistance of some chiefs to having Maori brought under the new laws. It is difficult not to conclude that, on the Tribunal's statement of the matter, any consensus of Maori in the 'overriding power' of the Crown in excess of what was ceded must have been reached very much later and that, if and to the extent that it was reached, it was part of a process of legitimation.

That process is the subject of chapter 6. In the meantime we have to consider in chapter 5 how the revolution was carried out and the limits to which the imperial-colonial revolutionaries carried it; and also the temporary success of what may be seen as Maori counter-revolutions in the New Zealand wars.

Chapter 5: REVOLUTIONS AND COUNTER-REVOLUTIONS 1840–1986

The 1840 revolution

The revolutionary nature of the Crown's seizure of power in pursuance of the proclamations of sovereignty of May 1840 is clear from the first constitutional steps taken by it. To give effect to the Treaty, if it did not create the protectorate of later imperial practice,[1] the Crown ought to have created a colony with a written constitution in which Maori rights were identified and received entrenched protection. That kind of solution was not part of the constitutional thinking of the time. What the Crown in fact and law did was to create a Crown colony on the general model (at first as a dependency of New South Wales). The country was given by the New Zealand Constitution Act 1852 (UK) the same kind of representative government as New South Wales, Victoria and other Australian colonies (where there were of course no treaties with the indigenous peoples).

Before that it had been realized, at least by the first Attorney-General, William Swainson, that there was a discrepancy between the authority the Crown claimed over the whole country and what it could properly claim under the Treaty of Waitangi. He seems to have assumed that the supreme power of actual sovereignty had been ceded, but he was alive to the problem of the non-signatories, who of course had ceded nothing. Hence his opinion to Acting Governor Shortland in 1842, that '[a]s regards the aborigines, our title to the sovereignty over the whole of New Zealand appears to be incomplete'.[2]

But the Crown, through the Under-Secretary of State for the Colonies, Sir James Stephen, was prompt to reject this understanding of the matter. His minute on the opinion asserted the acts of state by which the Crown had claimed government of the whole of the country, commenting that 'Mr Swainston [sic] may think this is unjust — or impolitic — or inconsistent with the former acts. But still it is *done*'.[3]

Then came a rebuke to Swainson by the Secretary of State:

> I do not think it necessary or convenient to discuss with Mr Swainson the justice or the policy of the course which the Queen has been advised to pursue.

For the present purpose, it is sufficient to say that Her Majesty has pursued it.[4]

One should note carefully what the Secretary and Under-Secretary were in effect saying. The Queen on the advice of her ministers had asserted her sovereignty over the whole of New Zealand by acts of state that were revolutionary at least in relation both to the hapu of non-signatory chiefs and (on our consideration of the matter) those of the signatory chiefs also insofar as the absolute sovereignty claimed went beyond what they respectively had ceded. And, as with all revolutions, whatever ideological justification the revolutionaries may claim, the revolution must rest finally upon its success, upon what is 'done', rather than what is just or moral or legal (since the revolution is by definition illegal, in this case in relation to the customary legal orders of Maori). As both ministers recognized, the justice and morality of what was 'done' might be defective; but they would presumably also have thought that (in terms that are familiar to us) the passage of time, if nothing else, would in part at least cure any such defect.

But there are complications here. In the 1840s, and for decades after, the revolution was far from completely effective throughout the country, notwithstanding that persons in the Queen's service (like Swainson), and for that matter her subjects generally, were in law bound to regard it as if it were. What Sir James Stephen asserted was 'done' was in part only notionally done. The Court of Appeal noted in *Hohepa Wi Neera v Bishop of Wellington* (1902) that '[t]he Queen's writ did not run throughout all districts of New Zealand till long after 1865';[5] and indeed it did not so run until about the end of the century when the seizure of power by the Crown, partly through ultimately successful warfare or (as at Parihaka) other employment of force or pressure, became generally complete.

Thus for long the new imperial-colonial order was 'by and large effective' in parts of the country only. It had for competitors in other parts the continuing customary legal orders of Maori and also more developed Maori legal orders, notably that established under the central government of the Maori King in what came to be called the King Country. Before we consider further these competitors and their nature, more must be said about the Crown's own revolution and its relationship to the legal orders that it superseded as the revolution progressively fulfilled the Kelsenian condition[6] in becoming effective throughout New Zealand.

Rules of the 1840 revolution

The General Assembly established by the New Zealand Constitution Act 1852 of the imperial Parliament consisted of the Governor, Legislative Council and House of Representatives. It had under section 53 the usual power of a colonial legislature to make laws for the peace, order and good government of the colony, which was, as we have seen, a plenary power subject only to territorial and repugnancy limitations; and the exercise of this power could not be called in question in the courts on the grounds that a particular piece of legislation was not in fact for the peace, order or good government of the colony.[7] Again, on the colonial model, the Governor had (under section 56) power to give the royal assent to a bill passed by the Legislative Council and the House of Representatives, with the alternative of reserving the bill for the signification of the Queen's pleasure. In exercise of those powers the Governor had (under section 57) to act on the Queen's instructions. (He was under such instructions generally in carrying out his office.) By section 58, the Queen was empowered to disallow any bill to which the Governor had given the royal assent, within two years from when the Secretary of State received an official copy of the bill. By convention the Queen would in all these matters act on the advice of her United Kingdom ministers.

Finally, the General Assembly was given a limited power to amend the provisions of the 1852 Act, by the New Zealand Constitution Amendment Act 1857 (UK). The power of amendment did not extend to certain basic provisions, including section 71 (to be considered in detail later) which made provision empowering the Crown to create districts where Maori customary law would continue subject to certain limitations.

The above is a sufficient sketch for our purposes of the provisions of the representative constitution provided for New Zealand by the Queen in Parliament of the United Kingdom, after the country's initial period as a Crown colony. In effect the Constitution of 1852 provided rules for the exercise of the supreme power or sovereignty which the Crown had by Hobson's proclamations of May 1840 asserted over the whole country and was gradually enforcing by progressively bringing the country under its effective rule.

Maori as British subjects

Whatever the intended effect of article 3 of the Maori version of the Treaty of Waitangi, it has been widely accepted that in imperial-colonial law all Maori became British subjects by virtue of the Crown's assumption of sovereignty over New Zealand proclaimed in May 1840. We have already noted the contrary opinion of the Attorney-General in 1842. The rejection of his advice by the Colonial Office did not in itself conclude the matter. But recent Australian authority[8] adds support to the view of the Under-Secretary of State and his superior: immediately on the proclaimed assumption of sovereignty all those who were members of the tribes or polities whose territories were thus annexed became British subjects. But some doubt remains. A possible basis for it (different from that suggested by the Attorney-General) is that over very large areas of the country the Queen's writ did not run. In those areas, whether or not the chiefs of the hapu concerned had signed the Treaty, Maori autonomy prevailed in fact; and Maori were outside the protection of the Crown, hence (it may be argued) owing it no allegiance. This co-relation between protection and allegiance established by *Calvin's Case* (1608)[9] would support an argument that allegiance was not owed except as the Crown progressively made its claim to sovereignty effective and provided protection to its new subjects. So too would the Crown's practice of treating residents of the lost French provinces (claimed in right of England until 1802) as persons owing no allegiance.

The doubts, whatever the reasons for them, were in any event removed by the Native Rights Act 1865, which (among other things) declared that every Maori whenever born was deemed to be a natural-born British subject. Hence, when the question of the legal status of Maori in arms against the Crown was referred to James Prendergast, as Attorney-General in 1869, he had no hesitation in advising (though even apart from the Act of 1865) that they were British subjects, who in his view had no claim to be treated as belligerents entitled to the usages of war, as distinct from being treated as rebels.[10] Even if and where they were 'rebels', his view on the latter point need not be accepted, based as it was on the assumption that, of the two sides in the fighting, Maori alone committed atrocities. But, on the status of Maori as British subjects in the new imperial-colonial order, his opinion, based essentially on the Crown's assertion of its sovereignty through acts of state, concurs with the accepted view.

However, the Secretary of State for the Colonies (the Duke of Newcastle), in a despatch to Governor Grey in 1863, accepted as 'quite notorious' that 'the allegiance of the natives has never been more than nominal'.[11] In the same year J. C. Richmond, debating the Suppression of Rebellion Bill, said that '[s]ubstantially the Natives never had been subject to the Crown'.[12] Those statements were true generally of the areas of Maori autonomy that existed in the 19th century. The Crown's acts of state of 1840 that in law annexed New Zealand anticipated the imperial-colonial exercises of power that brought those areas to an end and that enforced the Crown's claim to the allegiance of Maori and established their status as subjects in fact as well as law. Professor James Belich writes of the Taranaki and Waikato conflicts that they were 'more akin to classic wars of conquest than we would like to believe'.[13] No doubt the observation may be true of the New Zealand wars generally, especially when they were waged against hapu whose chiefs had not signed the Treaty of Waitangi.

In these matters legal difficulties abound. Governor Grey achieved the 'pacification' of the Wairarapa in 1847 by a use of martial law that in important respects appears to have been illegal by the rules of the system he was attempting to impose. It appears so at least in the detention of Te Rauparaha without trial and in the condemnation by court martial of 'rebels' charged with treason. In neither matter did Grey give good reason for not proceeding in the regular courts.[14]

Then there was the matter of the Waitara purchase in Taranaki.[15] The Crown, in claiming the allegiance of Maori and asserting their status as British subjects under the new revolutionary legal order, was entitled to treat them as rebels only where they made war on the Crown (so that martial law could be used against them) and not where its forces gratuitously made war on *them*. Wiremu Kingi's chiefly veto of the Waitara purchase, which precipitated the attack by government troops on the Te Atiawa people that began the First Taranaki War in 1860, may be upheld as a matter of common law, as an incident of the aboriginal customary title recognized in *R v Symonds*.[16] (That it may be upheld also as an exercise of rangatiratanga guaranteed by article 2 of the Treaty of Waitangi, which did not give a *legal* basis for the veto, is another matter.) Maori resistance at Waitara was then, at least initially, self-defence against unlawful attacks by the armed forces of the Crown, and not rebellion. So also (though the matter may be more complicated) in the Bay of Plenty hostilities that followed the killings, by Maori, of the Revd Carl Volkner and of James Fulloon, in 1865;[17] on the facts the Crown's use of its forces to apprehend the killers appears to have gone beyond that limited purpose to extend to waging war on the Ngati Awa and Tuwharetoa people.[18]

The Crown's concern to secure its sovereignty — to carry out and complete the revolution begun in 1840 — could lead it to make war on those it claimed as its subjects when they were not actually in rebellion, so that they, in terms of the very legal system that was being imposed on them, were entitled to resist in self-defence. No doubt the nature of Maori participation in the hostilities was always likely to change from self-defence within common law principles to counter-aggression. Where it did so, then in the colonial legal system being imposed Maori came into rebellion and force could lawfully be used against them. That the rebellion might nevertheless be justified (for example as an exercise of the right to rebel discussed in chapter 3) is another matter. The immediate point is that the Crown, in carrying out the revolutionary seizure of New Zealand, had by the very proclamations of sovereignty in 1840 bound itself to treat Maori as its subjects and under its own municipal law did not have the same free hand to deal with them by acts of state that it would have had if it had simply embarked on a war of conquest. This should have been to the practical advantage of the Maori. But on the other hand, in what were in many cases really wars of conquest, Maori whose status as subjects was nominal were (to their certain disadvantage) liable on capture to be treated and punished as if the status were real, and to be denied the protection which, as enemies and not subjects, they might claim under the laws of war.

Undoubtedly because of the unreality of the Crown's claim to Maori allegiance and to sovereignty over the whole country, those captured in arms were not always treated as rebels but, at least in later stages of the Taranaki and Waikato wars of the 1860s, were generally treated as prisoners of war (as would be appropriate in a war between nations).[19] That is, the unreality of the claim to their allegiance was recognized. But this was not so on all occasions. The Disturbed Districts Act 1869,[20] after referring unambiguously in the preamble to the 'open rebellion' of 'certain aboriginal Native subjects of Her Majesty', made special provisions for prompt trial (in the regular courts, not by court martial) of persons charged with certain offences including high treason. Under the Act a large number of prisoners taken in the war against Te Kooti were tried and about a hundred of them sentenced to death. Except in two cases the sentences were commuted to imprisonment. The nominal or notional allegiance was certainly enforced.

Because (at least under the Native Rights Act 1865 and whatever the political realities in parts of the country) all Maori were from the assumption of sovereignty in 1840 British subjects in law, every Crown dealing with Maori over their land should have been in accordance with the common law doctrine of aboriginal title. That meant that such dealings were not acts of state beyond the examination of the courts. Prendergast C.J. (who as Attorney-General advised in 1869 that all Maori were subjects) should have so ruled in *Wi Parata v Bishop of Welllington* (1877).[21] That he and Richmond J. in that case did not do so had important consequences for the development of that doctrine.[22]

Maori autonomy

We have noted the Court of Appeal's observation that '[t]he Queen's writ did not run throughout all districts of New Zealand till long after 1865'.[23]

The areas of autonomy, such as the King Country, persisted into the late 19th century, areas in which the allegiance of Maori to the Queen was nominal or notional only and Maori customary legal systems continued and, significantly, tended at least in some of the areas to become more developed. James Belich has described the King Country as 'an independent Maori state nearly two-thirds the size of Belgium exist[ing] in the middle of the North Island'.[24] He refers to it as

> ...making and enforcing its own laws, conducting its own affairs, sheltering fugitives from *Pakeha* justice, and killing Europeans who crossed its borders without permission.[25]

And in the 1890s, even after actual resistance to the Crown had 'ceased to be realistic ... [t]he King Movement was still collecting taxes, administering justice, and discouraging land-sales in the 1890s'.[26]

Although he had earlier been somewhat sceptical about the effectiveness of the rule of the Maori King,[27] in one of his last writings Sir Keith Sinclair quoted with implied approval Belich's territorial comparison of the King Country with Belgium.[28] And he quoted James Cowan's description of another of the autonomous areas, Parihaka, run by the prophets Te Whiti and Tohu, as 'a little republic,' and an 1881 visitor's description of it as 'New Zealand's Andorra'.[29] Sinclair added:

> ...the government's relations with the Maori King and the prophet Te Whiti did not involve governing them. Rather, relations were more like those of diplomacy between independent European states[30]

— and went on to give a detailed account of those relations in the latter part of the century.

The Maori King governed with the aid of his runanga or council. There were also runanga in individual iwi or hapu,[31] providing (with the King's government) a means of Maori self-government and apparently marking the evolution of more developed legal systems in which Hart's 'secondary rules'[32] (here, rules for the changing and making of rules) became more clearly discernible; and runanga assumed some legislative and judicial functions. An example, recorded by Alan Ward, was the runanga of the Ngatimahuta, which, terming itself a 'Sanhedrin', in 1859 promulgated a brief code of criminal offences.[33] Ward notes the clear Biblical influence here and the tendency of Maori to 'see themselves as analogous to the Jews'; specifically one may speculate that the Ngatimahuta had in mind the autonomy allowed by Rome to the Jews (as to other peoples of its empire) of which the Sanhedrin was an institution and which is shown in the New Testament accounts of the trials of Jesus and St Paul.[34]

In the King Country itself, much of the organization of the kingdom, whatever its extent, survived the King's making of peace with the colonial government in 1881 and came to include the establishment of the King's Kauhanganui or House of Assembly in 1892. The King's establishment of a bank in about 1886 (cheques and bank notes of which survive) indicates that, unless special rules were made, the English common law as to negotiable instruments must have been adopted or received by the King's government.[35] The laws of the King, though apparently primarily applicable to Maori, were to some extent at any rate enforced among Pakeha residents 'within the sphere of influence of the King'.[36]

Sir Keith Sinclair's account of the relations between the colonial government and King Tawhiao mentions two offers made to him, one in 1875 and one in 1878, to recognize his authority within his district.[37] But the King accepted neither offer because the government would not also return the Waikato land confiscated by it under the New Zealand Settlements Act 1863. Despite the instances of official recognition that the areas of autonomy existed (there were other such areas among the Ngapuhi in the North and the Tuhoe in the Urewera country), their legal status remained de facto — indeed counter-revolutionary — in relation to the Crown's claims to a sovereignty nominally extending throughout the country. In reality, of course, they were simply areas to which the Crown's revolution, begun in 1840, had not extended; and where, even after active resistance ceased, Maori self-government, claimed under pre-revolutionary legal orders and article 2 of the Treaty of Waitangi, persisted until the areas finally ceased to exist about the end of the century.

Section 71 of the New Zealand Constitution Act

Yet questions remain, questions linked with the often-referred-to but seldom closely examined section 71 of the New Zealand Constitution Act 1852. The Crown might have been wrong in law (quite apart from the reservation of tino rangatiratanga in article 2 of the Treaty of Waitangi) in its view that Maori self-government in the King Country and elsewhere had at the most no more than de facto status. There were two closely related possibilities of argument on the point. It might have been argued that the Crown's dealings with iwi, hapu or other Maori polities (such as the Kingitanga or the Parihaka community) gave them the status of domestic dependent nations after the North American model in United States law.[38] Sir Keith Sinclair's account would give some support to that. Then it might also be argued on slightly different ground that the common law doctrine of aboriginal rights was received in New Zealand as 'part of a body of fundamental constitutional law' necessarily incident to the acquisition of British sovereignty, and that it included limited rights of Maori self-government.[39]

Whether or not those arguments could have been maintained will appear from the close consideration that section 71 of the 1852 Act requires. The section was one of the remaining provisions of that Act in force until repeal by the Constitution Act 1986 (NZ) and had been one of those beyond the General Assembly's power of repeal or amendment until 1947. Section 71 read:

> 'And whereas it may be expedient that the Laws, Customs, and Usages of the aboriginal or native Inhabitants of *New Zealand*, so far as they are not repugnant to the general Principles of Humanity, should for the present be maintained for the Government of themselves, in all their Relations to and Dealings with each other, and that particular Districts should be set apart within which such Laws, Customs, or Usages should be so observed:'
>
> It shall be lawful for Her Majesty, by any Letters Patent to be issued under the Great Seal of the United Kingdom, from Time to Time to make Provision for the Purposes aforesaid, any repugnancy of any such native Laws, Customs, or Usages to the Law of *England,* or any Law, Statute, or Usage in force in *New Zealand,* or in any Part thereof, in anywise notwithstanding.

The view that section 71 of itself permitted the continuation of areas of Maori autonomy has been held by some. Indeed it has been recently argued in the Court of Appeal that the section has that effect today (apparently even despite repeal by the Constitution Act 1986) by an appellant claiming a customary right to be tried in accordance with Maori law and tikanga for an alleged drug offence.[40] The Court rejected the argument. Quite apart from the effect of the repeal, the 'continued application [of Maori laws, customs and usages under section 71] required the issuing of letters patent by the Queen. . . .' And it appeared that none had ever been issued.

Section 71, together with its implications and its history, is important despite its never having been given effect either by the Sovereign or (on delegation) by the Governor. The power under the section was, in its terms, exercisable by the Sovereign, necessarily on the advice of a United Kingdom Secretary of State. The provision for delegation to the Governor was in section 79, and delegation in fact occurred at least once (in favour of Governor Gore-Browne in 1858).[41] But section 79 was repealed by the Statute Law Revision Act 1892 (UK). There is no doubt that, from then until section 71 was itself repealed by the Act of 1986, the New Zealand Prime Minister could have requested that a British Secretary of State advise the Sovereign to exercise the power. But apparently there was never such a request (and without the request the power would not be exercised). Indeed even before 1892, the passing of the control of Maori affairs, from the Governor on his own gubernatorial responsibility to (in effect) his ministers in 1863, made it highly unlikely that the power would ever be exercised except at their request. What I have just described is the result of evolving constitutional conventions,[42] which affected the Crown and its legal powers under section 71. (It will be necessary to refer shortly to the more general effect of those conventions on the relationship between Maori and the Crown.)

Then consider the scope of the power and the effect that an exercise of it would have had. It would have overridden any conflicting local New Zealand legislation and could, on a reasonable interpretation, have enabled limited Maori self-government to develop beyond existing customary forms, within the districts set apart for the purpose. But Maori laws, customs and usages (even if part of the rangatiratanga preserved by article 2 of the Treaty of Waitangi) that were 'repugnant to the general Principles of Humanity' would not be preserved; so that, for example, slavery could not exist in any of the districts. We noticed earlier that such a limitation was usual in legislation of this type.[43] Either the Letters Patent exercising the power would have specified what laws etc. were not preserved or, possibly, the role of determining that question would have been assumed by the colonial courts. The degree of autonomy that would have been preserved was not slight, even though necessarily remaining subject to the continuing paramount authority and power of the United Kingdom Parliament.

But there were indications that the section was a temporary measure only. Robert Stout advised Governor Jervois in 1885 that it was (pointing to the phrases 'it may be expedient' and 'should for the present be maintained') and (in effect) that the Native Land Court Act 1880, in dealing with Maori customary ownership of land, now covered the concerns of section 71.[44] The occasion of Stout's advice was King Tawhiao's petition to Queen Victoria in 1884 for Maori self-government in the King Country and the Secretary of State's consequent suggestion to the Governor that provision could properly be made accordingly for the 'Native Territory', by Letters Patent under section 71.

Stout was wrong about the relationship of the Native Land Court Act to section 71. The matter of Maori customary title to land, dealt with however inadequately and improperly in the native land legislation, was the subject of specific provisions in the New Zealand Constitution Act (particularly in sections 72 and 73) which set it apart from the general preservation of Maori laws, customs and usages under section 71. There was no basis for reading down that section so that it should not be used to preserve a limited Maori autonomy in the districts contemplated by it. Indeed, Stout's interpretation left very little scope for the section to operate at all. He was right, though, about the apparently temporary purpose of the section. Nevertheless it was not subject to any time limit and could, if implemented, have modified the results of the revolution begun in 1840, giving districts such as the King Country a domestic, dependent nation status that might in the event have lasted at least long enough to result, as suggested by Alan Ward, in 'an essentially Maori New Zealand'.[45]

There were at least two occasions when it seems that section 71 came close to being used or where provision similar to it would have been required. In 1875 the colonial government, under Grey as Premier, offered to recognize King Tawhiao's authority over the district, much reduced by the Waikato war and the confiscations, of which he was still head.[46] A similar offer was made by the government in 1878.[47] Tawhiao did not accept the proposals, holding out for the return of the confiscated land. Had he accepted them, either the General Assembly would have had to pass legislation to give effect to the arrangement or, preferably from the Maori point of view, section 71 would have been used for the purpose.

Section 71 has somewhat adverse implications for the possibilities, mentioned above, that Maori polities may have (independently of the section) acquired in law 'domestic dependent nation' status and that the doctrine of aboriginal rights received in New Zealand law included a limited right to autonomy. Despite a degree of practical recognition given by officers of the colonial government in their dealings with rulers of some of the areas of Maori autonomy, the status of those areas (including the King Country) seems to have remained de facto without the kind of legal recognition under section 71 that could have resulted in their having that status. There is the implication also that, without effect given to the section, Maori laws, customs and usages relating to self-government were not preserved as part of the received doctrine of aboriginal rights, specifically recognized in respect of title to land in section 73 and other sections of the Act of 1852.

The division of the Crown: another revolution?

> They ... clearly distinguished between the Crown and the current government, and were adamant that the treaty was not an acceptance of the subsequent settler controlled structures of 'responsible government' which te iwi Maori had never authorised.

So wrote Jane Kelsey[48] of the kaumatua whose affidavits were before the Court of Appeal in the celebrated case of *New Zealand Maori Council v Attorney-General* (the *SOE* case).[49]

On the same matter I have myself written:

> ... the chiefs could scarcely be expected to understand that they were making a pact with a Sovereign ... whose political capacity was exercised by ministers responsible to ... [the imperial] Parliament but then also, as would become the case with the advance of colonial self-government, by ministers in New Zealand responsible to the colonial General Assembly.[50]

The effect of the Treaty of Waitangi was that Maori did, so to speak, marry unknowingly into the complicated British constitutional order. Half of the problem was, as we have seen, that the Queen in her imperial Parliament claimed sovereign power even over the Treaty itself. The other half is that without Maori consent the imperial Crown's responsibilities under the Treaty passed through constitutional convention to (in effect) the local New Zealand government and ultimately, in law, to a separate Crown in right of New Zealand. How did this happen?

The Crown with which the Treaty of Waitangi was made, and which by revolution in relation to the Maori tribal legal orders assumed sovereignty over New Zealand, was an imperial unity. To put the matter so far as possible in the personal terms that fit traditional constitutional theory and are consistent with the Maori understanding of the matter, the Queen was an imperial constitutional entity and, generally on acquiring sovereignty in her colonies, remained that. But in general she could act only on the advice of ministers who, by the convention that had developed, had to command the confidence of the House of Commons as the elected House. As long as her Governor of New Zealand, appointed by her on the advice of a United Kingdom Secretary of State, was responsible to her through her United Kingdom ministers for the governing (kawanatanga) of Maori, the constitutional fact that her personal role in relation to Maori was really a fiction did not matter much in the colonial context taken as a whole (and putting aside questions about the legitimacy of the whole enterprise of colonization). That was the state of affairs when the Treaty was signed and the colony began. What did matter and was (on any interpretation) not contemplated by the Treaty was the switching in 1863 of the conventions of responsible government in Maori matters from, to put it briefly, the Queen's administration in the United Kingdom to her administration in New Zealand; so that in future the Governor as the Queen's delegate would under the convention now applicable deal with such matters on the advice of the Crown's local ministers responsible to the General Assembly, rather than on behalf of ministers responsible to the imperial Parliament.

But the Governor still remained subject to Royal Instructions — in effect of course those of the imperial government. When the switch took place, the Secretary of State (the Duke of Newcastle) was at pains to inform Governor Grey that, although now the constitutional position in native policies was generally to be the same as for other colonial matters (in respect of which there had been local responsible government since 1856), nevertheless

> ...you would be bound to exercise the negative powers which you possess by preventing any step which... was at variance with the pledges on the faith of which Her Majesty's Government acquired the sovereignty of New Zealand, or in any other way marked by evident injustice towards Her Majesty's subjects of the native race.[51]

The negative powers referred to were those standard in the Royal Instructions to colonial Governors, that the Governor was to be guided by the advice of his Executive Council but, if he saw 'sufficient cause', might act in opposition to the Council's opinion, and was then to report that he had done so to the Secretary of State.[52]

But there was progressively less and less possibility that any Governor (or Governor-General) would ever exercise the negative powers in the way contemplated in the despatch just quoted.

Yet these developments, though obviously of great importance, were matters of convention only. There was as yet no Crown in right of New Zealand as a separate constitutional entity to which the imperial Crown's obligations under the Treaty of Waitangi (whatever their nature) had passed. As late as 1912 Williams J. in the Court of Appeal in *Tamihana Korokai v Solicitor-General*,[53] in rejecting the Solicitor-General's contention that he could exercise a prerogative power to prevent certain proceedings from being taken in the Native Land Court, said:

> If the Crown has this power it is exercised on the advice of the Responsible Minister of the Crown. Whether it should be so exercised or not is a matter affecting the honour of the Crown, not merely as the Sovereign of this Dominion, but as the Sovereign of the British Empire. It was with the Sovereign of the British Empire that the Treaty of Waitangi was entered into. Whether Imperial obligations should or should not be observed is a matter of Imperial concern for the Responsible Advisers of the Crown in Great Britain to decide upon, and not for the Advisers of the Governor here, unless the power of deciding has been expressly delegated to the Governor.[54]

That passage appears consistent with the Duke of Newcastle's instruction to Grey quoted above, at least to the extent that, even though generally in Maori matters the Governor must act on the advice of the colonial ministers, yet in extreme circumstances he should on behalf of the Crown use his 'negative powers' to prevent the colonial government from acting in breach of the Treaty of Waitangi.

Such a suggestion would admittedly be difficult to reconcile with the imperial government's practice of referring Maori deputations to the monarch (at least those of 1882 and 1884 to Queen Victoria)[55] to the colonial government in Wellington, except on the ground that extreme circumstances had not arisen to justify intervention by the imperial government. However that may be, the passage indicates the Judge's view — undoubtedly correct at the time — that in 1912 the Crown was still an imperial unity with its responsibilities under the Treaty (whatever their exact nature) still intact and not relegated to a separate New Zealand Crown. No such separate legal entity existed. The Crown indeed had its imperial government in Westminster and a local colonial government in Wellington but remained a constitutional unity.

Obviously things have changed since then. Maori recourse to the United Kingdom — no longer imperial — government for the remedying of grievances has long been legally and constitutionally barred, even were the most extreme circumstances of Pakeha oppression alleged. Maori have recourse to the New Zealand government only. The 'settler controlled structures of "responsible government"' to which Jane Kelsey referred only partly explain this development, for those conventions left in the hands of the Crown acting on the advice of its United Kingdom ministers a residue of legal powers in respect of New Zealand. There has been an actual change in the law, that has divided the Crown, so that those powers have been annulled. The change has come about quite apart from, though consistently with, the constitutional steps that were taken in the evolution of New Zealand from one of the self-governing colonies of the Crown to one of its several independent realms. I must briefly trace those steps before suggesting that it is by yet another revolution that the Crown has been divided.

The adoption of the conventions of responsible government in 1856 (generally extended to Maori matters in 1863), and the development of a convention that the imperial Parliament would not legislate for New Zealand (as one of the major self-governing colonies or 'Dominions') without its request or consent, meant that, as in the case of the other Dominions, the facts of the country's autonomy were apparently not matched in the relevant law, under which the status of the Dominions was still colonial. Hence the Statute of Westminster 1931 which, though in not very clear terms, brought the law more in line with the facts by, among other things, freeing the Dominions from the restrictions of the Colonial Laws Validity Act 1865.[56] New Zealand belatedly adopted the Statute of Westminster in 1947. The combined effect of its doing so and of the New Zealand Constitution (Amendment) Act 1947[57] was to confer on the General Assembly full legislative power, including full power to amend the remaining sections of the New Zealand Constitution Act 1852. Exercises of that power culminated in the enactment of the Constitution Act 1986 now in force.

That Act has replaced the remains of the old Act of 1852 and severed all dependence on legislation of the United Kingdom Parliament by declaring the New Zealand Parliament's own supreme power and providing that not only the Act of 1852 but also the Statute of Westminster and the New Zealand Constitution (Amendment) Act 1947 are no longer in force in New Zealand.

In the meantime, in 1983, new Letters Patent reconstituting the office of Governor-General[58] had been issued by the Queen on the advice of her New Zealand Prime Minister, omitting the subordination of the Governor-General to the United Kingdom government (evidenced, for example, by the 'negative powers' referred to by the Secretary of State in his 1863 despatch to Governor Grey) that had been carried over from previous, colonial-type Letters Patent.

The result of all this is that New Zealand is an independent constitutional monarchy, with the Crown in right of New Zealand an entity separate from what used to be the unitary imperial Crown. The country's Parliament, unfettered by a basic written constitution (since the Act of 1986 is repealable like any other), claims the sovereign power that Diceyan orthodoxy ascribes to the United Kingdom Parliament.

I have argued elsewhere that the Constitution Act 1986 made a revolutionary break with the old imperial legal order and in Kelsen's terms a change in the *grundnorm* or basic norm of New Zealand law.[59] More accurately perhaps, that Act completed a revolutionary break already taking place in the facts of the movement of paramount power from London to Wellington and the revolutionary emergence of the Crown in right of New Zealand as a separate legal entity. The constitutional legislation (including the 1983 Letters Patent) referred to above is *consistent* with the division of the once unitary imperial Crown: that is, a division that creates a separate New Zealand Crown, leaving the Crown in right of the United Kingdom and its dependent territories as, so to speak, a residual imperial Crown. But there is nothing in that or other legislation that even by implication *creates* the division.[60]

Section 2 of the Constitution Act 1986, which might be supposed to deal with the matter, simply provides, in subsection (1), that '[t]he Sovereign in right of New Zealand is the head of State of New Zealand, and shall be known by the royal style and titles proclaimed from time to time'. That section, the Royal Titles Act 1974 to which it refers and the Letters Patent of 1983 at the most do no more than acknowledge that the Crown in right of New Zealand as a separate constitutional entity has come into existence.

When and how did it come into existence? As late as 1976[61] I argued that the older doctrine of the Crown as a legal and constitutional unity but with separate governments in its various territories was legally correct and still adequate to explain what long before then had become the real independence of New Zealand and the other former Dominions still acknowledging the Queen as Head of State. That view, however, did not take sufficient account of the problem of treaty and other obligations undertaken by the Crown as an imperial unity in relation to the aboriginal inhabitants of the territories it acquired as colonies. Did those obligations (whatever their exact nature) still bind the Crown's government in the United Kingdom? If they had passed, and passed wholly and exclusively, to the government of the ex-colony in question, when and how did that happen? Those questions, when asked in the New Zealand context, are obviously important for the Treaty of Waitangi.

The answer comes mainly from a consideration of the judgments of the English Court of Appeal in *R v Secretary of State ex parte Indian Association of Alberta* (1982).[62] In that case aboriginal groups attempted to hold the Crown in right of the United Kingdom to obligations under George III's proclamation of 1763 and under treaties entered into with the Indian Nations at times before this century, when the Crown was an imperial unity. The action could not have succeeded save as a bare assertion of legal principle, for there was nothing the United Kingdom could do effectively — there had long been nothing it could do — to perform the Crown's obligations under the treaties. The obligations must have passed exclusively to the Crown in right of Canada as a constitutional entity distinct from the Crown in right of the United Kingdom as the residual imperial Crown. The Court of Appeal so held but the Judges differed among themselves as to the reasons.

The Master of the Rolls, Lord Denning, held that the Crown, originally single and indivisible, had become separate and divisible 'according to the particular territory in which it was sovereign', in the first half of this century; so that the obligations of the Crown had become divided and those in question no longer binding on the Crown in right of the United Kingdom. This change he based simply on 'constitutional usage and practice'.[63] Kerr L.J., on the other hand, found the division much earlier and in law rather than convention recently become law, in the long-established distinction between the separate governments of the Crown in its various territories.[64] That is, the setting up of a local colonial government was in itself sufficient to create in law a separate local Crown upon which the obligations of the imperial Crown to the indigenous people immediately devolved. But that is to formulate a quite unjust general rule which would allow the old imperial Crown to shed generally its obligations to the indigenous people on to the colonial government (to be satisfied exclusively out of local funds which the colonial legislature might be unwilling or financially unable to grant), long before imperial control had ceased to be a reality. Lord Denning's judgment by contrast has the merit of being much more closely related to the facts of imperial control and developing colonial independence.

Essentially the same question came again before an English Court in *Noltcho v Attorney-General*[65] in regard to treaties entered into with the Indian Nations. Vice-Chancellor Megarry followed the *Alberta* case, albeit in some puzzlement, noting that on Lord Denning's view there is 'nothing to explain just how constitutional usage and practice changed the law'[66] nor when exactly the change was made. (Indeed there is a general rule that constitutional conventions — usages or practices that have acquired that status — cannot crystallize into law; a necessary rule since without it the formal legal rules for changing the constitution could be by-passed simply by the less certain development of constitutional conventions.)[67] However, the House of Lords, in refusing leave to appeal against the *Alberta* judgments, had endorsed the 'accumulated reasons'[68] given by the Court of Appeal. Megarry V.-C. accordingly stated the position as best he could, in terms closer to those of Lord Denning's judgment than those of Kerr L.J.:

> The Crown's promises [under the treaties] were made by the Crown as sovereign. If sovereignty is transferred, the obligation to do sovereign acts can no longer remain with the sovereign which no longer has sovereignty over the territory where the acts are to be performed. ... *Just how the doctrine works may seem to be obscure, but that is no doubt due to our frail vision: what the* Alberta *case shows is that somehow it does work, and work beyond a peradventure.*[69]

The only explanation of the mystery referred to in the words I have emphasized lies in the concept of revolutionary change. It can only be that the facts of constitutional life[70] — in this case the facts of the long-standing autonomy of the Dominions that made them independent states (recognized as such in international law), where the imperial government was politically powerless to intervene — had added such weight to custom and usage that the originally indivisible Crown had divided with the legal consequences we are discussing.

When did the division occur? The precise time may be impossible to determine. One may be reasonably sure that, in the case of New Zealand, it had not occurred when in 1882 and 1884 the imperial government referred Maori deputations to Queen Victoria back to the colonial government,[71] so that the only justification for its doing so was that extreme circumstances warranting its intervention on behalf of the Queen had not arisen. In light of Williams J.'s opinion in *Tamihana Korokai's* case in 1912 to the effect that the Crown was then still an imperial unity,[72] the same may be the case with the similarly treated Maori deputation to George V in 1914; perhaps on the other hand the 1924 deputation to him came after the division and too late to invoke London intervention however extreme the circumstances. One can only speculate. But that it has occurred, probably (as Lord Denning thought) some time in the first half of the century, is beyond doubt, and only a quiet revolution can adequately explain the occurrence. The important consequence of this revolution is that, as the Privy Council stated in *New Zealand Maori Council v Attorney-General* (1993),[73] after quoting the English version of the Treaty of Waitangi, 'the obligations of Her Majesty, the Queen of England, under the Treaty are now those of the Crown in right of New Zealand' — and by implication not those of the Crown in right of the United Kingdom (so to speak, the residual imperial Crown).

The imperial government's willingness to shed its Treaty responsibilities on to the colonial government in Wellington was, as we have seen, given effect through the extension to Maori matters of the conventions of responsible government already established in the colony. As long as the Crown remained an imperial unity, the former government might still have attempted to exercise a residual legal power (unaffected by the conventions) to protect Maori from breaches of the Treaty but only, one must suppose, in most extreme circumstances that were presumably never thought to arise. Then the division of the Crown removed even that remote possibility. All this occurred without the consent of Maori, whose Treaty was with the Crown as an imperial unity. The shift in paramount power from London to Wellington, which culminated in a division of the Crown that was revolutionary in that no legislation provided for it, was something beyond Maori control. Whether or not the Constitution Act 1986, in severing completely the New Zealand Parliament's constitutional links with its United Kingdom creator, effected (as in my view it did) a 'quiet revolution', the division of the Crown clearly did effect one, as a kind of sequel to the revolutionary seizure of power which, as an imperial unity, the Crown began in 1840.

The personal identity of the monarch necessarily remains despite the revolutionary division of the Crown. Though the constitutional entities are separate, the Queen of the United Kingdom is also the Queen of New Zealand. The Maori perception of Queen Victoria and her successors as personally bound by a Treaty, made by her in her political capacity on ministerial advice, was the understandable consequence of the archaic forms of government in a constitutional monarchy. The perception has always been unrealistic (except insofar as Queen Victoria herself may perhaps have had sufficient personal influence to insist on receiving the deputations of 1882 and 1884 had she wished).[74] But this particular difficulty is unconnected with the revolutionary division of the Crown — that is, of the monarch's political capacities.

Chapter 4 began with a reference to Dr David Williams's initially Kelsenian approach to New Zealand constitutional origins. Taking up and adapting the same approach (with some mention too of H. L. A. Hart) we postulated a succession of revolutions, the first one begun by the Crown in 1840, which in the end superseded throughout the country the Maori customary legal orders that had existed. In that the Crown asserted in 1840 a sovereignty over New Zealand that was nominal in regard to vast areas of it, the Maori resistance to the revolution could be seen as counter-revolutionary. The Maori areas of autonomy showed legal systems developing from an originally customary base, as in the King Country. But the areas of autonomy ceased to exist about the turn of the century. In Kelsen's terms, the systems of norms which constituted the Maori legal orders in the areas of autonomy ceased to be by and large effective, and the basic norm for each such area could no longer be presupposed to accord legal validity to the system.

Is the position still the same today or does a Maori legal order exist based on the tino rangatiratanga reserved by article 2 of the Treaty of Waitangi? Professor Paul Havemann, in discussing the views of the radical nationalist writers Moana Jackson and Annie Mikaere, apparently intends to adopt a Kelsenian analysis when he writes of their rejection of the orthodox notion that there is a single *grundnorm* (he uses the untranslated term) 'for testing the validity of law in New Zealand', one which results on his account from the alleged cession of sovereignty under the Treaty.[75] On the account I offer in this book the *grundnorm* of the original colonial legal order was established not so much by the Treaty as by the facts of the British assumption of power. But however that may be (and whatever the revolutionary history since), there is no doubt that the *grundnorm* of the present New Zealand constitutional order does not include the rangatiratanga reserved by article 2 or any part of it. Indeed, as Havemann in effect shows, the writers he is discussing really postulate an altogether separate *grundnorm*, for a separate Maori legal system, giving full effect to tino rangatiratanga. But until there is a separate Maori system of norms, based in tino rangatiratanga and functioning by and large effectively to constitute a new and separate legal order, Mr Jackson, Mrs Mikaere and similar writers are appealing to a *grundnorm* that does not exist.

That is not to deny that their writings raise serious questions about the legitimacy, as distinct from legality, of parts of the present legal order. We turn to such questions in chapter 6.

The revolution and the land: the Legislature and common law Maori title

The New Zealand Constitution Act 1852, creating and empowering the General Assembly of the colony, recognized in section 73 that the 'aboriginal Natives' had rights in the land. That was a clear recognition of the common law doctrine discussed in an earlier chapter; and indeed section 73 is in accordance with that doctrine, as well as with article 2 of the Treaty of Waitangi, in providing that the Crown alone may extinguish the Maori customary title. Following Brian Slattery, we may take the doctrine to have come to New Zealand as 'part of a body of fundamental constitutional law that was logically prior to the introduction of English common law' as a whole.[76] I accept that distinction myself but it is not essential: one may simply see the doctrine as part of the English common law received in New Zealand as at 14 January 1840, which by statute became the general date of reception.[77]

As the Court of Appeal explained in *Te Runanganui o Te Ika Whenua Inc Soc v Attorney-General* (1994) (in terms that once applied generally throughout the Crown's possessions):

> Aboriginal title is a compendious expression to cover the rights over land and water enjoyed by the indigenous or established inhabitants of a country up to the time of its colonization. On the acquisition of the territory, whether by settlement, cession or annexation, the colonizing power acquires a radical or underlying title which goes with sovereignty. Where the colonizing power has been the United Kingdom, that title vests in the Crown. But, at least in the absence of special circumstances displacing the principle, the radical title is subject to the existing native rights.[78]

The doctrine limited in certain respects the Crown's revolutionary seizure of Aotearoa New Zealand and hence provides one of the factors partly legitimating that seizure; much as it has done historically as one of the means of partly fulfilling the just expectations of those who have had to submit to conquest or imperialist revolution.

That history, as is well known, has been somewhat patchy. In *R v Symonds* (1847)[79] Martin C.J. and H.S. Chapman J. applied the doctrine, following a persuasive line of authority from the United States Supreme Court. In effect, Maori customary title was recognized as a legal encumbrance on the radical or allodial title that the Crown acquired on assuming sovereignty over New Zealand and it would last until extinguished either by purchase by the Crown or by other legal means. Then further recognition followed in a dictum of the Colony's Court of Appeal, *In re 'The Lundon and Whitaker Claims Act, 1871'* (1872):

> The Crown is bound, both by the common law of England and by its own solemn engagements, to a full recognition of Native proprietary right.[80]

Apparently overlooking or misunderstanding that dictum, and misunderstanding both the judgments in the *Symonds* case and also the American authorities, Prendergast C.J. and Richmond J. in *Wi Parata v Bishop of Wellington*[81] reached the quite different conclusion that such rights existed (to anticipate North J.'s statement of the matter 90 years later *In re the Ninety Mile Beach* (1963), quoted below), only by 'grace and favour' of the Crown, being cognizable by the courts only if they were given effect in statute law. Notwithstanding decisions of the Privy Council in cases around the turn of the century, which substantially recognized the common law doctrine, the *Wi Parata* view prevailed; until, dealing with customary fishing rights (to which the doctrine applies as well as to land), the judgment of Williamson J. in *Te Weehi v Regional Fisheries Officer* (1986)[82] began the New Zealand revival of the doctrine. The revival is now complete, as shown by the passage quoted above from the Court of Appeal's judgment in *Te Runanganui o Te Ika Whenua Inc Soc v Attorney-General*.[83]

In early controversies in the colony it was argued that the doctrine was limited to land effectively possessed (actually cultivated or lived upon) by Maori. But the New Zealand courts, even when rejecting the common law nature of the doctrine and applying it only under statute, held that no part of the country was outside Maori customary ownership noting that this was the position accepted by the 'Governor and Legislature of New Zealand . . . [and in] numerous Ordinances and Acts of Parliament passed to enable the Maoris to transmute their customary title into freehold'.[84]

I do not attempt a full study of the doctrine here but concentrate on the Crown's power, and the power of Parliament (i.e., of the Crown in Parliament) to extinguish the customary title. As to the former, the Crown could extinguish the title by purchase or by acts of state when asserting sovereignty by the proclamations of May 1840 (though I know of no instances of the latter).

What, though, of later seizures of Maori land by the Crown? In the century or so when the doctrine was substantially rejected or misunderstood, New Zealand cases, beginning with *Wi Parata v Bishop of Wellington* (1877), treated all grants of land by the Crown as implying conclusive declarations by it that the Maori rights had been properly extinguished; the Crown's dealings with Maori were, it was held, acts of state, even (it was clearly implied) when occurring after the assumption of sovereignty. Hence they were unexaminable by the courts. Consistently with that, North J. remarked *In re the Ninety Mile Beach (*1963)[85] that 'on the assumption of British sovereignty — apart from the Treaty of Waitangi — the rights of the Maoris to their tribal lands depended wholly on the grace and favour of Her Majesty Queen Victoria.. .'. Somewhat similarly but without recourse to the act of state doctrine, and according a degree of recognition to customary title denied in *Wi Parata's* case and *In re the Ninety Mile Beach*, it was held by the High Court of Australia in *Mabo's* case [86] that the aboriginal title could be extinguished by a Crown grant inconsistent with it.

But as we have seen,[87] any such views — even in the latter case — are criticizable on the ground that (to refer to the New Zealand context) the Crown by its assumption of sovereignty claimed Maori as its subjects; so that thereafter their property rights, including customary title to land, could not be infringed under the prerogative. That is, the Crown could not and cannot, without legislative authority, extinguish the customary title; and it has (though without reference to the reason just given) recently been so held.[88]

If there was some doubt about the Crown's prerogative power in this matter, there was and is none about the power of the Crown *in Parliament.* That is, in the imperial-colonial legal system introduced by the Crown's revolutionary assumption of sovereignty, legislation of the United Kingdom Parliament could legally extinguish Maori customary title or give the Crown as the executive the authority to do that. It was at first more doubtful whether the New Zealand General Assembly, under the 1852 Constitution Act that created it, had the same power as its United Kingdom parent. To take the most obvious instance, did the General Assembly have the power to enact the confiscatory provisions of the New Zealand Settlements Act 1863, that enabled the Governor to carry out the raupatu?

At the time, the repugnancy proviso in section 53 of the Act of 1852 — that the General Assembly must not make laws 'repugnant to the laws of England' — had not been effectively clarified and narrowed, by sections 2 and 3 of the Colonial Laws Validity Act 1865, to apply only to Acts of the United Kingdom Parliament that extended 'by express words or necessary intendment' to New Zealand. The repugnancy proviso, until so clarified and narrowed, was very vague. The English Law Officers of the Crown were asked to advise the

Secretary of State for the Colonies in effect whether the phrase would invalidate the New Zealand Settlements Act and its companion the Suppression of Rebellion Act 1863. Their advice was, in short, that both were justified as emergency legislation, for '. . . the laws of England have repeatedly recognized the necessity for exceptional legislation, to suppress a rebellion threatening the existence of the State'.[89] (There were precedents in both English and Irish legislation.) At least so far as the New Zealand Settlements Act was concerned, I think their advice was correct, however doubtful some of the instances of its implementation were. Which is really to say that that Act, an important instrument of the Crown's partly revolutionary seizure of power, was valid within the rules which (so to speak) the revolution imposed on itself; and which were applicable at the time as part of the legal order progressively imposed on the country.

It is also clear that other legislation, enabling Maori proprietary rights to be extinguished and the revolution begun in 1840 to be carried forward, has likewise been valid; such as the provisions in successive Acts under which the Native Land Court and then the Maori Land Court have made orders converting the Maori customary title to freehold. One must include also a number of provisions in those Acts (last contained in the Maori Affairs Act 1953) designed, in certain circumstances, also to extinguish the customary title or to prevent its assertion against the Crown.[90]

The power of the New Zealand legislature to enact legislation such as that just discussed was clearer still after that body, freed by the constitutional steps taken in 1947, 1973 and 1986 of any constitutional dependency on the United Kingdom Parliament,[91] became itself a Parliament claiming and exercising supreme power, uncontrolled by a written constitution and subject only to the uncertain common law limitations that we have discussed. If, discarding what has been the orthodox doctrine of parliamentary sovereignty, we test parliamentary power by the record of what Parliament has effectively done, we are unable to impugn the *legal* validity of New Zealand legislation extinguishing Maori title or other customary proprietary rights or rendering them unenforceable against the Crown.

When Sir Hugh Kawharu wrote of the Native Land Court as a 'veritable engine of destruction' for separating Maori from their land,[92] he was referring to operations of that Court which were, like the confiscations under the New Zealand Settlements Act 1863, incidental to the carrying out of the revolution. The operations resulted in the 'freeholding' of Maori land into individual titles of common law co-ownership as distinct from the essentially communal ownership of customary law. Legislation valid under the imperial-colonial legal order authorized them; but again questions of legitimacy remain. Largely in its later history, the revolutionary role of the Native Land Court was admittedly qualified by its protective functions, insufficient though they were. However, under Te Ture Whenua Maori Act 1993 the protective functions are now a dominant characteristic of the present Maori Land Court. Far from being a 'veritable engine of destruction' of Maori land ownership, the Court must as part of its 'primary objective . . . promote and assist in . . . [t]he retention of Maori land and General land owned by Maori . . .'.[93] But in the period of which Sir Hugh Kawharu writes the general role of the Court in furthering the revolution appears clear enough.[94]

The confiscations under the New Zealand Settlements Act 1863, purchases from Maori that were other than fair or occurred under heavy political pressure, the operations of the Native Land Court so far as these were essentially a means of furthering colonization, and statutory provisions directed against the customary title, may all be seen as giving effect to a revolutionary seizure of power over New Zealand. In particular, the 'opening up' of the King Country and of the tribal lands of Tuhoe in the Urewera country, through the work of the Court or through sales under heavy government pressure, show the revolution at work in establishing the settler government's control over areas where Maori autonomy had long survived the Crown's originally nominal assertion of sovereignty.[95]

More recently, one must see the revolutionary power of Parliament exercised where, as by the Treaty of Waitangi (Fisheries Claims) Settlement Act 1992 (dealing with sea fishing), it extinguishes customary common law title or other proprietary rights, in giving effect to a settlement reached with most but not all iwi or hapu over Maori claims that are based on the legal rights as such as well as on confirmation of those rights by article 2 of the Treaty of Waitangi.[96] In relation to dissenting iwi or hapu such legislation might be seen as carrying the Crown's revolution further. That it might be seen as a proper (legitimate) exercise of the kawanatanga claimed by the Crown would, strictly, not be relevant to hapu who dissented from the settlement and who were not party to the Treaty.

It will be seen that in relation to land the revolution was twofold. First, there was the vesting of the radical title to the land in the Crown, in accordance with the theory of English land law; but the vesting was subject to the Maori customary title, which was recognized to exist throughout the country, there being owners for every part of it. Secondly, there was the extinguishment of that customary title by revolutionary means; which is in effect to say, wherever and however it was extinguished otherwise than by fair means and with Maori consent.

Land under water as customary land

Where the customary title remains unextinguished, the land is 'customary land' for the purposes of Te Ture Whenua Maori Act 1993: that is, it is land held by Maori in accordance with tikanga Maori, defined in the Act as 'Maori customary values and practices'[97] and equivalent in our terms to Maori customary law. Very little customary land remains; very little, that is, if one has regard only to land not under water. As to land under water, it may be that much of it remains customary land, in which the Maori title (where it existed) has never been extinguished either by fair means or by means that (as we have seen) were part of the Crown's giving effect to its revolutionary assertion of sovereignty over New Zealand. Here we must note a necessary requirement to the exercise of the power of extinguishment. In words quoted with approval by Blanchard J. in *Faulkner v Tauranga District Council* (1995),[98] Brennan J. said in the High Court of Australia in *Mabo v State of Queensland (No 2)* (1992):

> However, the exercise of a power to extinguish native title must reveal a clear and plain intention to do so, whether the action be taken by the Legislature or by the Executive. This requirement, which flows from the seriousness of the consequences to indigenous inhabitants of extinguishing their traditional rights and interests in land, has been repeatedly emphasized by courts dealing with the extinguishing of the native title of Indian bands in North America.... [R]eference to the leading cases in each [Canadian or United States] jurisdiction reveals that... native title is not extinguished unless there be a clear and plain intention to do so. That approach has been followed in New Zealand. It is patently the right rule.[99]

The Judge's reference to New Zealand is to *Te Weehi v Regional Fisheries Officer (*1986) where Williamson J. remarked of the Canadian cases (and of some United States cases to the same effect) that they

> follow the general approach that customary rights of native or aboriginal peoples may not be extinguished except by way of specific legislation that clearly and plainly takes away the right.[100]

This strict requirement is, so to speak, a limit which the revolution has imposed upon itself. (It is obviously complied with in such a statute as the Treaty of Waitangi (Fisheries Claims) Settlement Act 1992.) We have to take account of it when considering certain types of land under water: river and stream beds, lake beds, foreshore and seabed; at least some areas of which may still be Maori customary land. The issues are complex: not all of them are covered in what follows.

There are general statutory provisions respectively declaring the Crown's ownership of (i) the beds of navigable rivers,[101] (ii) some areas of the foreshore[102] and (iii) the seabed of the internal waters of New Zealand (such as beds of harbours) and of the 12-mile New Zealand territorial sea.[103] But in each case the statutory declaration of vesting appears to be insufficiently specific to extinguish the Maori customary title where it could exist and (but for the question of the effect of the vesting) is shown to exist;[104] except in the case of minerals in the beds of navigable rivers, which are particularly declared to be the absolute property of the Crown.

In the case of most of the foreshore (land between high and low water mark) the bed is vested in the Crown not by statute but at common law. The Court of Appeal held *In re the Ninety Mile Beach* (1963)[105] that a freehold order of the Maori Land Court fixing the seaward boundary of coastal Maori land at high water mark has the effect of extinguishing the Maori customary title in the adjoining portion of foreshore. But, at common law, title to the foreshore or seabed was not necessarily related to title to the adjacent coastal land. There was no reason (other than the avoidance of apprehended inconvenience) for the Court of Appeal to treat a Land Court determination in respect of the latter as affecting the former also. The decision is in any event not consistent in principle with more recent cases recognizing Maori customary title and may well be overruled if and when the matter comes before the Court of Appeal again. In any event, the decision does not apply where the customary title in the coastal land in question was extinguished otherwise than by an order of the Land Court.

The beds of some large lakes, notably Lake Taupo and the Arawa lakes (Lake Rotorua and others), have been declared by statute to be vested in the Crown expressly freed of the Maori customary title.[106] Where that has not been done, and at least if the Crown has not specifically granted any part of the lake bed, its radical or allodial title to the bed will remain subject to the Maori customary title until it is legally extinguished. The customary title to the beds of a number of lakes has been investigated by the Maori Land Court separately from the surrounding riparian land.[107]

In the case of non-navigable rivers and streams, Crown grants of riparian land (that is, land bounded by the river or stream) were at common law presumed to include half the river or stream bed, to the middle line (the *ad medium filum aquae* rule).[108] This presumption was applied by the Court of Appeal to orders of the Maori Land Court extinguishing the customary title in the riparian land. But the former Court has now noted in *Te Runanganui o Te Ika Whenua Inc Soc v Attorney-General (*1994)[109] that the presumption is inconsistent with the Maori conception of a river as a taonga, 'as a whole and indivisible entity, not separated into bed, banks and waters'[110] and 'may well be unreliable in determining what Maori have agreed to part with'.[111] It is uncertain how far, if at all, the observations in this case may raise uncertainty in particular cases as to whether the customary title in a non-navigable stream bed has been extinguished.[112] There would, for example, be no uncertainty in the areas covered by the raupatu, where statutory extinguishment is plain.

Chapter 6: LEGITIMATION OF THE 1840 REVOLUTION; AND THE SPECIAL CASE OF THE CHATHAMS

Walker, Kelsey and the 1840 revolution

The account in chapters 4 and 5 of the revolutions and counter-revolutions that have left in place the present New Zealand legal order dealt with questions of legality. Questions of legitimacy remain. As earlier chapters have shown, success in the seizure of power may attain legality for the revolutionary order and regime, as it has done in New Zealand. But legitimation of the revolution, always assured in the eyes of the successful revolutionaries, may need, among other things, the passage of time to complete it at least partially. In the New Zealand context the Crown's revolution was that, in the seizure of power that it began in 1840, it took more than was ceded by the Treaty of Waitangi by taking more than kawanatanga from the signatories and taking from the hapu who, not being parties to the Treaty, had ceded nothing. The legitimation over time that has ensued has been partial only, in that the just expectations of Maori remain to be fulfilled, in particular by the Crown's fulfilling its obligations under the Treaty, modified though they have been by time and circumstance.

This chapter considers the process by which the Crown's New Zealand revolution has been (as it is argued) thus partly legitimated and the considerations, some of them to be rejected or accepted only in modified form, which have been urged as legitimating it. The theme will be developed from previous writings of mine on the matter. We may begin by seeing how the case set out in those writings, to be more fully argued here, has been responded to by Professors Ranginui Walker and Jane Kelsey.

Their comments were made not directly on any of those writings but on the use made, in 1995, by two ministers of the Crown, of what was then the latest of them, the text of a valedictory lecture given in November 1993 and published the following year.[1] The Hon. Simon Upton[2] and then Sir Douglas Graham (as he now is)[3] both publicly accepted my general thesis of the revolutionary element in the country's constitutional origins and of the legitimating effects of time. Their doing so prompted strong reaction from

Legitimation of the 1840 Revolution

Walker and Kelsey, in comments which may be seen as 'counter-hegemonic discourse' in the Gramscian ideological war of position[4] in which both appear to be engaged.

Professor Walker's comments are in the report of an interview with him by Hineani Melbourne in *Maori Sovereignty: The Maori Perspective*. She reported him to be 'disgusted by the stance taken by Simon Upton and Doug Graham on sovereignty'[5] and quoted him thus:

> They [i.e., the ministers] are finally admitting that the Treaty was a sham document — that we didn't cede mana under the Treaty. We ceded kawanatanga which is not the same thing. They have finally admitted that the Treaty isn't the basis of the Crown's sovereignty — rather it was taken by military force. And they say that over time that becomes legal! What a thing to say![6]

In her important book *The New Zealand Experiment* Kelsey linked the ministers' statements with what she termed 'threats' by 'the government' to charge two radical controversialists, Mike Smith and Annette Sykes, with 'sedition' for predicting violence if radical demands of Maori are not met.[7] In her view the threats were hypocritical in light of the government's now admittedly revolutionary origins:

> Here were two Ministers of the Crown legitimising revolution — indeed, privileging it over other constitutional processes. Yet the same Crown was claiming the moral and legal authority to indict for sedition those Maori who promoted 'revolutionary' means to recover what the colonial state had forcibly taken away.[8]

The statements of both professors are blatantly populist, Walker's no more than an outburst showing no sign he had actually read the material on which the ministers' statements were expressly based. Kelsey's treatment of the possibility of sedition proceedings against Smith and Sykes is facile and imprecise and does not warrant comment here.[9] But more importantly, on the main issue she joins Walker in stating in the New Zealand context a viewpoint directly opposed to that of this book. Though there was no attempt on the part of either to argue the matter carefully with reference to my writings, there is some value in commenting on what they said, by way of leading up to the particular issues of legitimacy to be dealt with in this chapter and without responding in kind to populist polemic.[10]

Walker does no more than state his position baldly, no doubt using the word 'legal' to include the notion of legitimacy. Kelsey apparently draws a distinction between moral and legal authority, between, one may take it, legitimacy and legality. It is useful to consider her linking of the issues with the theoretical question (as distinct from the possibility of proceedings in the particular cases mentioned) of a Maori dissident's liability for sedition, or for that matter treason, in a legal order established substantially by revolutionary overthrow of the Maori customary legal orders.

Chapter 5 showed the partly notional nature of the revolution of 1840, notional in that the Crown's claim to sovereignty extended to vast parts of New Zealand outside its control, so that the allegiance of Maori within those areas was nominal or notional only. In reality it was a revolution that was only begun in that year. There was no doubt that treating those Maori, whom the Crown had never protected, as subjects owing it allegiance and hence liable for treason if they resisted was morally wrong.[11] But where a revolution or conquest has succeeded, historical precedents (one as recent as the Fiji revolutions of 1987)[12] showed clearly that the revolutionary regime is likely to hold the defeated to a new allegiance and do so in most circumstances with at least arguable justification. To repeat the condition laid down in the Pennsylvanian case of *Respublica v Chapman* (1781),[13] those who have opposed the revolution must have a reasonable time to leave the country before they can be so liable. Inevitably that condition must often be illusory, for withdrawal from the country may for many reasons be impossible (though the regime must not impede it). Nevertheless it is difficult to dispute the claim of the Crown, as a regime established by successful revolution, to the allegiance of Maori, dissident or not, who last century in fact came under its protection and effectively subject to its laws, as the Queen's writ progressively came to run throughout the country.

The position will be similar if the future for New Zealand is (as Kelsey sometimes suggests it may be if radical demands are not met)[14] one of a further revolutionary seizure of power. If it is, no doubt the regime of the new order will be as swift to claim the allegiance of defeated dissidents as was the revolutionary regime in Fiji after the revolutions of 1987. That is the way of successful revolutionaries. If ideologically inspired, they will be convinced that they are right to make that claim; and anyway securing revolutionary success with the aid of the newly available instrument of the law is likely to be a matter of necessity.

The Crown's claim to allegiance is obviously the stronger in respect of present-day Maori dissidents, for the revolution has been complete now at least for a century and for much of the country for longer. But that is to introduce the effect of the passage of time as a legitimating factor (which Walker expressly rejects and Kelsey appears to ignore). More of that and of factors associated with it in the New Zealand context will be said below.

In all of this the analysis of earlier chapters is applicable; Aotearoa New Zealand as a whole presents no special case.[15] The legality established by the revolution begun in 1840 acquired in the areas progressively subject to it the minimal legitimacy of a working legal order.[16] But the other considerations relating to legitimacy, ideological, moral, and prescriptive — i.e., involving the passage of time — remain to be considered and applied in the New Zealand context.

The ideologies of colonization

The legitimacy of the constitutional order that the Crown brought, by revolutionary extension, to New Zealand in 1840 rested on 'among other things, the acceptance of the results, over centuries, of civil conflict, successful assertions of political power and the evolutionary force of constitutional custom'.[17] Distinguishing here between issues of legality and legitimacy is unnecessary for our purpose. In any event, the criteria have changed, in that legitimacy has long depended less on the once all-important rules of succession to the Crown (where the concepts of legality and legitimacy coincide) than on the participation of the people in democratic government through extensions of the franchise and on the democratizing of the law itself that we noted in chapter 3.

The institutions and practices that legitimated the imperial legal order in the country of its origin would, from the point of view of the settlers, legitimate a subordinate colonial legal order like that of New Zealand, as imported into the colony in forms adapted to local circumstances. But, as William Renwick has written of the evolution of colonial autonomy in which the Governor came to be subject locally to the conventions of responsible government:

> In the standard Pakeha reading of our history this was celebrated as a quite proper transition to internal political self-determination. But to Maori, it meant that, instead of standing between Maori and settler, the Crown had been annexed by the settlers' duly elected representatives.[18]

The imperial Crown had assumed the role of protecting and securing the rights and interests of Maori under the Treaty. Indeed, if one has regard to the historical instances and the common law doctrines, Maori might properly have claimed their rights to property and expected a limited autonomy, even without the Treaty. At all events, acts done by the Crown in performance of the protective role would have been legitimate as well as legal, beyond the minimal legitimacy attaching to acts done as part of a working legal order,[19] even though the actual seizure of power at least partly lacked legitimacy. In fact, as we have seen, the Crown in effect abdicated from the protective role in favour of its colonial government, without first leaving in place a secure constitutional structure that would enable Maori expectations to be fulfilled so far as was possible within the polity created by the revolution.

How far those expectations are being fulfilled today and how they may be fulfilled in the future are matters dealt with later in this and in the final chapter. First I want to consider the respects in which the Crown's seizure of power, begun in 1840 and carried through by the colonial government, did lack legitimacy and what factors apart from the Crown's fulfilment of obligations under the Treaty of Waitangi might have partly remedied that lack. So far as it took more than was ceded by the Treaty, the seizure was in James Fenton's words, 'an immense intrusion into other people's business'[20] or the 'fair thievish purchase' or large-scale robbery (*magnum latrocinium*) of St Augustine's story of the pirate and the emperor.[21] That is, unless one accepts any of the ideological justifications that have been put forward for it as for other imperialist enterprises.

To Christianize and civilize

In New Zealand one of the principal ideologies of British imperialism, that of Christianizing and civilizing, was thought to support the Crown's seizure of power as strongly as elsewhere in the empire. The duty to Christianize 'the poor benighted Heathens',[22] thought to be imposed by divine command, the universalist claims of Christianity and the particular conviction (at least in the case of evangelicals) that one could be saved only through personal conversion inspired the missionaries; and those that were British (the majority) 'identified themselves with British colonial expansion . . .',[23] though they often defended Maori against colonialist excesses. They diminished rangatiratanga by requiring chiefs to free their slaves before being baptized.[24] Their activities must be seen as part of the 'colonization of Maori philosophy' bitterly deplored by Moana Jackson.[25]

More generally the 'Protestant worldview' and the 'sense of superior difference' which it engendered, described by Linda Colley,[26] was a large part of this ideology of the British imperialist revolutions. Today few (even within the Christian churches, where the duty of mission now appears to be differently understood and in many parts of which universalist claims are much modified) would see the purposes of 'Christianizing and civilizing' as sufficient to justify — to legitimate — seizures of power through which colonization took place. On the other hand, some of the consequences of colonization, in the revolutionary carrying out of those purposes, must be said to have been legitimated and serve to partly legitimate the present order.

'Use or lose'

The Lockean ideology of the moral rightness of expropriating indigenous peoples' lands that were regarded as unoccupied or insufficiently used[27] was abandoned early in New Zealand colonial history, in that it became accepted that for all parts of the country there were Maori owners. Stout C.J. in *Tamihana Korokai v Solicitor-General* (1912)[28] referred to '[a]ll the old authorities' as being unanimous on this, citing Bishop Selwyn and Chief Justice Martin and noting the legislature's recognition of the position in the Maori land legislation. However the Lockean position reappears in a different form in the 'relatively simple view' to which, Tom Brooking writes, 'most settlers adhered', that 'if you did not use your land you deserved to lose it'.[29] This is the ideology of the 1840 revolution in relation to Maori land and the moral justification for the various measures taken by warfare, confiscation, the work of the Native Land Court and unduly heavy pressure upon Maori to sell, that carried out this aspect of the revolution; and which led, for example, to the 'opening up' of the King Country[30] and of the lands of the Tuhoe in the Urewera country.[31] This settlers' view is still widely held, at least to the extent that any doubts about its original moral rightness are removed by consideration of the economic development that has ensued. As in the less controversial matters discussed in the next section, such a justification is ex post facto. What is in effect the original Lockean view has been revived recently by Stuart Scott.[32]

A legitimated consequence of the revolution: the end of Maori slavery

Enslavement of those of the defeated whom the victors permitted to survive was a normal sequel to a Maori tribal victory. Slaves 'by definition, had no mana at all'[33] and could be arbitrarily killed. It appears that at least by the early 19th century they could be traded as property.[34] But they could 'regain status either for themselves or for their children, by inter-marriage or by particular acts of courage or contribution to the community'.[35] Such a process must have corresponded to the formal emancipation of slaves in legally more developed societies. However good the possibilities of regaining status and freedom, the institution was not one which could survive the success of the Crown's revolution. The freeing of a chief's slaves, where insisted on by the missionaries, was a loss to his rangatiratanga which, in the new legal order superseding the customary orders of iwi and hapu, could not be restored. The freeing of other slaves came about gradually, again with the loss of rangatiratanga over them. In a letter to Governor Grey, asking for the Governor's help in controlling his slaves, the chief Tamati Ngapora wrote in 1848: 'Formerly, if slaves were disobedient, they would be killed. If a slave disobeys now we cannot kill him, lest the laws of the Europeans should be infringed upon.'[36]

It is clear that for Tamati Ngapora his authority over his slaves was a part of his rangatiratanga that he had expected to maintain at least in some measure, and just as clear that, under rules imposed through either the Crown's proper exercise of its kawanatanga or its revolutionary seizure of power, he would lose that authority in the new order. It is worth considering for a moment why he would. In England the unfree status of villeinage, which was akin to slavery, had never been formally abolished by Parliament but had disappeared largely through the use of common law remedies enabling a villein to obtain or enforce his or her personal freedom.[37] But local laws had provided for the slavery of blacks in certain of the British colonies and the status of those persons when they were brought to England had been uncertain. Lord Mansfield's judgment in *Somerset v Stewart* (1772)[38] appears not to have been the clear holding against the principle of slavery that it has been thought to be; but rather to have decided the narrower point that the black slave before the Court could not be sent out of the country against his will.

However a Scottish decision followed shortly, *Knight v Wedderburn* (1778)[39] in which slavery was declared contrary to the law of Scotland; and the imperial Act of 1833,[40] generally abolishing slavery throughout the colonies, appears to assume the unlawfulness of the institution in the United Kingdom as a whole. There is no doubt that when the Crown assumed sovereignty over New Zealand, the common law received into the colony, confirmed by the Act of 1833 if it applied here, could have been invoked by any Maori slave living within an area where the Queen's writ ran, to effect his or her release from a status which the superseded Maori customary law had recognized. To put it another way, the common law principle under which Maori proprietary rights were to be recognized could not have extended to property in slaves held under rangatiratanga. But it appears that Maori slavery was permitted to die out gradually through the consent or acquiescence of Maori under missionary influence, and little if any intervention of the law may have been needed. (That no doubt helped to reduce the disruption to Maori society, which was the occasion of Tamati Ngapora's asking for the Governor's help, and which would have been the greater had abolition been sudden.) But the effect of the new law was important also, as Tamati Ngapora's letter shows. After all, if rangatiratanga had been left completely intact, as Moana Jackson and (with less certainty) Jane Kelsey contend it should have been,[41] a chief would have remained free to kill his disobedient slaves if he wished to.[42]

I do not suggest great moral superiority for the Crown's attitudes to slavery over those of Maori. The Crown's long toleration of slavery in colonies where it had been established, and of the gross evils of the slave trade (abolished in the British Empire by Act of 1807),[43] limits the credit the Crown can claim. Nevertheless the trade and the institution were abolished and the common law was libertarian on this matter. No doubt slavery might have ultimately ended in Maori society without Western intervention. But end it did through the intervention of the missionaries and at least indirectly through the imposition of the new legal order. The ending is in the New Zealand context one legacy of Western imperialism that must be regarded as benign, legitimated (if for no other reason) by what came to be a sharing of values by colonizers and colonized. That that process of sharing itself came about through what Moana Jackson deplores as the 'colonization of Maori philosophy'[44] merely points to the conclusion that this was one aspect of the philosophic colonization that was itself beneficent.

'General principles of humanity', transcultural principles, and legitimation

That last sentence suggests that a transcultural principle applies, by which one may judge slavery to be an evil and its abolition, even by the exercise of usurped power, to be legitimate. I am conscious of Professor Dame Anne Salmond's warning[45] that the making of any claim to a

> 'proper superiority' (for one side or the other, or ourselves, for that matter) is

a perilous act of politics, for scholars as well as for the protagonists whose lives they try to understand.

To explain the process of legitimation fully appears to involve an appeal to transcultural principles (one of them, already much referred to, being the principle of prescription). I think we may do this in respect of particular institutions and practices, in whatever culture they occur, without necessarily claiming the superiority against which Salmond warns, but still rejecting a fashionable relativism that seeks to render beliefs, values and practices of any culture beyond outside criticism.[46] Admittedly, a claim to cultural superiority was a large part of the ideology of Christianizing and civilizing and lay behind the limiting words in section 71 of the New Zealand Constitution Act 1852 that the 'Laws, Customs, and Usages' of Maori should be maintained so far as 'not repugnant to the general Principles of Humanity'.[47] Those principles would have required the ending of slavery, even if allowed to take place gradually, in districts (had there been any) proclaimed under the section. But the principles themselves were independent of the claim to superiority and were necessarily inconsistent with slavery everywhere, including the slavery in other colonies of the Crown that, together with the slave trade, had been tolerated so long and only so recently abolished. The condemnation, after all, is transcultural. But, if this appeal to a meta-narrative is unacceptable to relativists, possibly they may still agree that the coming of freedom must have generally been experienced as a benefit (at least in the long run), whether by black slaves in the colonies of the Caribbean or by Maori slaves in Aotearoa.

Two violent societies

Salmond makes her warning a general one, in a context where, after referring to James Cook and his companions (in course of the third voyage) on the 'proper superiority' to be asserted over violent Polynesians, she remarks that 'both sides were violent':

> Maori fought often (although rather less so than popular mythology suggests) at that time, and punishment was physically harsh (including killing, captivity and torture); while in eighteenth century Europe there were endless wars, and punishment included floggings, hangings, the cropping of ears, slavery in the galleys and judicial torture.[48]

The comparison, which she develops in a later passage[49] on the 'extreme physicality of punishment in eighteenth-century Europe' and the horrors of European warfare as the technology of weaponry developed, is a valid one in many respects; though it might legitimately (sic) be narrowed to relate to Britain only, where things were in some respects becoming rather better than Salmond suggests.

Certainly any comparison of the severities of English law with those of the Maori customary legal orders would warrant a more detailed treatment and some revision or qualification of Salmond's list. In England, the imposition of torture in the obtaining of evidence, which had been lawful when authorized under the emergency prerogative of the Crown, ceased in 1640.[50] Though apparently never formally abolished, undoubtedly it cannot be revived, except (on the orthodox view) by statute. There had been other cruelties in the legal system, some of them extreme,[51] but the longest-lasting were greatly mitigated in practice before being reformed or abolished by statute in the late 18th or the early 19th century. Amongst the punishments or procedures so affected were the hanging, drawing and quartering (including disembowelment while the offender was still alive) of men convicted of high treason,[52] and the pressing to death of prisoners who refused to accept jury trial (*peine forte et dure*).[53] Punishment by 'slavery' in the galleys (imposed by the Star Chamber), apparently a forerunner of penal servitude, belonged to 16th-century England[54] rather than 18th-century Britain. The cropping of ears, admittedly referred to by Blackstone in his exhaustive list of punishments,[55] is (with other mutilations) noted by him as 'rare' and is regarded by J. H. Baker as one of the heavy discretionary punishments prohibited by the Bill of Rights 1688.[56]

All that strengthens in some respects and modifies in others Professor Salmond's comparison. British society, with its hangings[57] and floggings and external aggressions was violent enough; as apparently was Maori society, in its own ways. Both societies, like many at the time, could be criticized under 'general principles of humanity'. But one can add that, partly under the Enlightenment influences that Salmond notes, British society was in course of becoming somewhat less cruel and violent than it had been.

Pakeha rule of law: end of Maori feuding: greater protection of the individual?

The rule of law as it existed under traditional Maori customary legal orders, and the more developed legal orders that came into existence in areas of Maori autonomy during the 19th century, came to be superseded by that of the legal order imposed by the Crown in part by an arguably proper exercise of kawanatanga ceded by the tribes signatory to the Treaty of Waitangi and in part simply by the revolutionary seizure of power that began in 1840. The ending of Maori slavery is one change that occurred under the new order and which, I have argued, implied a legitimate exercise of the Crown's power over Maori even if the power was usurped. Can it be said more generally that the rule of law established under the new order has, at least to a large extent, been legitimated in the same way?

To urge this is to face the strong opposition of Professor Jane Kelsey who does not see the rule of law of the Western type, as introduced by the Crown's assumption of power, as of much, if any, benefit to Maori.[58] Again, in arguing otherwise, I do not suggest that what most people would see as benefits of the new legal order legitimate the actual seizure of power, which was in excess of what was ceded. I do suggest that, as with the ending of slavery, even if the power was entirely usurped (as in the view that kawanatanga was to be over Pakeha alone and not Maori as well), certain exercises of it in the establishment and administration of the new order — to be seen as consequences of the revolution — have been benign and have been among the factors partly legitimating the present order.

That is supported by the work of writers far from hostile to Maori. Before I turn to those writers, it is necessary to make the point first that, insofar as the new order was oppressive to Maori, it has never been legitimated (except to the extent that time and associated considerations have neutralized some of the effects of original wrongs). That is, the principle of prescription has applied, and new rights have arisen that should not now be annulled by steps taken to correct the original wrong. Where successful claims are made to the Waitangi Tribunal, the legislation or other acts of government found (to put it briefly) to affect the claimants prejudicially and to be 'inconsistent with the principles of the Treaty [of Waitangi]',[59] have never been legitimated. They may be lawful, as in the case of the New Zealand Settlements Act 1863 and the confiscations that took place under it, but where so the law has simply been, in E. P. Thompson's words, 'an instrument of imperialism'.[60] That is what it was in the case of much of the legislation of the General Assembly dealing with Maori matters, including the native lands legislation designed and used to separate Maori from their land. Nevertheless, again in Thompson's words, 'the rules and the rhetoric . . . imposed some inhibitions upon the imperial power'.[61] Thompson's description of the rule of law imposed by imperialism as a 'cultural achievement of universal significance'[62] applies to New Zealand as to the British empire generally. I suggest that Maori not only suffered from the law which as an instrument of imperialism was imposed upon them but also benefited by the restrictions on arbitrary power, the protection of individual life and (again to quote Thompson) the 'elaboration of rules and procedures which, on occasion, made some approximate approach towards the ideal',[63] that are part of (though not exclusive to) a Western rule of law. Writers either confirm this or provide material to support it.

Some years ago, Professor Salmond wrote that utu (the Maori customary remedy of self-help by which mana was protected), though sometimes taken by a tohunga's exercise of black magic or makutu, was

> [u]sually . . . exacted on the battlefield, where it was difficult to mete out precisely the right amount of punishment, and after every such encounter, new utu accounts were established. As a consequence groups were forever skirmishing. . . .[64]

That of course changed under the new legal order, of which Alan Ward, in his strongly critical account of the role of the law in depriving Maori of land and mana, nevertheless writes that:

> The rule of British law in general involved a respect for individual life probably greater than old Maori society had known, and few Maori seemed to regret the passing of infanticide, the casual killing of secondary wives by chiefs displeased with them, or the repeated obligation to engage in blood feud often precipitated by their own 'wild men'.[65]

In effect, to adapt James Belich's recent words,[66] the new 'sovereign power' ultimately 'remove[d] the capacity of its subjects to make war among themselves'. Before that happened, the 'persistence of tribal feuding' had been an indicator of the 'persistence of Maori independence' in the areas affected. Belich referred especially to the feuding of Ngapuhi that took place from the 1860s to 1888 and to the loss of at least eighteen lives in the course of it — which he had earlier described as 'a salutary reminder of the unattractive side of Maori autonomy, which also included customary killings for sorcery and adultery'.[67]

Belich has contrasted the last of the Ngapuhi feuds, that of 1888 (possibly, he says, the last tribal battle in Maoridom) with a near battle in the North in 1903 where the Ngapuhi chief Iraia Kuao had invoked Maori customary law and his rangatiratanga to justify his threat of armed force in a land dispute

Waitangi and Indigenous Rights: Revolution, Law and Legitimation

with rival claimants.[68] In the event a modest intervention of colonial law prevented the battle: Kuao and his principal followers were bound over to keep the peace under the Justices of the Peace Act 1882.

Another such intervention occurred in *R v Niramoana* (1880)[69] in which, in a dispute between Maori over customary land in the Tauranga district, some were fined under the Statutes of Forcible Entry of the English Parliament (1381–1429)[70] for forcibly taking possession. This intervention of the law, like that against Iraia Kuao, was clearly quite unjustified under the Treaty of Waitangi if kawanatanga did not extend to Maori.

As to respect for individual life, the opening words of the passage quoted above from Alan Ward's *A Show of Justice* contain a cautious comparison and judgment. One may rest on the probability that he mentions. The emphasis on the individual, characteristic of the new legal order as of Western culture generally, had its bad side in its claims to an all-embracing and universal validity and its intolerance of communal aspects of indigenous cultures (for example, in relation to land ownership) that in no way conflicted with proper respect for the individual. Nevertheless its good side, despite the violence in Western societies, lay in a degree of protection of individual life that the rule of law accorded, at least in normal times.

The accounts of both Ward and Belich indicate a lack of such protection in Maori customary law, in certain respects. The point they both make is illustrated further by the incident, recorded in a different context by Angela Ballara,[71] of the woman of Ngati Kurapoto, who was seen to take tubers from land claimed by Ngati Whiti. Pursuers from the latter hapu, believing the tubers to be kumara, killed her before discovering that she had in fact taken wild perei root, to which no proprietary right would have been so drastically asserted. Aside from the severity of the penalty (which a culture that used to hang thieves could scarcely criticize), the lack of due process caused an admitted and serious mistake. Due process was something which, with all its faults, the legal order established by the revolution begun in 1840 did generally provide.

Kelsey and the colonial courts

In New Zealand the legislature had, as we have seen,[72] plenary power within the limits fixed by its parent body, the United Kingdom Parliament. Its exercises of power within those limits was beyond review by the courts, so that, for example, the New Zealand Settlements Act 1863 was within the legislature's power of enactment. It will follow that in general the responsibility for the acts of government that prejudicially affected Maori lies with the Crown in its legislative and executive branches, and not with the courts. Professor Kelsey has written of the latter that they

> had consistently enforced settler government laws which sought to dispossess Maori of their resources, suppress Maori resistance, repress Maori culture and spirituality and denigrate Maori values from 1840 to the present day. At times they contributed their own creative solutions. But always they could claim they had done so within the rule(s) of law.[73]

That the courts enforced the statutes of the General Assembly should surprise no one: the surprise would have been if, in view of their well-defined position in the Constitution, the New Zealand courts had claimed a power of judicial review to enable them to hold legislation void if it conflicted with the Treaty of Waitangi. The courts admittedly long neglected or misunderstood the common law doctrine of aboriginal property rights and for that they could be criticized; but not simply for their obedience to the legislature in Treaty as in other matters. On the other hand, if in interpreting statutes or in applying the common law, judges manipulated the law against Maori, they could be strongly condemned for that. Jane Kelsey cited three cases in which she thinks the judges did that, in providing the 'creative solutions' mentioned at the end of the quotation. There is something to support her criticism in one of them (*Rua's case of 1916*)[74] but otherwise the examination of the three is faulty, as I have shown elsewhere, and makes a thin argument. Her indictment of the courts also rests on cases where they 'contemptuously dismissed the treaty as a nullity or as not binding on the Crown unless recognised by it in colonial statute'.[75] That criticism is correct of the judgment in *Wi Parata v Bishop of Wellington* (1877)[76] but scarcely so of those in the other cases she cites where, in neutral language, the Judges simply applied orthodox doctrine that the Treaty could be enforceable in municipal law only so far as made so by statute.

It is likely that Kelsey's reference to 'creative solutions' should be understood more precisely in general comment she has made (referring to *Rua's* case as a 'classic instance') about 'the overt partiality of the Judges, their Eurocentric values and priorities, their eagerness to bend legal principles to provide the desired outcome'.[77]

That is a strong general condemnation. We have yet to see adequate legal-historical research to support it.

It may be that judges have many times, consciously or unconsciously, manipulated the law or applied it unfairly against Maori, and that (a related matter) the criminal justice system has been (as in the 'clear perception of many Maori', reported by Moana Jackson in 1988) 'institutionally racist'.[78] But Jackson also noted that 'little research had been done' to support the perception.[79]

The legal order introduced by the Crown was necessarily a means by which the Crown's power was asserted and maintained and in that respect an instrument of the imperialist revolution. One cannot avoid that. Nevertheless the claim made here is that the new rule of law limited the exercise of arbitrary power by Maori chiefs more effectively than the old rule of law in the superseded customary orders, and gave greater protection to individual life. These were (*pace* Kelsey) substantive benefits to Maori which to some extent countered or balanced colonialist oppression in the use of law, even if the means to achieve them included the exercise of usurped power.

Partial recognition of rangatiratanga

So far as rangatiratanga has been recognized in the revolutionary legal order, the Crown's seizure of power has to that extent been legitimated. In essence the case against the Crown is that this recognition has never amounted to much, owing to the reluctance of the colonial Government to share power with Maori (notwithstanding article 2 of the Treaty) and the reluctance or inability of the imperial Government to compel it to do so. As we have seen, section 71 of the New Zealand Constitution Act 1852 was never used to provide for areas of Maori partial autonomy;[80] and the colonial government's offer to recognize King Tawhiao's authority in what was left of the King Country foundered when it refused his request that, also, Waikato land confiscated in the raupatu be returned.[81] The Urewera District Native Reserve Act 1896 provided for, among other things, local self-government for the Tuhoe but the government never gave the scheme proper effect.[82]

Otherwise the attempts at, in minor ways, accommodating Maori custom or sharing power with Maori included the creation of Maori structures by legislation: in particular, district runanga under the Native Districts Regulation Act 1858, the Councils under the Maori Councils 1900, and the New Zealand Maori Council and other Maori Associations under the Maori Community Development Act 1962.[83] Ironically, these very limited recognitions of rangatiratanga necessarily occurred as exercises of kawanatanga. Thus, notwithstanding its political effectiveness as a Maori national body, the New Zealand Maori Council has 'links with the state' that it 'has not been able to shrug off' and apparently is seen by some Maori as a manifestation of the latter rather than the former.[84] By contrast, institutions set up by Maori themselves, such as the tribal runanga of the 19th century, the de facto parliaments (the Kauhanganui of the Maori King and the rival Kotahitanga) and, latterly, the National Maori Congress set up in 1990, may be seen as clear manifestations of rangatiratanga. Such institutions could be tolerated by the Crown where kawanatanga was effective (as it became throughout the country) only if they were not part of a rival legal system (which of course the Maori kingship originally was).

The problem of empowering Maori institutions so that their legal authority does not depend on, and is not at the mercy of, a parliamentary claim to supreme power is one we turn to in the final chapter.

Legislative recognition of 'principles' of the Treaty of Waitangi

Some means to give effect to rangatiratanga — but, as in the instances mentioned above, necessarily by Parliament's exercise of kawanatanga — has been provided by legislation recognizing the 'principles of the Treaty of Waitangi' and by subsequent work of courts and tribunals in defining and applying those principles.

The Waitangi Tribunal, set up by the Treaty of Waitangi Act 1975 to inquire into and to make recommendations to the Crown in respect of (in brief) both legislative and executive acts of government 'inconsistent with the principles of the Treaty' that have 'prejudicially affected' Maori,[85] had its jurisdiction retroactively extended by the Amendment Act of 1985 to matters of complaint arising since 6 February 1840. In effect what the Tribunal does is to inquire into acts of government which may be lawful but which, even if lawful, breach the principles of the Treaty and are therefore not legitimate acts of government.[86] There is perhaps a certain paradox about the Tribunal's position, in that it has been set up as part of a legal order which itself rests on breaches of the Treaty so far as the Crown by revolution claimed power in excess of that ceded by the Treaty. A creature of statute, the Tribunal is subject to the supremacy of Parliament and as such has had to work out and apply the 'principles' with proper regard to that supremacy, so that the autonomy to which Maori are entitled is *necessarily* a 'qualified' one (though on a tenable interpretation of the terms of the Treaty it is that anyway).[87] Some radical critics have made the fact that the Tribunal necessarily functions in this way, instead of as some sort of potentially revolutionary body, a matter of unjustified complaint.[88]

Consistently with that explanation of its position, the Tribunal has, as we noted at the beginning of this book, affirmed that, in the rectifying of Treaty grievances, 'the resolution of one injustice should [not] be seen to create another'.[89] 'Rightly or wrongly, new circumstances now apply and a number of conflicting private interests, honestly obtained, must be weighed in the balance'.[90] That sentence refers to matters, arising in the conduct of affairs under the Crown's revolutionary legal order, which, especially with the passage of time, become morally relevant in the Tribunal's determinations.

The courts, the Treaty and its principles

The phrase 'principles of the Treaty of Waitangi' has been much criticized. To some radicals it is a watering-down of the Treaty, obscuring the reservation of tino rangatiratanga under article 2.[91] This criticism ignores the likelihood — indeed virtual certainty — that had the Treaty of Waitangi Act 1975, and the other statutes which use the phrase, referred baldly to the Treaty or its 'terms', the spare provisions, the two versions and the difficulties (at least in the Maori version) of reconciling the first two articles with each other would still have entailed a search for principles. In light of that one may understand the Privy Council's opinion in *New Zealand Maori Council v Attorney-General* (1994)[92] that the 'principles' are

> the underlying mutual obligations and responsibilities which the Treaty places on the parties. They reflect the intent of the Treaty as a whole and include, but are not confined to, the express terms of the Treaty. (Bearing in mind the period of time which has elapsed since the date of the Treaty and the very different circumstances to which it now applies, it is not surprising that the Acts do not refer to the terms of the Treaty.) With the passage of time, the 'principles' which underlie the Treaty have become much more important than its precise terms.[93]

To interpret the 'precise terms' is difficult indeed. In this matter the Treaty is not unlike Magna Carta, even some articles of the United States Bill of Rights, or (in a similar context to that of the Treaty) George III's proclamation to the Indian Nations of 1763.[94] For many reasons, historic constitutional instruments have often been drafted in general terms to which content has to be given and the scope of which has to be determined, in accordance with the principles that are perceived to underlie the instrument. The Treaty could have been better drafted and the relationship between articles 1 and 2, between the kawanatanga ceded and the rangatiratanga retained, made clearer. Nevertheless one should bear in mind that the 'principles' should be those that should apply in any event in the conduct of affairs between (to put it briefly) colonizers and colonized and support both the property rights and qualified autonomy of the latter. The failure to give effect to the principles in the 19th century has made the task more difficult today.

However that may be, Parliament has used the phrase and the task of giving it content in the conditions of today has fallen to the courts and the Waitangi Tribunal under their guidance. Which has prompted a criticism (quite different from that of radicals) that the phrase has been seized upon by 'activist' judges to legislate, usurping the role of Parliament.[95] The criticism has been directed most against the Court of Appeal, especially when it was under the presidency of Sir Robin Cooke (as he then was). I would willingly defend the activist judicial role but here am concerned rather to see how the exercise of that role, in relation to the principles of the Treaty, has contributed to the partial legitimating of the Crown's seizure of power.

The role, criticized as 'activist' by some but as insufficiently activist by the radical others, can be explained in light of the constitutional position of the courts, a position very different from that of the Waitangi Tribunal. The latter is simply the creation of Parliament and could be abolished by it. The High Court (together with the Court of Appeal), though provided for and regulated by the Judicature Act 1908, is the judicial arm of government, functioning in law independently of the executive and legislative branches and ultimately, as I have suggested, beyond the power of the legislative arm to abolish.[96] The courts' basic independence of the legislative arm means that, were they to apply the common law limits to Parliamentary supremacy of the sort contemplated by Lord Cooke,[97] there would (contrary to the orthodox view) be nothing unlawful or unconstitutional about that.

One cannot however apply similar limits based on the Treaty of Waitangi. As we have seen, apart from the ultimate common law limits just mentioned, a Parliament, unfettered by a written constitution and claiming plenary power, has its powers in particular matters defined by what it has successfully and effectively done in the past.[98] Such a power was claimed and exercised, over the Treaty and over Maori, by the imperial Parliament and then by the General

Assembly of New Zealand which it created by the Constitution Act of 1852. The same power is exercised now by the successor of the General Assembly, the Parliament of New Zealand, claiming to be a supreme legislature under the Constitution Act 1986. Against the background of even a qualified Parliamentary supremacy, it is extravagant to suggest (as some have done)[99] that judges, from the first holders of office in colonial times to their present-day successors, should have assumed the power to hold legislation, either of the imperial Parliament or the local legislature, to be invalid as conflicting with the Treaty or its principles.

Further reasons for rejecting such a suggestion need be stated only briefly here. The court, originally established by Ordinance of 1841 as the Supreme Court of New Zealand, was a revolutionary court to the extent that it was set up, to have jurisdiction over the whole of New Zealand, in exercise of the power seized by the Crown in 1840 in excess of what was ceded by the Treaty. The first judges and their successors, right up to the present in the (now) High Court of New Zealand and Court of Appeal, have held office as the monarch's judges, exercising the judicial part of that power. Neither at the original establishment nor since have the courts functioned in a situation of 'multiple sovereignty' (in Charles Tilly's terms),[100] in which Maori contenders for power constituted a competing government over the country and in which the court was required to decide between the competitors. (In circumstances hypothetically considered in chapter 7 that may change, but it has been the case hitherto.) The New Zealand courts have been part of a constitutional order originally established by the Crown as its revolution became progressively effective throughout the country. The normal principle that a court must uphold the order of which it is part has applied and that order has never been expressly or impliedly based on the Treaty. That being so, and given the repeated exercise of power by the imperial and then New Zealand legislature in relation to (and even in despite of) the Treaty, the suggestion is extravagant indeed.

All that is of course consistent with the orthodoxy of *Te Heuheu Tukino v Aotea District Maori Land Board* (1941)[101] and might be thought to ignore the Court of Appeal's suggestion that *some* judicial redefinition of the Treaty's position might be possible. Cooke P. had observed of that case in *New Zealand Maori Council v Attorney-General* (1987; the 'SOE' case):

> By past standards it could have been called the leading case on the Treaty of Waitangi. The Privy Council . . . held that without statutory rights Maoris could

not rely on the Treaty in the Courts. That judgment represented wholly orthodox legal thinking, at any rate from a 1941 standpoint....[102]

Then in *Te Runanga o Wharekauri Rekohu Inc v Attorney-General* (1993; the 'Sealord' case)[103] Cooke P. (for himself and Richardson and Gault JJ.) noted that in cases dealing with the statutory recognition of the 'principles' of the Treaty '... more fundamental questions of the place of the Treaty in the New Zealand constitutional system were left open...'.[104]

The possible reconsideration to which those passages point was not excluded by the Privy Council in *New Zealand Maori Council v Attorney-General* (1994)[105] when, though noting that the appellants had not challenged its decision in *Te Heuheu Tukino's* case, it referred to the Treaty as 'of the greatest constitutional importance to New Zealand'.[106] That acknowledgment places the Treaty in some sort of unique constitutional position, whereas in 1941 it had appeared as no different from any other treaty that, as an act of state, added territory to the British Empire. Yet what the courts can do to give effect to that importance is limited.

So far the effect given by the courts to the Treaty in judicial review of administrative or official action has generally depended on the express statutory recognition of its 'principles' or on the context in which the legislation operates. A number of Acts of Parliament, such as the much litigated State-Owned Enterprises Act 1986, have recognized the principles and, in formulae of varying strength,[107] required some effect to be given to them by those empowered or authorized by the legislation. Where an Act does not mention the principles, account may still have to taken of them by the empowered or authorized, if the Act operates in a context where Maori interests under the Treaty are concerned.[108] It is likely that such contextual judicial review will become established generally, and that all Acts will be interpreted and applied against the background of the Treaty where it is relevant to the legislative subject matter; except where there is express provision to the contrary.

But it is likely too that this process of 'constitutionalizing' of the Treaty can be carried no further than that by the courts. In the now celebrated words of Chilwell J., in founding contextual judicial review in relation to the Treaty principles, the Treaty 'has a status perceivable, whether or not enforceable, in law'.[109] That status and the degree of recognition given to the Treaty in legislation have provided a sufficient basis for what the courts have done. But any expectation that, in the absence of a written constitution of which the Treaty or its principles are a secure part, the courts will subordinate the authority of Parliament to that of the Treaty is almost as extravagant now as it would have been in the 1840s in the case of the first judges appointed to hold office under the Crown and exercise its judicial power.

As to the principles themselves, defined or given effect to by the courts (including the Environment Court and its predecessor the Planning Tribunal) or by the Waitangi Tribunal, the general statement of them by the Privy Council in *New Zealand Maori Council v Attorney-General* (1994),[110] quoted above, may be filled out with specific examples such as (in the Crown's relationship with Maori) the principles of partnership, of fiduciary duty, of the duty to consult and the duty to protect taonga, and the principle of qualified Maori autonomy at least in the management of resources. I do not attempt to give any full account here of the principles; or of the cases, many of which are under the State-Owned Enterprises Act 1986 or the Resource Management Act 1991.[111] It must be said of all of the principles that at present they exist and can only be applied against the background of the supreme power claimed by the Parliament, which as the Constitution stands, is free to legislate in despite of the principles even if the courts require the Parliament's intention to do that to be expressly made out. The partnership between the Crown (with its recourse to parliamentary powers) and Maori is necessarily an unequal one.

One general constitutional point should be made about the respective positions in relation to the Treaty of the Crown as the executive and of other authorities having statutory powers, in the exercise of which the principles of the Treaty are required to be taken into account or otherwise given effect. The kawanatanga ceded to Queen Victoria is exercised not only by the Crown itself in its executive capacity but by statutory bodies or officers created or empowered (as, for example, in the case of a local authority under the Local Government Act 1974), again in the exercise of kawanatanga, by the Crown in Parliament. It follows that, where an obligation (such as the obligation to consult) exists under the principles, no distinction should be drawn between the Crown and its ministers and other officers on the one hand and those statutory bodies and officers on the other. In giving effect to the principles the latter as well as the former should (unless the statute clearly provides otherwise) be bound by the obligations under them (or at least bound to take account of those obligations), for both are exercising kawanatanga.[112] The point is an important one, if the constitutional position of the Treaty and its principles, already scarcely strong, is to be maintained.

The courts and legitimation of the revolution

The critics of the role assumed by the courts in defining and applying the principles of the Treaty are divided between those who see them as usurping the legislature's functions and those who see them as not going far enough. Jane Kelsey, for example, who saw the courts' role in the SOE and other cases as having to resolve a dilemma in which the government found itself through its economic policies and 'treaty rhetoric', wrote in *A Question of Honour* that they resolved the dilemma 'without undermining the essential legitimacy and stability of the state'.[113] She emphasized that it was not a matter of the courts' deliberately intervening by applying biased rules to assist the government and that in fact the decisions temporarily checked government policies in requiring Treaty principles to be complied with. But the limited victories accorded by the courts to Maori in the end left the policies free to operate in denial of te tino rangatiratanga reserved by article 2 of the Treaty. In her view the courts, together with the Waitangi Tribunal, have played an essential part in the Gramscian 'passive revolution',[114] by which the organs of the 'colonialist' state achieve and maintain hegemony over Maori. In particular, writing in 1991, she saw the Courts and Tribunal of the 1980s (but her words would presumably have some application to them in the years since) as

> ...diverting and diffusing challenges which potentially undermined the state, not through any conspiracy of individuals, but by an astute reading of the signs of the times combined with an instinct for survival. This was legal imperialism in its modern, more subtle guise, but legal imperialism just the same.[115]

The last sentence shows clearly how the whole matter appears from Kelsey's neo-Marxist perspective. The courts, which on occasion provided 'creative solutions' in bending the law to assist the imperialist seizure of power, together with the Waitangi Tribunal now function in the more subtle role required by the passive revolution, by assisting a partial satisfying of Maori demands that will still leave the oppressive power of the 'colonialist' state largely intact.

One may find some common ground with Kelsey but in the course of a very different approach. Despite their relative independence of the Crown, the courts will uphold the constitutional order of which they are part: no one should expect them to 'undermine' it. That order limits the extent to which they can recognize and give effect to the interests of those whose legal orders were superseded by it. The judges have been able to correct the error of their predecessors that began with *Wi Parata v Bishop of Wellington*[116] by restoring the doctrine of aboriginal property rights as part of the New Zealand common law, and they have given effect to the principles of the Treaty both where Parliament has expressly recognized the principles and where it has legislated in statutory contexts to which they apply. Parliament has empowered the Waitangi Tribunal to review not only executive but also legislative acts of government against the standard set by the principles and has reformed the law to promote Maori retention of their land by Te Ture Whenua Maori Act 1993. All this, together with the Crown's redressing, largely through legislation, of some of the specific Maori grievances, has supplemented the deficient legitimacy of the legal order based on the revolutionary seizure of power that began in 1840. Maori expectations, both based on the Treaty and also in some measure on the historical record of dealings between colonizers and colonized,[117] have been partly fulfilled. Further legitimation remains possible through constitutional change that could accord and secure a qualified autonomy to Maori, based on article 2 of the Treaty.

All those are matters that, in Kelsey's Gramscian analysis, come within the passive revolution,[118] which of course is not a revolution at all but simply the means by which the Crown attempts in part to legitimate *its* revolution, of 1840. To the extent that such legitimation is insufficient, the Crown can supplement it by pointing to benefits that have accrued to Maori, ex post facto, under the constitutional and legal order that began to be established in that year (as in the ending of Maori slavery and other incidents of the rule of law). But since those consequential benefits of the exercise of usurped power do not legitimate the revolution itself,[119] the Crown must invoke also, in accordance with *R v Walker* (1989),[120] the durability of that order — the principle of prescription.

Revolutions on the Chathams: 1835–36; 1842: legitimation?

The Moriori, culturally distinct from Maori, were the indigenous people of the part of New Zealand known as the Chatham Islands.[121] It is probable that those islands were settled from New Zealand, in the view of one authority as early as towards the end of the first millennium.[122] The settlers lost contact with the mainland and were a separate people from Maori by the 16th century, their culture evolving in isolation, as that of the Moriori, until they were subjugated by Maori invaders in 1835–36. Speculations on their previous relationship with Maori led to the early 20th-century Great New Zealand Myth.

According to that the Moriori were the refugee remnant of the original occupants of the mainland, a people racially distinct from and inferior to Maori whom Maori with their superior warlike skills had overcome, only to be overcome in their turn by the still more advanced Europeans. The myth has long been authoritatively rejected by scholars (though something like it tends to linger popularly among older New Zealanders).

The present study in no way depends on any version of the myth. But it does depend on the scholars' certain identification of the Moriori as an indigenous people distinct from Maori so that, in Professor Douglas Sutton's words, 'the homeland of Moriori language and culture lies in the Chathams, not in distant New Zealand'.[123] For our purposes the successful invasion of the islands by Ngati Tama and Ngati Mutunga colonists (expelled by tribal warfare from their Taranaki lands) constituted a revolution, in which the distinct customary legal order of the Moriori was superseded by that of the invaders, to be superseded in turn by the colonial legal order imposed by the Crown in a further revolution. Queen Victoria's Letters Patent of 1842[124] redefined the colony of New Zealand to include the Chathams but apparently were not followed by any real attempt to exercise the authority so asserted until a first resident magistrate was appointed in 1854. After that, if slowly, the revolution proceeding on the mainland was effectively extended to the Chathams.

The Chatham Islands events show clearly a revolutionary succession of legal orders, that (or those) of the Maori invaders becoming by and large effective until superseded by that of the Crown. The events also raise questions of legitimation, which have to be considered in light of a little more detail. Conquest was not a source of title to land for Moriori (whose culture appears to have been peaceful) whereas it was for Maori.[125] The conquest carried out by the latter, and the killing of many of the unresisting Moriori that accompanied it, were justified specifically on customary grounds by the Ngati Mutunga chief Rakatau in evidence before the Native Land Court in 1870:

> ... we took possession of the lands in accordance with our customs.... We caught all the people, not one escaped. Some ran away from us, these we killed, and others were killed — but what of that? It was in accordance with our custom.[126]

The enslavement of most of the surviving Moriori that followed was also in accordance with the custom of the revolutionary invaders (but not that of the invaded). The customs and the ideology of conquest so invoked (like the ideologies of Western imperialism) merely explain or, at the most, excuse what was done; they do not justify it. Like the Crown's revolutionary venture on the mainland, the invasion was an 'intrusion into other people's business'[127] — or indeed, a 'fair thievish purchase'[128] — and needed to be legitimated. For legitimation of the Maori conquest one has to turn to the principle of prescription which in this case had scarcely long enough to operate. Maori did not on the Chathams have the centuries of established rule that fortified their claims as tangata whenua on the mainland. (Nevertheless their conquest was in some respects given effect under the new colonial order and, as will be suggested below, the passage of time may affect the question of its legitimacy accordingly.)

Then too the extension of the Crown's revolution to the Islands required to be legitimated. Here the particular considerations, obviously more complicated than those applicable to the mainland, are among the matters upon which historians have differed in their evidence to the Waitangi Tribunal in the Chatham Islands Claims. I am not competent to resolve the differences (which in any event must await the decisions of the Tribunal) and I trust I largely avoid them in what follows.

On the Chathams two distinct peoples, one of them non-indigenous and having very recently subjugated the other, had come under the Crown's rule nominally asserted in 1842. The Moriori were in decline, suffering from the diseases brought by early European contact and from slaughter and enslavement at the hands of the Maori invaders. The Crown's formal assertion of its authority in 1842 appears to have been premature, for it was not given substantial effect until the arrival of the first Resident Magistrate in 1855. Even then there was no swift exercise of power that might have helped to arrest that decline (and helped to legitimate the further revolution), for example, by a prompt freeing of the slaves. The lot of the Moriori slaves had improved under missionary influence and may have improved significantly in 1858. But the continuation of even an ameliorated form of slavery (possibly into the early 1860s)[129] could not be justified, as on the mainland, by the consideration that Maori society would be disrupted if the institution were not allowed to die out gradually, officially discouraged but not ended directly by active legal intervention.[130] There was no reason why customs as to slavery that applied among Maori should have applied as between them and the Moriori, to the oppression of the latter. Even at the expense of the rangatiratanga of the invaders of 1835–36, their slaves should have been promptly freed by the Crown, once it had assumed responsibility for the government of the islands.

Legitimation of the 1840 Revolution

If in the Crown's colonial legal order the issue of slavery on the Chathams was treated much as on the mainland, that was the case also with title to the land. Through decisions of the Native Land Court in 1870 and 1885, recognizing the Maori conquest as giving title, by far the greater part of the land lost by Moriori at 1835–36 was not restored to them but was awarded to their conquerors.[131] The custom the Court applied was Maori, not Moriori. The Court awarded a tiny percentage of land (2.7 per cent of the 60,156 hectares before the Court in 1870 hearings) to the Moriori by reason of the 'permissive right' under which they were occupying 'certain portions of land for their maintenance'.[132]

It is strongly arguable that in those proceedings the Court was legally wrong in the circumstances to apply Maori custom and the established 1840 rule[133] or, even if it was right in doing so, that the result was unjust. However that may be, the state of affairs recognized by the Court, in which Maori dominated the Moriori, persisted under British colonial rule and has given rise to Moriori claims now before the Waitangi Tribunal[134] that the Crown failed to protect their ancestors from slavery and to protect Moriori customary rights to land. The Chathams Islands Claims appear unique in that the Tribunal must resolve complex issues which involve not only Maori (Ngati Mutunga) and Pakeha but as well a third and distinct people whom the former had subjugated; and in which the claims of Ngati Mutunga[135] are largely based on a revolutionary seizure of the land that preceded the beginning of the Crown's revolution on the mainland by only five years.

In brief, the legitimating effect of the passage of time (the principle of prescription, operating in morality)[136] should be much the same in mainland New Zealand and in the Chathams and it operates over periods of comparable length. The Crown's revolution on the mainland and the respective revolutions of Maori and the Crown on the Chatham Islands are alike in need of the principle. In the case of the Crown there have been (I have argued) *ex post facto* benefits from its revolution, notably in the ending of Maori slavery and generally the introduction of the rule of law, which affect (so to speak) the legitimacy calculations. Those were benefits which the Crown apparently failed (for whatever reason) to extend soon enough to the Moriori. But, in the case of each of the three revolutions, we have not only the intrusive exercise of power by the successful revolutionaries, the large-scale robberies of St Augustine's story, that required to be legitimated, but also the never entirely extinguished expectations of the defeated of justice in the new order imposed on them.

Yet the Crown could not now do justice on the Chathams without account being taken not only of the Moriori claims but the success of the Maori revolution of 1835–36 and the effect given to it in the colonial legal order (essentially in the work of the Native Land Court in — though wrongly — applying Maori custom against the Moriori). The result of that consideration would be that prescription works (morally) in favour of Maori on the Chathams, in that the 7-year period that preceded the Crown's formal assertion of sovereignty in 1842 has been augmented by the years since. But just as prescription has modified but not extinguished Maori claims on the mainland as against the Crown's revolutionary seizure of power, so on the Chathams it has modified but not extinguished Moriori claims both as against the Maori revolution and that begun by the Crown in 1842.

In the case of the Moriori, any expectations that their Maori conquerors would treat them justly must have been fulfilled only as regards the 'permissive right' to occupy a little land (noted above) and presumably the possibility that they would be ultimately assimilated into Maori culture (if that were just). Their expectations of the Crown, perhaps never completely extinguished and certainly now revived, have been in effect that it would as the later invader correct in some measure the injustices done to them by the Maori.

Chapter 7: CONCLUSION: CONTROVERSIAL PRESENT AND (QUIETLY?) REVOLUTIONARY FUTURE

The case of the Chathams is obviously a special one, important because it shows the need to apply principles of legitimation on those islands, not only as between Maori and the Crown (as on the mainland), but as between Moriori and Maori and Moriori and the Crown. Where there are successive revolutionary assertions of power, in this case those of Maori against the indigenous Moriori and of the Crown against both those peoples, the process of legitimation is complex indeed. Maori cannot support their claims on the Chathams without employing against the Moriori the arguments which, invoked to legitimate in part the legal order established by the Crown's revolution on the mainland, are either summarily dismissed or ignored by Professors Walker and Kelsey[1] and other radical controversialists. As against the Crown Maori had the prior and therefore better legal right on the Chathams, for their legal order had effectively superseded that of the subjugated Moriori. But their prescriptive claim to legitimacy, by the passage of time, as against the latter was slight indeed in 1842 when the Crown's revolution began, only seven years after the Maori revolution on the Islands. (There would be a North African parallel to the whole case if the Ottoman subjugation of the Arabs in the 16th century had been followed almost immediately, instead of four hundred years later, by the invasion of the French.)[2]

I move on from the difficult yet illuminating case of the Chathams to a final consideration of the issues between Maori and the Crown in the comparatively straightforward form they take on the mainland. In one matter, Maori customary title, there is little controversy in principle among scholars, with the important exception that some radicals see it (in Gramscian terminology) as merely part of the Crown's 'passive revolution' designed to defeat claims to tino rangatiratanga. Outside the radical camp, the place of the doctrine in the New Zealand common law seems to be generally accepted, both by those to whom the Treaty of Waitangi is constitutionally relevant in some way and by those to whom it is not. Thus, of the latter, Professor Kenneth Minogue accepts it as arguable that 'earlier lawyers simply made a mistake in regarding indigenous custom and law as being of no legal force.'[3] He continues:

> The business of law must be to supply a continuity of legal framework which bridges not only circumstances but also regimes, as when British law came to dominate New Zealand.[4]

And David Round, sweepingly critical of Treaty jurisprudence and those he terms 'Treatyists', accepts the doctrine as independent of the Treaty.[5]

In view of the accumulation of judicial authority in New Zealand, Australia, Canada and the United States (the original source), it would indeed be late to dispute the doctrine of aboriginal title. In New Zealand little land remains subject to it except, in particular cases, for land under water as discussed in chapter 5. The application of the doctrine may, because of its possible impact, still be controversial in a particular case where Maori customary title is claimed to foreshore, seabed, river bed or lake bed.

But it is over the Treaty that present controversies, both scholarly and popular, largely rage. Revisionist views of the Treaty and judicial willingness to give effect to its 'principles' have been strongly criticized not only in populist writing, such as the inept (but bestselling) work of Stuart Scott,[6] but also in writings that demand close consideration, notably those of Minogue and Round (despite in the latter's case a certain wildness and lack of balance). Both writers fear for the future of a New Zealand divided by a perpetuation of the present controversies, that may lead to anarchy. Both reject or would reject any separate and protected constitutional status for Maori.[7]

Minogue resorts, as I have done in this book, to 'historical perspective',[8] but we come in the end to very different conclusions. Remarking that '*every political unity has been the result of violence*',[9] he gives the example (among others) of Britain 'unified over the resistance — the dead bodies even — of the English, Welsh, Scots and so on'.[10] But, significant as this instance may be, it is no more so for the argument than the ultimate failure of British hegemony over Ireland, where a precarious unity with Great Britain collapsed despite much shedding of blood in the efforts to maintain it. Minogue's 'general principle', that 'unity comes only from blood, but once it has been achieved, it benefits everyone',[11] is of course supported by the passage of time, by the principle of prescription. But in my argument, there is another principle also applicable: account must be taken of the opposition of those who lost the struggle and also ceased to satisfy the criterion of geographical coherence that was found in the opposition to Islam in Spain (for example) and to Britain in Ireland; but who have kept alive claims for a measure of autonomy that it was reasonable for them to expect, especially when promised by Treaty.[12] To adapt Minogue's words on the continuation of indigenous customary law,[13] such a measure of autonomy would come as part of a (necessarily much modified) 'continuity of legal framework' that should have been supplied on the Crown's setting up of the New Zealand polity.

Both Minogue and Round needed specific mention but I do not intend to embark on a general review of writing on Treaty and associated matters. Professor Paul Havemann valuably undertook such a review in 1993[14] and this was followed in 1998 by another, from the point of view of critical jurisprudence, by K. Upston-Hooper.[15] I do need to take up briefly some of the latter's useful comments on criticisms I made in 1990[16] of Jane Kelsey's writing. Upston-Hooper writes that, in referring to 'the often counter-productive polemic of much of her work',

> [Brookfield] ignores the fact that the 'counter-productive' polemic is actually the point of Kelsey's writing. Kelsey is attempting through her demystification of legal liberalism to initiate a counter hegemonic revolution, thus her 'counter-productive polemic' is in fact the raison d'être of her thesis. This polemic is of course centred around Kelsey's view that the relationship between government, law and the interests of Pakeha and capital is not linear, but always in the long term interests of Pakeha capital.[17]

On this approach the detailed analysis and criticism I made in the 1990 article (and in other writings) of Kelsey's work are, I agree, beside the point insofar as her concern may simply be to wage the Gramscian ideological war of position.[18] One might still (as I do) ask questions about the place of the rule of law (which must presumably share in the 'demystification') in the new socialist, 'Treaty-based' society to be brought about by the revolution. One might also ask underlying moral questions: for example, about the moral justification for and implications of the undiminished rangatiratanga which Kelsey has tended to endorse — and which might in fact be denied Maori even in a revolutionary socialist New Zealand in which Pakeha capital has been destroyed. But then such moral questions too may be irrelevant in the war of position, which, following Gramsci, is in part a war of propaganda. Precise legal or moral analysis may simply get in the way of the serious business of revolution and is not required: populist polemic is. In post-modern times, discourses of the latter sort, 'long on attitude and short on argument',[19] may well be acceptable and convincing to many, and perhaps be an effective means of waging the war of position.

That war is being waged not only by the counter-hegemonic discourses of Kelsey, Walker, Jackson and others but also by radical Maori protest in the form, among others, of pleas rejecting the jurisdiction of the courts of the present legal system and the authority of at least parts of certain general Acts of Parliament, such as the Crimes Act 1961.[20] These pleas have been based on tino rangatiratanga, claimed either under article 2 of the Treaty of Waitangi or on the ground that the claimants are of hapu whose chiefs did not sign the Treaty and therefore ceded nothing. Inevitably the courts do not accept such pleas. For example Fisher J. did not accept a plea based on the latter ground in *Berkett v Tauranga District Court* (1992)[21] in respect of protest acts performed on Tuhua / Mayor Island. He held that 'the New Zealand Parliament must now be taken to exercise sovereignty over the entire territory of New Zealand'[22] and its legislation to be in force over even a non-signatory hapu such as that which claimed Tuhua. This drew the comment of Mrs Annie Mikaere that '[n]o particular reason is given why this *must* be so';[23] though she apparently accepted the inevitability of the rejection. She had already commented in relation to two earlier cases where the law was applied against protesters:

> ... it is apparent that when the rules of the legal system are obeyed to the letter, as in both of these cases, the law does no more than satisfy its own internal logic. While this may reassure many as to the legitimacy of the present legal system, it is wholly inadequate to establish that legitimacy in the context of Maori claims to tino rangatiratanga.[24]

If one puts aside any 'letter/spirit' contrast (for in this context the spirit of the rules can scarcely be any more generous than the letter), the issue is one explained early in this book.[25] There is no revolutionary government making a substantial claim to the control of the State, which the Court might be asked to recognize, in exercise of a supra-constitutional jurisdiction. That being so the Court can only uphold the legal order of which it is part. It is impossible to carry the matter further except to point out specifically that the position is likely to be the same in any future New Zealand legal order that is equipped with courts. The legal order desiderated by radicals, in which tino rangatiratanga is at least part of the basic norm in a dual Maori–Pakeha or Maori-dominated polity, is likely to be established only as the result of a (probably overt) revolution.[26] If and when it is established (any supra-constitutional questions being resolved in its favour), though possibly very different in many ways it will have in the present matter the same 'internal logic' as the one it has superseded. Courts sitting under it will inevitably reject any challenges to their jurisdiction based either on the superseded order or one visualized for the future by persons who, like Erskine Childers in the Irish troubles of the early 1920s, look for a further and more extreme revolution.

Nevertheless, as Mikaere indicates, there are questions of legitimacy, as well as legality that arise in the cases where Maori protesters challenge the jurisdiction of the courts or the authority of Acts of Parliament. But it is not a 'reassur[ance]' of the 'legitimacy of the present legal system' that the decisions she examines can be taken to offer, apart from the minimal legitimacy of a functioning legal order. That is simply because controversial issues of legitimacy, relating to the Treaty of Waitangi and claims to tino rangatiratanga and affecting the basis of the legal system, are generally not for judicial consideration by the present courts, except insofar as the legal system itself self-critically raises them through legislation giving some effect to Treaty principles. Courts typically assume the sufficient legitimacy of the legal order under which they sit; and that will be true of courts in any future New Zealand legal orders as well as the present one. The Queensland case *R v Walker* (1988)[27] was a rare instance of a court's going behind that assumption to point to the moral factors, such as durability, that make for much of the substantial legitimacy of a legal order and which have been much of our concern in this book.

The position of Maori radicals who reject the jurisdiction of the courts of the present legal system, or the authority of particular Acts of Parliament so far as they see them as impinging on tino rangatiratanga, is often thought by Pakeha adversaries to be weakened by the radicals' acceptance of and reliance on much of the present legal system.[28] But it will be clear from our earlier consideration of de facto authority and of the processes of legitimation that there is not necessarily any inconsistency here. Maori who regard the Crown as a usurper may still accept that government by it is better than no government at all and recognize its laws in day-to-day matters where Maori constitutional claims are not affected.[29] For example, when in 1995 at a press conference Annette Sykes referred to 'the present illegal government',[30] that would not be inconsistent with her accepting many of the laws of the present order as valid under the de facto principle. Nevertheless it was late for her to deny 'the present . . . government' a legality she presumably would have accorded to Maori tribal government on the Chatham Islands when it became established in 1835–36.

In terms of the distinction we have held to throughout this book, the question she was raising was one of legitimacy rather than legality; though even in that respect she could consistently with her objections based on tino rangatiratanga concede the minimal legitimacy of a functioning legal order,[31] including the functioning of its courts in matters that do not touch Maori claims. To deny legitimacy beyond that, and to take protest action to demonstrate that denial, would obviously tend to erode the general legitimacy claimed by the present order.

As long ago as 1989, Jane Kelsey had concluded that resort to 'the jurisdiction of the courts' (arguing for Treaty rights 'within the parameters of the Pakeha law') now merely 'reinforce[d] its legitimacy to determine Treaty questions',[32] a legitimacy which she necessarily denied. She argued that the strategies of resorting to the courts and the Waitangi Tribunal, useful in the 'early 1980s', had become no longer so and indeed were proving 'counter-productive'.[33] In light of that, and of the ultimate and continuing domination by 'the structural interests of capitalism and Pakeha power combined with the immediate political imperatives of a majority Pakeha electorate',[34] she urged as the best course 'effective and organised opposition to Pakeha capital outside the electoral and judicial arenas'.[35] She has made it clear that such opposition, which would be a means of achieving, among other things, the setting up of separate Maori constitutional structures in the hitherto 'colonial state', need not be violent.[36] But the possibility of violence would be there and at a Law Conference in 1990 she warned the legal profession to 'address' the questions of necessary constitutional reform either 'beginning that process ourselves, or facing the prospect of being forced to do so'.[37]

Later in this chapter I turn to some of the radical proposals for separate Maori constitutional structures that have been made and which, I think, it would require overt revolution to carry out. For the moment let us note the change in tactics which Kelsey has contemplated. She appears to be saying that the possibilities of exploiting effectively, in the interests of the non-violent Gramscian war of position, the 'passive revolution'[38] that has occurred (is still occurring?) in the 'colonial state', are at an end. The war of position now requires some more direct action, with the possibility of the violence of the war of manoeuvre not ruled out if it is necessary to carry out the revolutionary overthrow or transformation of the 'colonial state' and the setting up of a new legal order that includes the separate Maori structures.

A quiet revolution and a qualified Maori autonomy?

The revolution setting up a new legal order may be a quiet one, one of the kind that is the agreed means of effecting and securing a constitutional settlement when the legal order as it stands lacks the machinery to do that.[39] Let us consider that sort of revolution as the means of changing the present legal order, so that Maori customary property rights and a qualified autonomy for Maori are secured within it. The qualified autonomy within the New Zealand nation-state, to be suggested, would probably not satisfy even the most moderate of the radical proposals mentioned below (and in any case much of its detail would still have to be worked out). The changes and the quiet revolution effecting them might well be seen as simply a further step in the Gramscian 'passive revolution', leaving tino rangatiratanga far from adequately provided for. The changes would however in my view, together with the settling of specific Maori grievances, constitute the closest approximation to justice that is possible in contemporary Aotearoa New Zealand and would give proper effect to the right, in international law, of Maori as an indigenous people to self-determination.[40]

I want to consider the matter first in relation to some recent work of Dr Paul McHugh, whose early writing was strongly influential in re-establishing the common law doctrine of aboriginal title in New Zealand and whose *The Maori Magna Carta* was a landmark in Treaty studies. McHugh now writes, again influentially, of the historiography of the Treaty and of the Constitution.[41] He argues for the 'indigenization' of the Constitution[42] through a 'contemporary', 'inter-cultural' constitutionalism (as distinct from the 'modern' constitutionalism in which he and I and others have hitherto worked).[43]

He credits the possibility of these developments to the 'environment of political engagement', which the Court of Appeal brought about, initially in *New Zealand Maori Council v Attorney-General* (the SOE case),[44] by requiring the Crown to negotiate with Maori, as its partner under the Treaty of Waitangi, the means for giving effect to the policy of the State-Owned Enterprises Act 1986 and the protection of Maori claims under the Treaty of Waitangi in respect of lands that would pass from the Crown to the state-owned enterprises under that Act. In fostering this 'contemporary' constitutionalism, the Court of Appeal

> recognises the political status of Maori organised as tribes with legitimate claims against the Crown. Partnership, after all, is a form of mutual recognition and common enterprise. The Treaty relationship becomes seen as one in

which relations between Crown and tribe are continually reassessed and negotiated on the basis of consent rather than unilateral imposition.[45]

It is difficult to know what to make of this in terms of actual constitutional reform. McHugh does not visualize the abandonment of 'the technical constitutional doctrine of Parliament's ultimate sovereignty'.[46] He sees in the Treaty relationship an acknowledgment 'that Maori rights may in some cases have to defer to an overriding national weal (such as conservation)'.[47] That seems obviously an instance where the Leviathan of 'modern' constitutionalism must have the last say and the ultimate sovereignty must be exercised, free of formal constraints necessary to protect Maori rights and interests in a nation-state where they are a minority. Where I differ from Dr McHugh is on the need for such constraints in the new environment he describes. In my view Maori rights have to be accommodated securely within the constitutional structure of the polity originally created by the revolution of 1840, recreated or reorganized by whatever later revolutions can be discerned, and now an independent nation-state. And the securing is against their being abrogated in the future by the ordinary legislative process of a simple majority vote in the Parliament. Leviathan has to be tamed.

This can best be done by the process of a formal or 'quiet' revolution to give effect to a constitutional settlement of these matters, between the Crown and Maori, that should take place either within the monarchy or (much better) as part of a wider revolutionary change, from the New Zealand monarchy to the New Zealand republic.[48] Despite present public apathy, that wider change cannot be long delayed and, when it becomes imminent, radical consideration of the country's constitutional needs will be essential. Settlement of the Treaty's place in a new republican Constitution will be best treated as the most pressing of those needs.

The constitutional machinery to carry through these revolutionary changes will be considered shortly. But let us first recall, against the background set by earlier chapters, the basis for making those changes to provide for and protect Maori rights. Quite apart from the Treaty of Waitangi, Maori could have entertained a reasonable expectation that they would have under the Crown a qualified autonomy of some sort, such as (though obviously the model cannot be taken exactly) that allowed by the Romans to the Jews in the New Testament accounts familiar to missionary-educated Maori; and of which, had Maori been aware, there were other historical instances including some in the British colonial and the United States dealings with the Indian Nations.

Conclusion

On the view taken in this book, the rangatiratanga reserved by article 2 has to be seen as a qualified autonomy of this sort. What was in any event a reasonable expectation became an entitlement (albeit in uncertain terms) in the case of signatory hapu, under a Treaty which, in the legal system imposed by the Crown, required legislation to give effect to it. By contrast, the continuation of Maori customary property rights was better assured, under a common law doctrine that, though long misunderstood by New Zealand judges, was a basic part of that system. But both Maori autonomy and property rights suffered in the Crown's revolutionary seizure of a power greater than that ceded by the Treaty. The successive New Zealand legal orders at least historically based on that revolution (begun in 1840) have been deficient in legitimacy as a result, a deficiency only partly remedied, prescriptively by the passage of time, and by certain benefits of Crown rule (as in the ending of slavery and in the rule of law as a means of limiting arbitrary power) that followed the revolutionary seizure. Further legitimation requires not only the remedying of specific Maori grievances (notably as recommended by the Waitangi Tribunal) but basic constitutional reform as well, best carried out by a 'quiet', or technical, revolution.

That then is the background. But the need for basic constitutional reform is not one which the Crown has accepted yet, holding the view that Maori grievances can be redressed without limiting parliamentary supremacy and that tino rangatiratanga in the form of Maori self-management may adequately be provided for within that supremacy and the present constitutional structure (or, one supposes, that of a New Zealand republic of minimal change, in which the same supremacy is maintained).[49] But this is to fail to recognize the serious mistake made by the Crown (including its colonial government) in the 19th century in not giving effect to the qualified autonomy reserved in article 2 of the Treaty. If the mistake can now, at least to some extent, be remedied (and it can), then it ought to be. The original setting up of New Zealand as a Crown colony without some secured form of Maori autonomy may have been understandable in the constitutional thinking of the time, but it was still a failure on the Crown's part, as was the neglect to set up the semi-autonomous Maori districts in which modified Maori customary law would have continued and for which the Crown in Parliament had made provision in section 71 of the New Zealand Constitution Act 1852.[50] The failure was that of not even providing (save in certain minor respects) for a Maori qualified autonomy subject to the supremacy of the Crown in Parliament, let alone one that was constitutionally protected against the exercise of that supremacy by the ordinary legislative process.

How and how far can those constitutional failures be remedied? Because of the intermingling of Maori and Pakeha populations the setting apart of semi-autonomous Maori districts is generally not possible. Perhaps the only exception relates to the Urewera Country, where it appears it might still be possible to establish Tuhoe local self-government on a reserve, for which provision was originally made in the Urewera District Native Reserve Act 1896 but never given proper effect.[51] The unhappy history of the Crown's dealings with Tuhoe[52] make it especially appropriate to recognize now their rangatiratanga in this way. That it *may* not be possible to do this in the same way for Maori elsewhere ought not to be a reason for failing to do it where it can be done. But, even without reserves, some form of limited self-government for the 'many hundreds of traditional communities existing on land bases with marae as their institutional centrepiece'[53] should be possible.

Setting up a separate criminal justice system for Maori generally (as distinct from continuing to make the present system more culturally sensitive), urged by Moana Jackson and now supported by Professor Bruce Harris in regard to the trial and sentencing of offenders,[54] is a much more difficult matter. Harris makes it clear that the substantive criminal law as to what constitutes particular crimes and offences should not be changed, merely the processes.[55] But difficulty remains.[56] There is the possibility of disparate (and, *pace* Harris, perceivably unfair) sentencing, especially where Maori and Pakeha offenders, involved in the same criminal act, are sentenced under different systems. And there is the highly individualized nature of the pre-trial and trial procedures of the present criminal justice system, in which the protections given the citizen by the New Zealand Bill of Rights Act 1990 play so important a part. Presumably those protections, in their conception and detail very much the product of the dominant culture, would be retained in any separate Maori system. It is difficult to imagine that many Maori suspects or defendants would wish to forego them in favour of protection by what might be less certain or less specific procedures based on Maori custom. But that is said tentatively. I may be wrong.

By contrast the need for arrangements satisfactory to Maori, for officially recognized systems of iwi and hapu self-government and for some form of constitutional body that would function for Maori nationally, with at least that body constitutionally secured, ought to be less controversial and seen as a proper fulfilment of article 2 of the Treaty so far as that is now reasonably possible.[57] Although it is arguable that the concept of a partnership between the Crown and Maori has been inappropriate because of the unequal positions of strength, it becomes less so the more the Maori position is strengthened. As we saw in the discussion of the partial giving of effect to rangatiratanga, there has been the problem that, inevitably in the present legal order, this giving of effect is dependent on the parliamentary exercise of kawanatanga, so that article 2 is subordinate to article 1.[58] This is a difficulty that cannot entirely be overcome, because of the constitutional and political facts of the Crown's revolution. But the difficulty can be greatly lessened if the kawanatanga, now exercised by the Crown in Parliament which claims supreme power even over the Treaty itself, becomes balanced by a protected rangatiratanga which, though necessarily limited, is secured in a written constitution giving effect to (among other things) a settlement between Maori and Pakeha of the constitutional issues between them. That settlement would recognize, on the one hand, the facts of the Crown's revolutionary seizure of power and the partial legitimation of the order that is based on it; and, on the other, the validity of Maori expectation of (and Treaty entitlement to) a measure of autonomy that, if it were provided by the Parliament under the present legal order, could be repealed, by the normal legislative process, on a simple majority vote in the House of Representatives. In Professor Mason Durie's words:

> The essential tasks are for Maori to reach agreement about decision-making within Maori society and for Maori and the Crown to agree on the most appropriate constitutional arrangements that will enhance the standing of both.[59]

Assuming that Maori will desire a national representative body with secure position in the constitutional structure, the functions and powers of the body would have to be agreed on with the Crown. It would have to be at least a consultative body, to which all proposed legislation affecting Maori rights or interests would have to be referred and which would have an active role in the forming of Maori policy. The body might have a stronger position in the legislative process, perhaps as a revising chamber with power to delay for a limited period (but not ultimately reject) measures it resolves to be contrary to the principles of the Treaty of Waitangi.

Preferably, in my view, as an alternative to the body's having that power, the Treaty or its principles should be entrenched in the Constitution by a formula which would generally protect the principles of the Treaty (and Maori customary rights at common law) against unjustifiable infringement by legislative or administrative acts of government. The protection would be comparable to that accorded in Canada to aboriginal and treaty rights by section 35(1) of the Constitution Act 1982.[60] The entrenchment would extend also to protect the Maori national representative body; and possibly, if that is thought desirable, provisions for iwi and hapu government and for local territorially based autonomy where that is geographically possible.[61] It is likely that all this would be part of a new, republican, Constitution that provided for the powers and structure of New Zealand government in its legislative, executive and judicial branches.

In the judicial branch a special Constitutional Court is likely to be necessary as the final court for testing legislation or executive action against the applicable constitutional limits, including limits protecting the Treaty principles, Maori customary property rights and the Maori role in government (together called 'Maori matters').

Entrenchment: the machinery of the revolution

The entrenchment clauses in the new Constitution would be comparatively easy to devise, providing to the effect that the protected provisions could not be repealed or amended except by a measure passed (say) by a majority consisting of 75 per cent of the members of the House of Representatives (and by an appropriate majority in the Senate, if there is one); and approved by a simple majority of electors at a referendum or, in regard to Maori matters, at separate referendums of Maori and non-Maori electors.

The much greater problem is the machinery to set up the new Constitution, which, though also easy enough to devise on paper, to ensure its effectiveness will require the taking of technically revolutionary steps to limit the supremacy hitherto claimed by Parliament, so that the new Constitution will be protected against repeal or amendment except in the terms that it prescribes as to majorities and referendums. It is this break with the constitutional past that can be achieved satisfactorily and with certainty only by a formal revolution in which (since we are considering the change to a republic as well as the new protection in Maori matters) both the monarchical base of the Constitution and the Parliament's absolute power over the Treaty will be abolished.[62]

The two changes are related in that the Treaty, to be protected (in some measure) in the new Constitution, was made with Queen Victoria as personifying the monarchy now to be abolished. The continuing personal relationship perceived by many Maori between them and her successors is, as a matter of political morality affecting the legitimacy of the change, an obstacle to the monarchy's being abolished without Maori consent. In happy agreement with Ranginui Walker, Jane Kelsey and Andrea Tunks, one may see the imminence of a republic as the occasion for Maori to require constitutional recognition of the Treaty as a condition of such consent, however much one might differ from those writers about the extent of the recognition that Maori should expect.[63]

I have no doubt that a new republican Constitution (providing securely for Maori matters in the way discussed), established by Act of Parliament with the concurrence of a virtually unanimous House of Representatives and with the support of Maori and Pakeha voters, taken in separate referendums, and with that concurrence and support recited in the preamble to the Constitution, would be an effective technically revolutionary means of replacing the present Constitution and would be validated by the courts in exercise of the supra-constitutional jurisdiction discussed in chapter 1. There would be a revolution in our terms (though a quiet one),[64] based on an accumulation of the 'facts of constitutional life'[65] referred to in the preamble, as well as on compliance with the present rules of law making (requiring a simple majority vote in the House of Representatives); whereas compliance with those rules is likely to be insufficient in itself (whatever the Act might provide to the contrary by way of attempted entrenchment) to displace those rules for the future and to protect the new Constitution from repeal or amendment under them.

Alternatively, the Irish model of 1937,[66] more obviously revolutionary in breaking the links with the constitutional past, could be adapted and the new Constitution enacted by a constitutional convention of the New Zealand peoples (with a separate concurrence by Maori delegates), set up by an Act of Parliament that did not empower it to do this. The courts would undoubtedly validate a clearly revolutionary change made in that way and (as under the former alternative) in due course take their place as courts under the new Constitution.

The problem, however, if one refers back to the cases showing the exercise by modern courts of a supra-constitutional jurisdiction, is that a revolutionary change to a New Zealand republic might well depend mainly on the effectiveness of the change and that 'facts of constitutional life' (including presumably acceptance by the electorate in one general referendum) might well be sufficient to show that effectiveness without separate Maori concurrence.[67] In short, while I have no doubt that political morality requires that concurrence, it may well be that the change could be effective without it and receive the validation of the courts accordingly, at least if there has been consultation with Maori. But one cannot say more about those uncertainties here.

Further uncertainty attaches to the whole matter of establishing public support for the revolutionary changes that will be part of the 'facts of constitutional life' necessary to establish the new order, in which for the first time Treaty and associated rights will be constitutionally protected (even if the provision is far from adequate in the views of some). Professor W. H. Oliver has discerned an increasing 'fragility of Pakeha liberal support' for Maori aspirations, caused in part by unease at the development of 'tribal capitalism' and in part by the 'extremist acts' of some Maori radicals.[68] That there may be insufficient support among Pakeha for even moderate (though technically revolutionary) constitutional change in these matters is certainly possible. The changes might nevertheless be carried forward under political leadership which, with the support of liberal participants in the controversy, can convince doubtful or indifferent Pakeha of the justice of what is proposed.

Here it is necessary to refer again to the concept of justice and its application to the issues we are considering. Professor Andrew Sharp, carrying further the consideration he had given the matter in *Justice and the Maori*, sees justice in Aotearoa New Zealand as something impossible to achieve because of the conflicting expectations of Maori and Pakeha.[69] The rough approximation that is possible — which indeed in his view is 'not really justice but simply an expression of how a particular society orders its relations'[70] — is one which in the end has to be fixed and enforced by Leviathan, 'the currently-located sovereign power' as the 'final arbiter'.[71] The final arbiter's failure 'to deliver wise judgments' would result in the loss of its 'practical legitimacy with those it tries to govern'.[72] I agree with much of that analysis. I see the rough approximation to justice and the 'wise judgments' necessary to attain it as matters of objective reasoning, requiring all relevant factors to be considered and weighed. In the present context those factors include pre-eminently the continuing existence of Maori as a separate people and 'nation' and their strong assertion of identity as such, their rights under the Treaty of Waitangi and customary property rights at common law, the practical difficulty (save possibly in the Urewera country at least) of setting aside semi-autonomous Maori districts, the location of political power in the present 'sovereign' (resulting from the Crown's revolution begun in 1840), the fact of Pakeha numerical dominance in the population and consequently in the exercise of that power, and the partial legitimation over time (and through some shared values of Maori and Pakeha) of the present legal and constitutional order. In the light of those and other relevant matters, I suggest that justice, according to the transcultural standard that, in Professor Minogue's words, 'ought to regulate relations between peoples',[73] requires an arrangement such as that discussed above and the securing of it in a written constitution.

What though if Pakeha opposition prevents that? As long as it does (and but for the matters to be considered below), the doing of justice to Maori can only continue by way of the present ad hoc process of the Crown's meeting particular Maori grievances and dealing with Maori in the 'more horizontalised form' of 'Crown-tribe relations' of contemporary constitutionalism that Paul McHugh discerns to be developing, without 'abandoning the technical constitutional doctrine of Parliament's ultimate sovereignty'.[74] To relate this to Mason Durie's discussion of the matter, the 'constraints which the Maori nation imposes on parliamentary supremacy'[75] could then be provided only by the developing of constitutional conventions (such as, for example, a convention inhibiting Parliament from abolishing the Waitangi Tribunal) that Parliament could ultimately ignore, rather than properly secured 'fresh constitutional arrangements'[76] that Durie writes of and a form of which I have suggested above.

But there is the likelihood in any event that the arrangement suggested above, achieved by a quiet or technical revolution (in my terms), would be seen by some as merely another measure in the quite differently conceived Gramscian 'passive revolution' by which a measure of placatory reform is mediated that leaves the hegemony of the Pakeha capitalist state substantially undiminished and rangatiratanga insufficiently restored and still subject to that hegemony.[77] (A technical revolution such as I propose would be irrelevant in the Gramscian scheme.) I turn to the more radical constitutional arrangements which, again following Gramscian terminology, the war of position and any necessary element of the war of manoeuvre might yet bring about.

The radical alternatives and overt revolution

The 'extremist acts' of Maori radicals, which, in W. H. Oliver's account, are one of the causes of 'unease' among liberal Pakeha and render their support for Maori causes 'fragile', have in the polemic of Jane Kelsey the very different role of warning Pakeha of the possibility of (necessarily revolutionary) violence if more extreme Maori demands for rangatiratanga are not met. Liberal and for that matter all Pakeha are warned that radical change is needed if a grim future is to be avoided. There is some validity in the warning, for Pakeha motivation sufficient to meet Maori demands might well be provided in part by such a consideration. But on the other hand the fear of the grim future might also deter many Maori from the pressing of extreme demands that might lead to it if Pakeha do not yield.

However that might be, the range of radical claims needs our close attention. In Jane Kelsey's words, it covers variously, (i) 'sovereign Maori authority over the entire country', (ii) 'complete Maori independence from the colonial state', and (iii) 'co-existent and co-operative polities of equal status within one nation'.[78]

Of those claims, the second appears to require a geographical division of the country into separate Maori and Pakeha nation-states, something which Kelsey has also contemplated.[79] Perhaps possible in the 19th century at least in the case of the King Country, today it would necessitate population shifts that are unlikely to occur and which alone would justify it on our analysis in chapter 3. The third, described by Kelsey as 'more moderate', is one for which constitutional machinery could be devised (but would it work?) and which could perhaps be brought about by a quiet revolution if Maori and Pakeha came to a constitutional settlement going much further than the one briefly discussed above. The first two especially appear to make no allowance for the various matters that can be urged as partly legitimating the present legal and constitutional order. The third makes some allowance for those matters and comes nearer a transculturally just solution than the other two. But in any event even it, 'more moderate' as it is, is unlikely to come about without at least the prospect of revolutionary violence that might bring Pakeha (heeding Kelsey's warning) to a settlement on its terms. More likely, it would not come about (and certainly neither of the other two would) without the overt revolutionary overthrow of the present order.

That in fact is contemplated in Chris Trotter's speculative outline of a constitution for a republic of Aotearoa New Zealand that would meet the third claim and of the kind of crisis that might lead to its establishment.[80] Set against a Gramscian background of the Crown's attempts by passive revolution to contain Maori unrest, Trotter's 'revolutionary scenario' begins with the election of an extreme 'New Right' government which, through measures that would remove barriers based on the Treaty of Waitangi to 'transnational capital's bid for global supremacy' and make 'both Maori and Pakeha . . . victim'[81] to that bid, precipitates mass popular resistance. This culminates in rebellion, the overthrow of the government, and the setting up of a revolutionary republican regime. The draft constitution[82] Trotter devises in outline (for enactment by the Constituent Assembly of the new Republic) is in effect one for a dual state,

Conclusion

consisting of the Maori Nation and the Pakeha Nation, which are constitutionally embodied respectively in a National Maori Assembly and a House of Representatives. Legislation may originate in either of the Houses but must be passed by both, before going to a Senate (composed equally of elected Maori and Pakeha members) having power to delay but not reject legislation. There is a Council of State, a President, and a Supreme Court made up equally of Maori and Pakeha judges at the head of the judicial system. The property provisions include a massive restoration of Maori property rights over 'lands, forests and fisheries exploited for commercial gain'. There is to be a Citizens' Charter of Political, Economic and Social Rights.

I do not deal with the matter in further detail here except to mention that, in the Trotter scenario, the sharing of sovereignty provided for in the Constitution is insisted on by the 'armed forces of Maori Sovereignty',[83] made up of Maori elements in the New Zealand armed forces which have successfully mutinied and without which the revolution could not have taken place. (Bitter resistance in the South Island is mentioned.)

This revolution is a result of the effective assertion of force, of course ideologically justified to those who have carried it out (Pakeha political opponents of globalization, contenders for Maori Sovereignty, trades unionists, radical university students). But, as with many another revolution, the legal and constitutional order set up by this one might need its legitimacy to be supplemented by the passage of time and by some satisfying of the just expectations of those who have not supported the revolution. They, in accordance with *Respublica v Chapman* (1781),[84] must be allowed a reasonable time to leave New Zealand if they wish but if they stay the regime under whose protection they now live will swiftly claim their allegiance, whether or not they yet accord legitimacy to it.

We are not told in the scenario whether the existing courts are swept away by the revolution. If they are not, then their recognition of the new regime would be likely to follow on its secure establishment, in exercise of the supra-constitutional jurisdiction discussed in chapter 1. There might before that be interim recognition, under the de facto principle, of the regime's day-to-day acts of government.[85] But if the courts are swept away in the immediate turmoil of the revolution or if they decline any supra-constitutional function, the revolution will have to set up its own courts.

At all events, it appears from Chris Trotter's proposals that there will be a separation of powers[86] and one may assume that the independence of the judiciary, from the executive and legislative branches of the government, will be properly maintained. Apparently the full Gramscian revolution, with its 'essentially innovatory' conception of law and rejection of the separation of powers,[87] does not take place in this scenario. The rule of law, E. P. Thompson's favourable view[88] of it being apparently accepted, will continue to inhibit the exercise of arbitrary power in the new order.

Chris Trotter's revolutionary scenario and his outline of a revolutionary republican constitution for a dual-nation state affords a useful means of reviewing much of the ground we have covered in this book. The main difficulty with it (apart from its grimness) is one which in a more extreme form attaches to the other Maori claims mentioned by Jane Kelsey, for 'sovereign Maori authority over the entire country' or for 'complete Maori independence from the colonial state'; and which takes us back to differences earlier considered in chapter 4 about the extent of the kawanatanga ceded to the Crown under article 1 of the Treaty of Waitangi. Did it extend to Maori as well as Pakeha or was it limited to the latter? All three of the radical claims as described by Kelsey, including the third (which the Trotter draft would meet), appear to be premised upon an equality of the relationship created by the Treaty between the Crown and hapu who were party to it, which would be consistent with the view that kawanatanga did cover Pakeha alone and left the rangatiratanga of the signatory hapu, reserved by article 2, intact; as completely intact as that of the non-signatory hapu.

If, on the other hand, kawanatanga did extend to Maori, rangatiratanga seems to be unavoidably subordinate to it, and the relationship created by the Treaty an unequal one; at least in that exercises of kawanatanga, especially through parliamentary legislation, have been the necessary (but not always acceptable)[89] means of making any provision for rangatiratanga in the New Zealand legal order. Further, only a revolutionary limitation of the kawanatanga actually exercised would accord rangatiratanga constitutional protection. And as we have seen, whatever view is taken of articles 1 and 2 and their interrelationship, some of the restrictions that kawanatanga (even if seen as usurpation) has imposed on rangatiratanga, as in the ending of slavery and important aspects of the introduction of the rule of law, have been legitimated.[90]

Generally there is the fact of the Crown's effective exercises of power in the revolution begun in 1840 and their many direct or indirect consequences, that, to the extent that they have themselves been legitimated by the passage of time or other considerations, serve to support a legal and constitutional order *not* based on equality in the Treaty relationship (though that order remains far from legitimated entirely). Among those consequences is the imbalance in the population, Maori being a minority, though a large one, in a country that was originally theirs alone. The imbalance itself introduces considerations that may conflict in our arriving at (to echo Andrew Sharp) the 'wise judgment'[91] necessary to reach the closest approximation to justice possible, in the relations between Maori and Pakeha. On the one hand (I suggest), justice does not require the large majority to share power equally with the minority. But on the other hand, justice does require constitutionally secure provision for the minority within the nation-state; and that the power of the majority be limited accordingly.[92]

Yet all that may not dispose of the matter. As we have seen, in Trotter's revolutionary scenario the Maori armed forces demand a shared sovereignty. But what if they demanded and forcibly established 'sovereign Maori authority over the entire country', adopting the most radical of the three claims described by Kelsey and convinced that justice requires no less? (One remembers the observation that it is the perception of what is just (and of what justice requires) rather than objective injustice that prompts rebellion).[93] The Maori armed forces would, it is likely, establish a quite different republic with a quite different legal and constitutional order from that in Chris Trotter's outline, let alone of course from any that would meet my suggestions. The new order, ideologically legitimate to these more extreme revolutionaries and their supporters, would await a greater legitimation over time, which would no doubt much depend on how far the now-subject Pakeha majority were treated and accommodated within it. The successful ideological resurgence itself would have its historical parallels (more or less), in triumphing against an order which, largely imposed by the revolution begun in 1840, could make some claim to a legitimacy accorded by the passage of time (even if an ideological opponent might allow no other ground). The sovereign Maori authority might well of course, in its turn, sooner or later be overthrown and the issues and processes of legitimation arise afresh in respect of yet another revolutionary order.

Conclusion

The British Crown's revolutionary seizure of power in Aotearoa New Zealand, legitimated only in part by the Treaty of Waitangi, was otherwise an 'immense intrusion into other people's business' — or indeed a large-scale robbery. It had that in common not only with other such ventures of Western imperialist states but with conquests and seizures of territory generally, like those within Maoridom itself and the Maori conquest of the Chatham Islands. Further, all involved revolutions, in which legal orders hitherto existing were superseded by an order imposed by the successful seizers of power. Where such things happen within the same culture (as within Maoridom), the legitimation of the results of conquest or seizure may in some sense come comparatively quickly (though the utu account or its equivalent may remain unclosed), through the operation of well-understood custom within the culture. But it comes also in conquests that are transcultural, as with Maori over Moriori and Pakeha over Maori. That happens, if for no other reason, because principles of prescription operate between as well as within cultures. (Other possible reasons are that the new, revolutionary, order may by some means incorporate part of the old; and that some effects of conquest and colonization may be accepted as right and beneficial, such as the ending of slavery and other aspects of the rule of law under the new order.) That is to say briefly, revolutionary conquests, like internal revolutions, are usually legitimated at least ultimately. But claims and expectations, maintained by the losers of the struggle and insufficiently accommodated in the new revolutionary order to reconcile them to their defeat, may impede complete legitimation.

New Zealand, as we have seen, is not unique in these matters. Like other nation-states founded as colonist polities of the West, it is too closely placed in time to the founding revolution for the present order to be completely legitimated by prescription. Maori claims and expectations, based on the Treaty of Waitangi or on the revived common law of aboriginal rights, remain outstanding. That, in the case of the Treaty, is despite a degree of effect given to its principles by Parliament and by courts and tribunals.

New Zealand shares in the general repentance of the West for the wrongs done in imperialist activities — the repentance described by Bernard Lewis as unprecedented among conquerors;[94] though it is not the less valid on that account. The repentance is an acknowledgment that the ideologies of Western colonization were insufficient to legitimate it and that there survive grievances of the colonized that require to be redressed.

This has been an analytical book, considering the role of judges in dealing with revolutionary challenges based on such grievances, and the problem of Maori claims in a world context and from a historical and moral perspective. That perspective takes into account the wrongs done by revolutionary conquest or seizure of territory, whoever the conqueror and whether the polities involved are of the same or different cultures. But account is taken also of counter factors: especially the prescriptive effect of the passage of time and the benefits that partly balance the wrongs; so that legal orders based on such wrongs, and

Conclusion

whose legitimacy is in question because of them, are partly legitimated.

The processes of legitimation necessarily apply to the country's constitutional arrangements, as well as to private interests. This book makes the case for a settlement of Maori claims that extends to basic constitutional change secured by a technically revolutionary break with the present order, for the redressing of wrongs that go back to the revolution begun in 1840. But it does so in light of both the moral nature of particular exercises of even usurped power and also the moral consequences that, under general principle, over time may come to attach to such exercises, both within cultures and between them.

There we might leave the matter. But there is a difficulty which, though strictly out of the compass of this book, needs to be mentioned briefly. The constitutional settlement argued for here would result from a renegotiation of the constitutional arrangements under which Aotearoa New Zealand is governed — a renegotiation of the exercise of sovereignty within the New Zealand nation state. The difficulty is that, as Professor J. G. A. Pocock has recently commented,[95] Maori and Pakeha 'have been renegotiating sovereignty even as it is being sold out from under them' in the process of economic globalization to which the country has submitted itself since the mid-1980s. Some supporters of globalization policies are likely to oppose the kind of constitutional change I have suggested. They may prefer that the existing order be retained, in which such policies can be pursued free of any strong constitutional restraints protecting the Treaty of Waitangi. (Indeed, in Chris Trotter's revolutionary scenario considered earlier in this chapter, it is the present legal and constitutional vulnerability of Maori rights and interests to the state's enforcement of globalization that partly causes the revolution.)

Pocock in effect reinforces the warning we may take from the writings of Jane Kelsey[96] that the proclaimed eclipse of the nation-state under globalization may be inimical to the just resolution of the claims of indigenous peoples, and in particular of issues between the Crown and Maori that have been a main concern in this book. The serious doubts I have expressed over Kelsey's treatment of some aspects of those issues do not detract from the importance of the warning. The constitutional settlement I have suggested would depend on the New Zealand nation-state's having the political will and power, despite any adverse economic pressures, to put the settlement into effect and to carry through the quiet revolution needed to secure it.

Finally, one may speculate incidentally that globalization itself might lead ultimately to revolutions of one sort or another in many countries (including

New Zealand), that would establish a new global constitutional order. Like any other, the new order would be subject to the processes of legitimation that we have considered here; and, in circumstances we have considered, it would itself be vulnerable to revolutionary change or overthrow.

ABBREVIATIONS

AC	Appeal Cases (House of Lords and Judicial Committee of the Privy Council)
A.J.A	Acting Justice of Appeal
AJHR	Appendices to the Journals of the House of Representatives
BostCICLRev	*Boston College International and Comparative Law Review*
CA	Court of Appeal
CBRev	*Canadian Bar Review*
Ch	Chancery (Division of the English High Court)
C.J.	Chief Justice
C.J.C.	Chief Justice of Canada
CLJ	*Cambridge Law Journal*
CLR	Commonweath Law Reports (High Court of Australia)
CNLC	Canadian Native Law Cases
CNLR	Canadian Native Law Reporter
CO	*Colonial Office Papers*
GBPP	*Great Britain Parliamentary Papers*
HC	High Court
HCA	High Court of Australia
J.	Justice
J.A.	Justice of Appeal
Laws NZ, Water	The title Water in Butterworths' *Laws of New Zealand*
L Ed	Lawyer's Edition (United States; mostly USSC reports)
L J	*Law Journal*
L.J.	Lord Justice (English Court of Appeal)
LR	Law Reports
LRC	Law Reports of the Commonwealth (formerly the British Commonwealth)
LRC (Const)	Law Reports of the Commonwealth (Constitutional)
L Rev	*Law Review*
McGLJ	*McGill Law Journal*

NZLJ	*New Zealand Law Journal*
NZLR	New Zealand Law Reports
NZLRev	*New Zealand Law Review*
NZPCC	New Zealand Privy Council Cases (1840–1932)
NZRecLRev	*New Zealand Recent Law Review*
NZRMA	New Zealand Resource Management Appeals
NZULRev	*New Zealand Universities Law Review*
PLD	Pakistan Legal Decisions
QB[KB]	Queen's [King's] Bench (Division of the English High Court)
QdR	Queensland Reports
QLJ	*Queen's Law Journal*
R Regina [Rex]	Queen [King] (i.e. the Crown; usually in criminal proceedings)
SA	South African Law Reports
SALJ	*South African Law Journal*
SASR	South Australian State Reports
SC	Supreme Court
SCR	Supreme Court Reports (Canada)
St Tr	State Trials
US	United States (Supreme Court Reports)
USSC	United States Supreme Court
UTLJ	*University of Toronto Law Journal*
VUWLRev	*Victoria University of Wellington Law Review*

NOTES

Introduction
1 *Report of the Waitangi Tribunal on the Muriwhenua Fishing Claim* (Wai 22; 1988), p. xxi.
2 Created by the Treaty of Waitangi Act 1975. Its jurisdiction was made retroactive to the making of the Treaty of Waitangi (6 February 1840) by the Treaty of Waitangi Amendment Act 1985.

Chapter 1
1 *European Revolutions 1492–1992* (1993), p. 8.
2 Ibid., p. 10.
3 Ibid., p. 14.
4 Ibid., p. 15.
5 Ibid., p. 240.
6 Ibid., p. 9.
7 Ibid. See the definition of 'coup' in Luttwak, *Coup d'Etat* (1968), p. 27:

> A *coup* consists of the infiltration of a small but critical segment of the state apparatus, which is then used to displace the government from its control of the remainder.

8 Cf. the treatment of the great European revolutions and of the legal systems created by them in Berman, *Law and Revolution* (1983).
9 Conquest here includes the case where the territory concerned is formally ceded by the vanquished to the victor.
10 See further at pp. 17–18.
11 See the complicated example of the splitting of Ireland into the separate polities of what is (now) the Irish Republic and Northern Ireland. See further n. 12 below.
12 As in the establishment of the Constitution of Eire in 1937, enacted by referendum of the electorate without the authority of the existing Free State legislature. Because the latter was, arguably, and on the British view, the creation of the Westminster Parliament, the device of technical revolution was adopted to sever the constitutional links with the United Kingdom. See Wheare, *The Constitutional Structure of the Commonwealth* (1960), pp. 90–94, and Delany, 'The Constitution of Ireland' (1957–58) 12 *UTLJ* 1, pp. 6–8.
The process by which the British Imperial Crown became a plurality of Crowns (in right of New Zealand, in right of the United Kingdom, etc.) also appears to be a revolution of this type. See ch. 5, pp. 119ff.
13 As where the United Kingdom Parliament has passed legislation in breach of some of the fundamental provisions of the Union of 1707 between England and Scotland. On one (Scottish) view, these have been instances of 'revolution by consent': see Smith, 'The Union of 1707 as Fundamental Law' [1957] *Public Law* 99, p. 112. For brief discussion see my 'The Treaty of Waitangi, the Constitution and the Future' (1995) *British Review of New Zealand Studies*, No. 8, 4, pp. 4–5.
14 See ch. 4, pp. 104–106.
15 See ch. 7, pp. 177ff.

16 See ch. 6, pp. 157–158.
17 See ch. 7, pp. 169ff.
18 By 'constitutional structure' I mean both (i) the apparatus of government (cf. the definition of 'coup' in n. 7 above), referring collectively to the offices, legislative, executive and judicial, which make up that structure or apparatus in the developed state (provided for in most instances by a written constitution) and (ii) the authority structure established by custom in a tribal polity.
19 For the proposition that the acts of a de facto monarch are regarded as valid, see the old authorities discussed by Richmond J. in *Re Aldridge* (1893) 15 NZLR 361, pp. 368–371. The statute 1 Edw. IV, c. 1 (1460) confirmed generally the judicial acts of the Lancastrian kings (Henry IV, Henry V and Henry VI, all of whom were de facto monarchs in relation to the claims of the House of York); but this Act appears to be declaratory of the common law since it is the only example of validating legislation passed after a period of monarchical usurpation. On the other hand the Act 12 Car. II, c. 12, passed on the restoration of the monarchy in 1660 to validate generally the proceedings of the courts of the republican interregnum, was necessary, since the principle under discussion was applied to monarchical usurpation only. For the view that 1 Edw IV, c. 1 was declaratory, see *Re Aldridge*, pp. 369–370 (Richmond J.). (The contrary view of Simon P. in *Adams v Adams* [1971] P 188, p. 213 does not take into account the differing monarchical and republican contexts of the statutes.)
20 The distinction in the text between 'English' and 'British' is deliberate, since it was the common law of England that was received into the settled colonies of the British Empire.
21 See at pp. 22–23 below.
22 Each of the last three monarchs named was a usurper in relation to the line of succession disrupted by the coup which he carried out. (Henry V and Henry VI were lawful successors to Henry IV in the line that he established by his coup.) In the case of William and Mary the coup was largely carried out by means of foreign (i.e., Dutch) invasion but that circumstance does not affect the validity of the comparison.
   On the matters discussed, see my 'Kelsen, the Constitution and the Treaty' (1992) 15 NZULRev 163, pp. 164–165. A fuller exposition is to come. But the argument is sufficiently indicated here to set the 'de facto' monarch (as a monarch for the time being) apart from the generality of usurping officers and governments to which the de facto doctrines discussed later in this chapter apply.
23 See n. 19 above.
24 Such a change might of course be validated by tribal acceptance, either immediately or in time.
25 See Luttwak, *Coup d'Etat* (1968), p. 23. Cf. Yash Ghai, 'Constitutions and Governance in Africa' in Adelman and Paliwala (eds), *Law and Crisis in the Third World* (1993), 51, p. 70 (referring to 'coups, which are merely transfers of power among political elites' as 'common').
26 See the analysis of the coup d'état in Finnis, 'Revolutions and Continuity of Law' in Simpson (ed.), *Oxford Essays in Jurisprudence* (2nd series, 1973), 44, pp. 46–50. See further n. 32 below.
27 This would be by way of exception to the general position as analysed by Finnis (see nn. 26 above and 32 below).
28 See the cases cited and discussed at pp. 23ff.
29 See ch. 4, p. 85 and ch. 5, pp. 123, 127.
30 H. Kelsen, *General Theory of Law and State* (Wedberg's translation, 1945; reprinted 1999), pp. 115, 117–118; *Pure Theory of Law* (2nd edn; Knight's translation, 1967), p. 204. See the discussion in my 'The Courts, Kelsen, and the Rhodesian Revolution' (1969) 19 *UTLJ* 326

Notes

at 338ff. On the (now) fictitious nature of the *grundnorm* construct, see Kelsen, *General Theory of Norms* (1979; Hartney's translation, 1991), p. 256, and Paulson, 'Kelsen's Legal Theory' (1992), 12 *Oxford Journal of Legal Studies* 265, pp. 268–270.

31 Kelsen, *Pure Theory*, p. 212.
32 For Kelsen '[a] revolution in the broader sense of the word (that includes a coup d'état) is every not legitimate change of . . . [a] constitution or its replacement [in a manner other than that prescribed] by another constitution': *Pure Theory*, p. 209. I accept that definition as an alternative to mine (i) except so far as it appears to include *all* coups d'état (see above as to the non-revolutionary coup d'état) and (ii) with the qualification that it would appear artificial not to allow that a revolution involving a partial constitutional change may, depending on its extent, take place without involving notionally the *complete* change in the basis of the legal order (i.e., in the basic norm) that Kelsen's theory requires. But such a partial revolutionary change would, like the complete change in the basic norm, require to be by and large effective for it to be validated under the supra-constitutional principles discussed at pp. 23ff.
33 By the Articles of Union and the Acts of Union of the respective Parliaments (1706) and the Protestant Religion and Presbyterian Church Act 1707 (Scotland). For the Union as a revolution by consent, see Smith, n. 13 above, p. 111. The resultant basic norm for Great Britain is also the basic norm for Northern Ireland as the residual part of Ireland under the Crown. As to the Irish Republic see n. 12 above. (As to the creation of the basic norm simply by custom, see Kelsen, *General Theory of Norms*, p. 255. Cf. in the United Kingdom context Harris, 'When and Why Does the Grundnorm Change?' [1971] *CLJ* 103, p. 111.)
34 Probably most tribal legal orders, both within individual tribes and in the miniature international societies that they may constitute in a particular territory, are in varying degrees undeveloped or primitive, in lacking special legislative and judicial organs of government for the creation and application of law. They are comparable in that respect with the (originally western) international legal order which has only recently begun to develop legislative and judicial organs. See Kelsen's discussion of international law as a primitive legal order, in which the 'technique of self-help, characteristic of primitive law, prevails', in *Pure Theory*, p. 323. In a rudimentary tribal or inter-tribal legal order, consisting largely of customary law, the basic norm is of course likely to be created by custom (see n. 33 above); as in more developed legal orders lacking formal constitutions created by agreement.

For a general definition of customary law, see, e.g., Hamnett, *Chieftainship and Legitimacy* (1975), p. 14: '. . . a set of norms which the actors in a social situation abstract from practice and which they invest with binding authority'. It is distinguishable from mere practice — what people do — which is inevitably often contrary to the norms of customary law: see ibid., p. 12 and *Hlophe v Mahlalela* 1998 (1) SALR 449, pp. 457–458 (Transvaal Provincial Divn).

See further ch. 3, pp. 70–71 and ch. 4, p. 86.
35 See ch. 5.
36 See ch. 5, pp. 122ff.
37 See my 'The Fiji Revolutions of 1987' [1988] *NZLJ* 250.
38 See ch. 7, pp. 166ff. and 177ff.
39 See further ch. 4, p. 94.
40 See pp. 32–34.
41 [1923] 1 Irish Reports 5.
42 For brief mention see the Law Commission's Report No. 22, *Final Report on Emergencies* (1991), paras 4.45–4.48; and see below, ch. 5, p. 112.

43 See, e.g., de Smith and Brazier, *Constitutional and Administrative Law* (7th edn; 1994), pp. 567–569.
44 For references and discussion see my 'The Fiji Revolutions of 1987' [1988] *NZLJ* 250, p. 251.
45 See e.g. *Re Aldridge* (1893) 15 NZLR 361 (CA) and *Ararimu Farms Ltd v Stotter* (1992), unreported but noted [1993] *NZRecLRev* 286. For discussion and further references, see ibid. and my 'The MP and the De Facto Doctrine' [1983] *NZLJ* 86.
46 See Grotius, *De Jure Belli ac Pacis* (English edn; 1738, p. 121), 1. 4. 15:

> We have treated of him, who has now, or has had, a Right to govern; it now remains that we say something of him that usurps the government; not after he has either by long possession, or Agreement obtained a Right to it, but so long as the Cause of his unjust Possession continues. The Acts of Sovereignty exercised by such an Usurper may have an obligatory Force, not by virtue of his Right, (for he had none) but because it is very probable that the lawful Sovereign, whether it be the People themselves, or a King, or a Senate, chooses rather that the Usurper should be obeyed during that Time, than that the Exercise of the Laws and Justice should be interrupted and the State thereby exposed to all the disorders of anarchy.

47 7 Wallace 700.
48 171 US 388.
49 See dissenting judgments in *Madzimbamuto v Lardner-Burke* 1968 (2) SA 284 (High Court of Sthn Rhodesia; Appellate Divn), pp. 435ff. (Fieldsend A.J.A.), and [1969] 1 AC 645 (PC), pp. 732ff. (Lord Pearce). The passage from Grotius (n. 46 above) is quoted in the majority judgment of the Privy Council ([1969] 1 AC, pp. 728–729) with the comment: 'It may be that there is a general principle, depending on implied mandate from the lawful Sovereign, which recognises the need to preserve law and order in territory controlled by a usurper.'
50 *Jilani v Government of the Punjab* PLD 1972 SC 139; *Bhutto v Chief of Army Staff* PLD 1977 SC 657.
51 *Mitchell v DPP* [1986] LRC (Const) 35.
52 See n. 49 above.
53 *R v Ndhlovu* 1968 (4) SA 515.
54 See p. 13.
55 See pp. 15-16. Such a coup would depose the monarch for the time being in right of New Zealand, in favour of another claimant.
56 Briefly summarized, s. 5(1) provides that 'the death of the Sovereign' has the effect of transferring the powers and functions of the Crown to 'the Sovereign's successor, as determined in accordance with' the Act of Settlement 1701 (England) '*and any other law relating to the succession to the Throne*' but has no other effect in law. It is uncertain whether the emphasized words would include the law relating to the 'usurping' monarch for the time being. The difficulties cannot be considered further here.
57 7 Howard 1.
58 1968 (2) SA 284, pp. 426–428.
59 [1969] 1 AC 645, p. 732.
60 See Robinson, *Justice in Grey* (1941), pp. 3–5, 25–26.
61 [1969] 1 AC 645.
62 At p. 724.
63 *Uganda v Commissioner of Prisons, ex parte Matovu* [1966] EA 514.
64 *State v Dosso* [1958] 2 Pakistan Supreme Court Reports 180; *Jilani v Government of the Punjab* PLD 1972 SC 139; *Bhutto v Chief of Army Staff* PLD 1977 SC 657.
65 *Mitchell v Director of Public Prosecutions* [1986] LRC (Const) 35.

Notes

66 *Mokotso v HM King Moshoeshoe II* [1989] LRC (Const) 24.
67 *Mangope v Van der Walt* 1994 (3) SA 850 (Bophuthatswana General Divn).
68 *State v Dosso* (Pakistan), n. 64 above, *Matovu* (Uganda), n. 63 above, and *Madzimbamuto v Lardner-Burke* 1968 (2) SA 284, pp. 315-318 (Beadle C.J.). See also *Mokotso*, n. 66 above, pp. 124-127.
69 See my 'The Courts, Kelsen and the Rhodesian Revolution' (1969) 19 *UTLJ* 326, pp. 342-344.
70 Honoré, 'Reflections on Revolutions' (1967) 2 *Irish Jurist* (NS) 268, pp. 275-276. Cf. John Finnis's suggestion (in part adapting work of the Danish jurist, Alf Ross) of a 'general principle' accommodating in law revolutionary constitutional changes, except for those totally subverting the order of society. See Finnis, n. 26 above, pp. 63-65, and discussion in my 'Parliamentary Supremacy and Constitutional Entrenchment' (1984) 5 *Otago L Rev* 603, pp. 624-627.
71 *Jilani*, n. 64 above, p. 182 (Hamoodur Rahman C.J.), p. 258 (Sajjad Ahmed J.) and p. 267 (Salahudin Ahmed J.).
72 [1969] 1 AC 645, pp. 724-725.
73 See: *Mokotso*, n. 66 above, p. 133; *Matanzima v President of Transkei* 1989 (4) SA 989, pp. 996-997 (Transkei General Divn); *Mangope*, n. 67 above, pp. 865-866. The statements in these cases refer to the validation of legislation but the principle clearly applies generally to the acts of revolutionary governments.
74 See *Mokotso*, n. 66 above, p. 125.
75 At p. 128.
76 See *Mangope*, n. 67 above, p. 867 (Comrie J.), where however 'the risk of a premature recognition of legality *in mediis rebus*' — when the outcome of the revolution is not yet decided — is noted.
77 See *Mokotso*, n. 66 above, p. 139.
78 PLD 1977 SC 657, pp. 688, 692 and 721 (S Anwarul Haq C.J.). Of the other eight Judges only Qaisar Khan J. (pp. 740ff.) appears to have dissented on that point, applying a test of effectiveness only.
79 [1986] LRC (Const) 35.
80 At p. 72.
81 [1993] 3 LRC 13, p. 63.
82 At p. 63, quoting from *Mokotso*, n. 66 above, pp. 129-130.
83 *R v Walker* [1989] 2 Qd R 79. See ch. 2, pp. 38ff.
84 *After 1989: Morals, Revolution and Civil Society* (1997), p. 4.
85 11 Hen VII, c. 1.
86 The majority view is that of the older writers, such as Coke, *Institutes*, III, 7, and Hawkins, *Pleas of the Crown*, Book 1, ch. 17, pp. 35-36, accepted in *Harris's Criminal Law* (22nd edn (McLean and Morrish); 1973), p. 123, and *Russell on Crime* (6th edn (Turner); 1964), vol. i, p. 211. Blackstone (4 *Comm* 77-78) strongly dissented, maintaining that allegiance was not due to the de facto monarch as against the lawful claimant. In that he is supported by Honoré ('Allegiance and the Usurper' [1967] *CLJ* 214). For a detailed defence of the majority view, see Brookfield (forthcoming).
87 *R v Cook* (1660) 5 St Tr 1077, 114; *R v Vane* (1662) 6 St Tr 119.
88 [1969] 1 AC 645, p. 726.
89 18 Canadian Criminal Cases 495.
90 Both provisions followed the draft English Criminal Code of 1875.
91 [1993] 3 CNLR 209 (Ontario Prov. Divn.).
92 For the case on appeal (where s. 15 of the Criminal Code was not relied on) see *R v*

Pamajewon [1996] 2 SCR 821 (SCC) and n. 60, p. 196.
93 See, e.g., *Captain Streater's Case* (1653) 5 St Tr 365 and *Lord Protector v Mordant* (1658) 5 St Tr 907.
94 *The State v Eight Rotuman Chiefs*, Law Report, *Fiji Times*, 10 June 1988.
95 See (1990) 60 *Pacific Islands Monthly*, no. 12, p. 17.
96 1 Dallas 53.
97 At p. 57.
98 At p. 58.
99 De Smith and Brazier, n. 43 above, p. 74.
100 See p. 27.
101 Cf. *Jilani v Government of the Punjab* PLD 1972 SC 139 at p. 261 (Sajjad Ahmad J.), where the principle is stated specifically in the revolutionary context.
102 The term 'validate' (in the sense of uphold what is in itself unlawful) is appropriate for the exercise of this supra-constitutional function. See D. P. O'Connell's use of the term in discussing the abolition of the monarchy in Australia by purported amendment of the Constitution; which (in his view) would be beyond the amending power (and hence revolutionary) but which, he allowed, the High Court would 'validate'. See his 'Monarchy or Republic?' in Dutton (ed.), *Republican Australia?* (1977), 23, p. 38. For this type of revolution, see p. 15.
103 See ch. 5, pp. 123ff.
104 See pp. 13–14.
105 See pp. 19–20.
106 [1923] 1 Irish Reports 5.
107 At p. 9. See Ring, *Erskine Childers* (1996), pp. 283–284.
108 See ch. 7, pp. 166ff.
109 As in *R v Walker* [1989] 2 Qd R 79. See ch. 2, pp. 38ff.
110 See ch. 2, p. 38.
111 See ch. 4, pp. 93–95.
112 Sharp, 'Why be Bicultural?' in Wilson and Yeatman (eds), *Justice and Identity* (1995), 116, p. 129. I am using 'prescription' to include the concept of adverse possession, i.e., 'possession as of wrong' (see *Sze v Kung* [1997] 1 Weekly Law Reports 1232, p. 1235 (PC)), which is essentially the possession of the squatter in the common law. (For the technical prescription/adverse possession distinctions see, e.g., *Buckinghamshire County Council v Moran* [1990] Ch 623, p. 644.)
113 Twelve years (60 where the Limitation Act 1950 applies to Crown land) is the period which perfects a squatter's title under ss. 7 and 18 of that Act in the rare cases where they apply. The period is 20 years under s. 3 of the Land Transfer Amendment Act 1963. See my 'Prescription and Adverse Possession' in Hinde (ed.), *New Zealand Torrens System Centennial Essays* (1971), 162; and Hinde, McMorland and Sim, *Butterworths Land Law in New Zealand* (1997), para 2.027.
The Limitation Act 1950 does not apply to Maori customary land (s. 6(1)); except in favour of the Crown, so that the customary title cannot be enforced against it when the 12-year period has expired (s. 6(1)(A) and s. 7A). See further ch. 5, pp. 131, 133.
114 This is substantially the effect of Part I of the Land Transfer Amendment Act 1963 (Prescriptive Title to Land), qualifying the protection (against the adverse possessor) given to the registered proprietor by s. 64 of the Land Transfer Act 1952. See generally on the New Zealand position: Brookfield, n. 113 above, pp. 205ff.; and *Land Law*, n. 113 above, paras 2.004 and 2.179–2.191.
115 1968 (2) SA 284.

Notes

116 At p. 369. The 'adverse user' referred to by the Judge President means the use or exercise of powers of government by the usurper. It corresponds in effect to the 'adverse possession' of the squatter on land, as to which see n.112 above.
117 At pp. 368–369, quoting Bryce, *Studies in History and Jurisprudence* (1901 edn), vol. ii, p. 65.
118 See Brookfield, n. 113 above, pp. 163–165; and *Land Law*, n. 113 above, para 2.004.
119 This is the case as between squatters even on land in a New Zealand registered title. See Brookfield, n. 113 above, pp. 174ff.; and *Land Law*, n. 113 above, para 2.004.
120 As to the position in Maori society, see ch. 4 , p. 89 and n.41, p. 204.
121 For the traditional doctrine, see Korman, *The Right of Conquest* (1996), Part I.
122 Bartlett, *The Making of Europe* (1993), pp. 92–95; and see n. 123 below. At least in England, however, some did take by grant from William, in accordance with the traditional view: see Green, *The Aristocracy of Norman England* (1997), pp. 52–53.
123 The long-accepted proposition that on the conquest in 1066 William became the owner of all land in England, so that all titles were based on grants made by him to persons who then held as his tenants, is disputed by S. Reynolds, in her recent challenge to orthodox views of feudalism. See her *Fiefs and Vassals* (1994), esp. pp. 360–361. It is however too late to question the orthodox common law doctrine of the Crown as ultimate owner of all land. See ch. 2, p. 53 and in the New Zealand context ch. 5, p. 128.
124 See p. 35.
125 The end came about under the Covenant of the League of Nations, the General Treaty for the Renunciation of War (1928) and the Charter of the United Nations. See Korman, op. cit., pp. 179ff. But 'the modern prohibition against the acquisition of territory by conquest should not be construed as affecting titles to territory created prior to the Charter regime and valid under international law': Korman, op. cit., p. 13, fn. 17, quoting UN General Assembly Resolution 2625 (XXV), 24 Oct 1970.
126 See e.g. Korman, op. cit., pp. 281ff.
127 Ibid., pp. 16–17.
128 As to acts of state, see ch. 2, pp. 53–54.
129 The legality of such conquests has also been impugned, as by India in respect of the centuries-long Portuguese occupation of Goa by right of conquest, in order to justify India's own invasion and annexation of Goa in 1961. See Korman, op. cit., 267ff. and n. 125 above.

Chapter 2

1 See ch. 1, pp. 27–28.
2 See Passerin d'Entrèves, *The Notion of the State* (1967), pp. 141ff. See also ch. 3, pp. 57ff.
3 See Finnis, *Natural Law and Natural Rights* (1980), pp. 251–252. The responsibility being in the interests of the governed, the actions of the revolutionaries in discharging it are legitimated even if the seizure of power was morally wrong, and (generally) whatever the ideology of the revolutionaries. This does not legitimate the title to rule, except so far as it strengthens claims to legitimacy based on the durability of the revolutionary order. This minimal legitimacy is a moral parallel to the legal validity of the acts of government of a de facto regime (see ch. 1, pp. 20–22).
4 [1989] 2 Qd R 79.
5 At p. 83. See Wade, 'The Basis of Legal Sovereignty' [1955] *CLJ* 172, p. 189.
6 [1989] 2 Qd R, p. 83. See Kelsen, *Pure Theory of Law* (2nd edn; Knight's translation, 1967), p. 212.
7 [1989] 2 Qd R, p. 84. See Dias, 'Legal Politics: Norms behind the *Grundnorm*' [1968] *CLJ* 233, p. 237.

8   See ch. 1, pp. 34–36.
9   See ch. 1, p. 35.
10 *Justice and the Maori* (2nd edn, 1997), p. 286.
11 *Confusions and Revolutions* (1649), p. 32 (printed in Sharp, *Political Ideas of the English Civil Wars* (1983), p. 220).
12 Hume, *A Treatise of Human Nature,* Book III, part II, sect X, p. 255 (Everyman's edn).
13 See p. 45.
14 Dickinson, *Liberty and Property* (1977), p. 135 (his emphasis); Hume, op. cit., p. 255. Hume allowed for 'resistance in the more flagrant instances of tyranny and oppression': ibid., p. 252 (quoted by Dickinson, op. cit., p. 136).
15 David Beetham, dealing with the evidence of consent necessary to establish legitimacy, requires 'demonstrable expression' (such as swearing allegiance or taking part in elections) by those qualified to give consent in the particular society. See Beetham, *The Legitimation of Power* (1991), pp. 18–19. (By contrast, the dissenters' continuing to reside within the country after it has come under effective revolutionary rule and there has been reasonable opportunity for them to leave, is sufficient to make them subject to the new legal order: *Respublica v Chapman* 1 Dallas 53 (1781). See ch. 1, pp. 30–31.)
16 Actions taken in unlawful opposition to the government (unlawful, that is, under the revolutionary legal order of which the government is part), in withdrawal of consent, necessarily erode its legitimacy. See Beetham, op. cit., p. 19.
17 See ch. 1, p. 15.
18 Beetham, op. cit., pp. 101–102.
19 The need for some measure of consent of the governed, always a criterion of the legitimacy of the government and the political system and legal order, has in modern times become a need for their actual and controlling participation in the government, through universal suffrage and an elected legislature with substantial powers (though the powers may be properly limited to secure other elements in legitimacy such as individual freedoms).
20 Beetham, op. cit., pp. 138, 142.
21 See ch. 1, p. 27.
22 See pp. 38–39.
23 Fletcher and MacCullough, *Tudor Rebellions* (4th edn, 1997), p. 119, quoting Bercé, *Revolt and Revolution* (1987), p. 221.
24 See in the New Zealand context ch. 7, pp. 176–177.
25 See pp. 38–39.
26 *The Notion of the State* (1967), pp. 141–142.
27 See p. 41.
28 See p. 43.
29 Kelsen, *Pure Theory of Law,* pp. 48–49.
30 Ibid. 'Remota itaque iustitia, quid sunt regna, nisi magna latrocinia? Quia et latrocinia quid sunt, nisi parva regna?': Augustine, *De Civitate Dei,* iv, 4. Kelsen's translator uses Healey's translation (1610) but omits 'fair', losing the sense of large-scale robberies (*magna latrocinia*) of the Latin.
31 Augustine, loc. cit.: W. M. Green's translation, *The City of God against the Pagans,* Loeb Classical Library, vol ii (1963), p. 17. Augustine's editors cite as the likely origin of the story the fragmentary version in Cicero, *De Republica,* III, 14, 24.
32 Deane, *The Political and Social Ideas of St Augustine* (1963), pp. 126, 298. I am grateful to Professor Andrew Sharp for discussion on this point.
33 Burnell, 'Service to Unjust Regimes', in Donnelly (ed.), *The City of God: A Collection of Critical Essays* (1995), 37, p. 45 (on the 'important principle [in Augustine] that civil justice,

Notes

or rather some approximation to it, is basic to a governmental system's right to be left alone').

34 Of course in an extreme case the lack of legitimacy is likely in the end to prompt either radical reform of the political system and the legal order by constitutional means (if that is possible) or their revolutionary overthrow and replacement, as in the collapse of the Communist regimes in Eastern Europe.
35 Cf. Zion and Yazzie, 'Indigenous Law in North America', (1997) 20 *BostCICLRev* 55, p. 58.
36 See Kunkel, *Roman Legal and Constitutional History* (2nd edn; 1973), pp. 76ff., where the *ius civile* is distinguished from the *ius gentium* (law of nations), the body of law applied in Roman courts to both Romans and foreigners in their interrelationships in both public and private law.
37 Ibid., 77–78.
38 Winter, *On the Trial of Jesus* (1961), pp. 11, 14.
39 As to the proceedings against Jesus and for further references, see Watson, *The Trial of Jesus* (1995), esp. ch. 13 and Winter, op. cit., pp. 49–50, 146–148, 173–174, et passim. For those against Paul (who, invoking his citizenship, appealed to Rome), see, for example, Winter, op. cit., pp. 76–87. The respective accounts in the Gospels and in the Acts of the Apostles are not necessarily clear or accurate in detail as to the facts or the law. But they show the dual Roman–Jewish jurisdictions that undoubtedly existed and may be of some significance in the understanding of kawanatanga (governance) in the New Zealand context: see ch. 4, pp. 100ff.
40 Lewis, *Islam and the West* (1993), pp. 47–48. The relative tolerance of Islam to the *dhimmis*, though as second-class citizens, was carried over to the Ottoman empire: Canuel, 'Nationalism, Self-Determination, and Nationalist Movements', (1997) 20 *BostCICLRev* 85, p. 97).
41 Lewis, loc. cit.
42 Bartlett, *The Making of Europe* (1993), pp. 204ff. The book is an account of the expansion of Latin Europe (the area originally Roman Catholic, rather than Greek Orthodox or non-Christian), especially by Normans and Germans. The frontier zones treated are those of Wales and Ireland, eastern Europe, Spain in the course of the Reconquest, and of the eastern Mediterranean in the Crusades.
43 Ibid., p. 208. Compare the similar toleration of Christians and Jews in Muslim principalities: see n. 40 above and Lewis, *Cultures in Conflict* (1995), pp. 44–46.
44 O'Callaghan, *A History of Medieval Spain* (1976), pp. 669–672; Bartlett, op. cit., p. 220; Lewis, *Cultures in Conflict*, pp. 46ff.
45 Bartlett, op. cit., p. 211.
46 On what follows, see generally Roberts-Wray, *Commonwealth and Colonial Law* (1966), pp. 534–538.
47 See Anderson, 'Customary Law and Islamic Law in British African Territories' in *The Future of Customary Law in Africa* (1956), 70.
48 For the difficulties attaching to the term 'indigenous', see ch. 3, pp. 77ff.
49 See generally as to British colonies, Roberts-Wray, op. cit., pp. 534–535, 575–579; and see Allott, *Essays in African Law* (1960) 74, 197–201, and Anderson, n. 47 above, p. 71. See the rule stated by Holt C.J. to be applicable to a conquered 'infidel' country: '. . . their laws by conquest do not entirely cease, but only such as are against the law of God' (*Blankard v Galdy* (1693) 2 Salk 411, p. 412). The exception stated by the Chief Justice is in effect the morality and justice exception.

See, as to New Zealand, s. 71 of the New Zealand Constitution Act 1852 and ch. 5, p. 116.
50 For this class of the colonies of the former British empire, see Roberts-Wray, op. cit., pp.

45–47; and generally on the criteria for classification see McNeil, *Common Law Aboriginal Title* (1989), pp. 117–132. Since the decision of the High Court of Australia in *Mabo v Queensland (No 2)* (1992) 175 CLR 1 there is now no link between the concept of the settled colony and sparsely populated territory conceived (until that case) as *terra nullius*.
51 See n. 77, pp. 210–211 below.
52 *Campbell v Hall* (1774) 1 Cowp 204, p. 209. See Roberts-Wray, op, cit., pp. 541–543. See further at p. 51.
53 This to prefer the 'continuity doctrine' which rests firmly on a line of cases decided on aboriginal title and now accepted as authoritative (see pp. 52–53), as opposed to the 'recognition doctrine' (see, for example, *Vajesingji Joravarsingji v Secretary of State for India* (1924) LR 51 Indian Appeals 357), holding that the Crown was bound only by such pre-existing aboriginal rights as it *chose* to recognize). For discussion and analysis of the two doctrines, see McNeil, op. cit., pp. 165–179.
54 See *In re Southern Rhodesia* [1919] AC 211 at 233–234 (PC). Despite the tone of the passage quoted from, the substance of what is said is not irreconcilable with the Privy Council's later warning, in *Amodu Tijani v Secretary, Southern Rhodesia* [1921] 2 AC 399, pp. 402–403, against the 'tendency, operating at times unconsciously, to render ... [native] title conceptually in terms which are appropriate only to systems which have grown up under English law.'
55 *Walker v New South Wales* (1994) 182 CLR 45 (HCA).
56 For cases and for discussion, see, e.g., McNeil, op. cit., p. 181. For New Zealand cases in particular see ch. 5, pp. 128ff.
57 *Cherokee Nation v State of Georgia* 5 Peters 1 (1831), p. 17, and *Worcester v Georgia* 6 Peters 515 (1832). In the latter case see, especially at pp. 546–548, Marshall C.J.'s explaining of the historical position of the Indian nations in relation successively to the Crown and the United States. See p. 54.
58 See for example Newton, 'Federal Power over Indians' (1984) 132 *University of Pennsylvania L Rev* 195 and Zion and Yazzie, 'Indigenous Law in North America' (1997) 20 *BostCICLRev* 55.
59 See *Connolly v Woolrich* (1867) 1 CNLC 70 (Quebec SC), esp. at 79–82. (The decision of Monk J. in that case was affirmed in *Johnstone v Connolly* (1869) 1 CNLC 151 (Quebec QB) but see the discussion in Walters, 'British Imperial Constitutional Law and Aboriginal Rights', (1992) 17 *QLJ* 350, 379ff. Cf. Strong J.'s use of the domestic dependent nations concept in *St Catharines Milling and Lumber Co v The Queen* (1887) 13 SCR 577 at 610–612, in relation to aboriginal land rights.
60 *R v Pamajewon* [1996] 2 SCR 821 (SCC) and *Delgamuukw v British Columbia* [1997] 3 SCR 1010, p. 114 (Lamer C.J.C.) and p. 1134 (La Forest J.). For criticism of the *Pamajewon* decision, see Morse, 'Permafrost Rights' (1997) 42 *McG LJ* 1011. As to the constitutional protection afforded by s. 35(1), especially in respect of rights of self-government, see McNeil, 'Envisaging Constitutional Space for Aboriginal Governments' (1993) 19 *QLJ* 95 and n. 98, p. 199 below.
61 *Coe v Commonwealth* (1979) 24 ALR 118 (HCA) and *Coe v Commonwealth* (1993) 118 ALR 193 (HCA).
62 See ch. 5, pp. 116–119.
63 Slattery, 'Understanding Aboriginal Rights' (1987), 66 *CBRev* 727, pp. 737–738.
64 *R v Coté* [1996] 3 SCR 139, pp. 174–175 (Lamer C.J.C.).
65 Roberts-Wray, *Commonwealth and Colonial Law* (1966), p. 534.
66 Allott, *Essays in African Law* (1960), p. 155.
67 Roberts-Wray, op. cit., p. 535.
68 It is notable that both Tanzania and Kenya, after independence, legislated to limit African

Notes

customary law to civil matters: Bakari, 'Africa's Paradoxes of Legal Pluralism in Personal Laws' (1991) 3 *RADIC (African Journal of International and Comparative Law)* 545, p. 546.
69 See p. 53.
70 Vitoria, *De Indis*, 1.1–6, 3.8. For translation, see Pagden and Lawrance (eds), *Vitoria*, pp. 239–251, 291–292.
71 Vitoria, op. cit., 2.1–3.8. See Pagden and Lawrance (eds), op. cit., pp. 251–291.
72 Natural law (*ius naturale*) was, in the classification of the Roman jurists, a system of ideal law (by contrast with the *ius civile* and the *ius gentium*: see n. 36, p. 195 above) which was rationally knowable by and applicable to all humanity, and under which (for example) people may not be enslaved. Differing views of the application of natural law to the conquests of the Americas were held by Spanish writers: see Muldoon, *The Americas in the Spanish World Order* (1994), pp. 79ff. See also ch. 3, pp. 58–59.
73 See Slattery, 'Understanding Aboriginal Rights' (1987) 66 *CBRev* 727, p. 737, referring to the description of the process by which the common law principles developed in the judgment of Strong J. in *St Catharines Milling and Lumber Co v The Queen* (1887) 13 SCR 577, pp. 607–616. Strong J. described the practice as 'well understood and established' (at p. 607) and 'invariably acted [upon by the Crown] with reference to Indian lands, at least from the year 1756. . . .'
74 For example, Robert Gray, whose views are discussed by G. Mackenthun, *Metaphors of Dispossession* (1997), pp. 193ff. Such views had some support in an opinion by several eminent English lawyers in 1675 to the effect that, at least as against the Crown, the Indians (as 'heathens and barbarians') had no title to the lands they occupied and hence nothing to sell. See *St Catharines Milling and Lumber Co v The Queen* (1885) 10 OR 196, p. 206 and, for discussion, McNeil, *Common Law Aboriginal Title* (1989), pp. 222–224.
75 By this proclamation (7 October 1763) the Crown, among other things, bound itself, to reserve under its 'Sovereignty, Protection and Dominion, for the use of the said Indians, all the lands and territories' described. The geographical scope of the proclamation has been in some doubt but it appears to extend throughout Canada. For recent discussion (with special reference to Quebec), see Boivin, 'The *Coté* Decision' [1995] 1 *CNLR* 1. The proclamation has the effect of a statute (analogous to *Magna Carta*: *Calder v Attorney-General of British Columbia* [1973] SCR 313, p. 395 (Hall J.)) and secures Indian rights generally, not only those of title to land, in respect of which it appears to be declaratory of the common law doctrine. The precise effects of the proclamation are not all yet determined. It is now, together with the treaties made by the Crown with the Indian Nations, protected by s. 35(1) of the Constitution Act 1982 (as to which see nn. 97–98, p. 199 below).
76 See *Fletcher v Peck* 6 Cranch 87 (1810), *Johnson and Graham's Lessee v M'Intosh* 8 Wheaton 543 (1823), *Worcester v State of Georgia* 6 Peters 515 (1832) and *Mitchell v US* 9 Peters 711 (1835). For discussion see, e.g., McNeil, *Common Law Aboriginal Title* (1989), pp. 227–229, 250ff., and Slattery, *Ancestral Lands, Alien Laws* (1983), pp. 17ff. The line of Supreme Court authority recoginzang the doctrine has continued fairly consistently since (though see the partially aberrant *Tee-Hit-Ton Indians v US* 348 US 272 (1955), in which the Court held that Indian title was not a constitutionally protected property right). See *County of Oneida v Oneida Indian Nation of New York State* 470 US 226 (1985). And see Kaplan, Annotation, 'Proof of Extinguishment of Aboriginal Title to Indian Lands' 41 American Law Reports Federal 425 (1979).
77 See *R v Symonds* (1847) NZPCC 387 (Supreme Court) and *In re 'The Lundon and Whitaker Claims Act 1871'* (1872) NZ 2 CA 41. For those cases and the later New Zealand developments see ch. 5, pp. 128ff.
78 For the earlier differences contrast (i) the rejection of the doctrine in the respective

judgments of Chancellor Boyd at first instance in *St Catharines Milling and Lumber Co v The Queen* (1885) 10 OR 196, p. 206, and of Taschereau J. in the Supreme Court of Canada in the same case (1887) 13 SCR 577, pp. 647–650, with (ii) the acceptance of it in the Supreme Court in that case by Ritchie C.J., at p. 600, and Strong J. in his important judgment at pp. 605ff. The judgments in the various Courts in that case are summarized by Pugh, 'Are Northern Lands Reserved for the Indians?' (1982) 60 *CBRev* 36. Of the many important recent cases in that Court accepting and expounding the doctrine (though not without difficulties), see among others *Calder v Attorney-General of British Columbia* [1973] SCR 313, and (following the constitutional protection accorded to the doctrine by s. 35(1) of the Constitution Act 1982) *Guerin v The Queen* [1984] 2 SCR 335, *R v Sparrow* [1990] 1 SCR 1075, *R v Van der Peet* [1996] 2 SCR 507 and *Delgamuukw v British Columbia* [1997] 3 SCR 1010.

79 See, for example, *St Catherine's Milling and Lumber Co v The Queen* (1888) 14 App Cas 46, where however (p. 54) the Indian title in question is ascribed to the royal proclamation of 1763 (see n. 75, p. 197 above) without reference to the common law, and also *Nireaha Tamaki v Baker* (1901) NZPCC 371, *Wallis v Solicitor-General* (1903) NZPCC 23, *Amodu Tijani v Secretary, Southern Nigeria* [1921] 2 AC 399, and *Oyekan v Adele* [1957] 2 All England Law Reports 785.

80 *Mabo v Queensland (No 2)* (1992) 175 CLR 1. See also *Western Australia v The Commonwealth* (1995) 183 CLR 373 and *Wik Peoples v Queensland* (1996) 187 CLR 1.

81 See n. 53, p. 196 above. The cases now overwhelmingly support or assume the correctness of the 'continuity doctrine'.

82 See *R v Secretary of State for Foreign and Commonwealth Affairs, ex parte Indian Association of Alberta* [1982] QB 892, pp. 910–911 (Lord Denning M.R.; referring to the customary communal rights of villagers, existing from time immemorial, recognized by the Court in *New Windsor Corpn v Mellor* [1975] 1 Ch 380); and see McNeil, *Common Law Aboriginal Title* (1989), p. 183, fn. 83. An apparent difference between the two types of customary right is that, whereas local customary rights in England are held to be immutable, it appears that customs establishing aboriginal rights may be modified by tribal or intertribal consensus. See *Hineiti Rirerire Arani v Public Trustee of New Zealand* (1919) NZPCC 1, p. 6 (discussed by McNeil, loc. cit., and Walters, 'British Imperial Constitutional Law' (1992) 17 *QLJ* at 393.

83 *Campbell v Hall* (1774) 1 Cowper 204, pp. 209–210; and see, e.g., *Sirdar Bhagwan Singh v Secretary of State for India* (1874) LR 2 IA 38. See McNeil, op. cit., p. 162. Cf. *Coe v Commonwealth* (1979) 24 ALR 118 (annexation of the territory of the Australian continent by acts of state, but without simultaneous seizure of aboriginal property). Generally as to acts of state, see Joseph, *Constitutional and Administrative Law* (1993), pp. 575–583.

84 On the general limitation in respect of those owing allegiance, see Joseph, op. cit., 577–578.

85 See *R v Symonds* (1847) NZPCC 387 (SC), *Veale v Brown* (1868) 1 NZCA 152, *Te Runanganui o Te Ika Whenua Inc Soc v Attorney-General* [1994] 2 NZLR 20, pp. 23–24 and *Mabo v Queensland (No 2)* (1992) 17 CLR 1; and Hinde, McMorland and Sim, *Butterworths Land Law in New Zealand* (1997), paras 1.017 and 1.018. The result in theory is that in all territories where the English common law was received, such as New Zealand and Australia, persons who in common parlance are said to have the freehold of land, and thus to own it, technically hold it as the tenants of the Crown (in succession to those to whom the Crown originally granted it). For doubts as to the historical explanation of the theory, see n. 123, p. 193 above.

86 See the treatment of the matter in the New Zealand context in ch. 5, pp. 129ff.

Notes

87 *Mabo v Queensland (No 2)* (1992) 175 CLR 1, *Western Australia v The Commonwealth* (1995) 183 CLR 373. See n. 88 below.
88 Canadian authority differs from the Australian cases cited in n. 87 above. See, e.g., *R v Badger* [1996] 1 SCR 771 (SCC) and the discussion of the differing Canadian and Australian authorities by McNeil in 'Co-existence of Indigenous Rights . . . in Australia and Canada' [1997] 3 *CNLR* 1. McNeil holds the view (accepted in this book) that in principle the Crown cannot by its prerogative extinguish aboriginal rights, since these are property rights of its subjects. For the New Zealand position, see ch. 5, p. 130.
89 See ch. 5, pp. 128ff.
90 Hogg, *Canadian Constitutional Law* (3rd edn; 1992) pp. 682ff. 'An Indian treaty is unique; it is an agreement *sui generis* which is neither created nor terminated according to the rules of international law': *Simon v The Queen* [1985] 2 SCR 387, p. 404 (Dickson C.J.C.).
91 See n. 98 below.
92 See Newton, 'Federal Power over Indians' (1984) 132 *University of Pennsylvania L Rev* 195, pp. 200–201. Agreements between the United States and Indian tribes before the legislative change of 1871 are regarded as treaties made with sovereign entities (domestic dependent nations: see p. 50) whose sovereignty however 'exists only at the sufferance of Congress': *United States v Wheeler* 435 US 313 (1978), p. 323.
93 Article VI, making treaties the law of the land, applies to the Indian treaties: *Worcester v State of Georgia* 6 Peters 515 (1832), p. 559 (Marshall C.J.). For discussion of the plenary power doctrine, originating in that case, see, e.g., Newton, n. 92 above.
And see *Minnesota v Mille Lacs Band of Chippewa Indians* 526 US — (1999); 143 Lawyers' Edition 2d 270.
94 Brownlie, *Treaties and Indigenous Peoples* (1992), pp. 8–9; Sorrenson, 'Treaties in British Colonial Policy', in Renwick (ed.), *Sovereignty and Indigenous Rights* (1991), 15.
95 Brownlie, loc. cit., criticizing the opposed view of McNair, *The Law of Treaties* (1961), pp. 52–54.
96 [1941] NZLR 590. See further ch. 4, p. 99.
97 In order to be an aboriginal right protected by s. 35(1) an activity must be an element of a tradition, custom or practice integral to the distinctive culture of the aboriginal group claiming it: *R v Van der Peet* [1996] 2 SCR 507.
98 The protection given by s. 35(1) is not absolute but may be infringed by legislation where the person relying on the infringement shows (i) a valid legislative objective for the legislation (such as preserving Aboriginal rights by conserving a resource) and (ii) that the legislation is as consistent as possible in the circumstances with the recognition and affirmation accorded by s. 35(1): *R v Sparrow* [1990] 1 SCR 1075. See Kent McNeil's discussion in 'Envisaging Constitutional Space for Aboriginal Governments' (1993) 19 *QLJ* 95, p. 103. The more absolute approach to s. 35(1) favoured by McNeil would secure a substantial measure of self-government to the First Nations.
99 *Nowegijick v Canada* [1983] 1 SCR 29, p. 36; *Simon v The Queen* [1985] 2 SCR 387, pp. 401 402 (SCC); *R v Badger* [1996] 1 SCR 771, pp. 793–794 (SCC). Cf. *Jones v Meehan* 175 US 1 (1899) and *Minnesota v Mille Lacs Band of Chippewa Indian* (see n. 93 above).
100 See p. 48.
101 As in the North American context. See p. 50.

Chapter 3

1 I use 'ideology' in the 'neutral' sense of 'refer [ring] to belief structures that are discretely based and different from one another. . .': see J. T. Johnson, *Ideology, Reason, and the Limitation of War* (1975), pp. 11–12.

2   See pp. 14-15.
3   *Two Treatises of Government* (ed. Laslett; 1988); Second Treatise, paras 36-43 (pp. 292-296).
4   See ch. 1, p. 36.
5   See ch. 6, pp. 158ff.
6   For the doctrine and its development, see Johnson, op. cit.
7   See n. 72, p. 197.
8   See Muldoon, *The Americas in the Spanish World Order* (1994), p. 27.
9   Already mentioned in the context of aboriginal property rights: see ch. 2, p. 52.
10 Vitoria, *De Indis*, 3.2. For translation, see Pagden and Lawrance (eds), *Vitoria: Political Writings* (1991), p. 285.
11 Ibid., p. xxvii.
12 *De Jure Belli*, I, ch. 9, cited by Korman, *The Right of Conquest* (1996), p. 49.
13 *Mare Liberum*, ch. 4, cited by Korman, loc. cit.
14 Ibid.
15 *The Devastation of the Indies* (1552) (trans. Briffault; intro. Donovan; 1992); and *In Defense of the Indians* (ca. 1552) (trans. and ed. Stafford Poole; 1992). Further on Las Casas, see, e.g., Muldoon, *Popes, Lawyers, and Infidels* (1979), pp. 150-152.
16 As witness e.g. George III's proclamation of 1763. See n. 75, p. 197.
17 True at least of England and France. See the comparison of the terms used in Elizabeth I's letters patent authorizing colonization of lands not possessed by another Christian monarch, in Seed, 'Taking Possession' (1992) 49 *William and Mary Quarterly* 183, pp. 185-189, 201-202.
18 Lamin Sanneh, *The Crown and the Turban* (1997), p. 207.
19 Ibid.
20 See pp. 75ff.
21 See p. 58.
22 *The Wretched of the Earth* (trans Farrington; 1967) and other writings.
23 'Goodbye to All That?', *New York Review of Books*, 20 June 1996, 59, p. 62. The description may also apply to the kind of imperialism which is not necessarily carried out or accompanied by actual colonization or revolutionary violence, as (i) by the United States in Latin America (Ferro, *Colonization* (1997), p. 19) or (ii), arguably, in modern 'globalization' (see, e.g., Kelsey, 'Globalisation, State and Law' in Arup and Marks (eds), *Cross Currents: Internationalism, National Identity and Law* (1996), 31, p. 48 and generally her *The New Zealand Experiment* (1995; new edn 1997) and *Reclaiming the Future* (1999).
24 Lewis, *Cultures in Conflict* (1995), pp. 6-7.
25 In the introduction to *The Devastation of the Indies*, n. 15 above, p. 23.
26 Ibid., pp. 19-20.
27 Ibid., p. 16.
28 See ch. 1, pp. 36-37.
29 See ch. 1, p. 35 and ch. 2, pp. 39ff.
30 See Jackson, 'The Treaty and the Word', in Oddie and Perrett (eds), *Justice, Ethics, and New Zealand Society* (1992), 1, p. 6.
31 See the discussion of *R v Walker* [1989] 2 Qd R 79 in ch. 2pp. 38ff.
32 Similar issues have of course arisen dramatically in the Israeli-Palestinian conflict, in (respectively) the establishment and expansion of the state of Israel and the Palestinian struggle for a separate state. I mention the salient points only: the conflicting ideological claims, the historic claim of Israelis to their ancient homeland (despite the long passage of years) now legitimated in part by (revolutionary) military success and by international

recognition, and the Palestinian claim based on immediate recent prior title (residence in British Mandatory Palestine before the establishment of the state of Israel). See Weiner, 'The Palestine Refugees' "Right to Return"' (1997) 20 *BostCICLRev* 1. Generally and for further references, see Canuel, 'Nationalism, Self-Determination' (1997) 20 *BostCICLRev* 85, esp. pp. 97–107.

33 *Cultures in Conflict* (1995), pp. 62–63. And see his *Islam and the West* (1993), pp. 3ff.
34 Lewis, *Cultures in Conflict*, p. 20.
35 Prawer, *The Latin Kingdom of Jerusalem* (1972), p. 475 (his emphasis).
36 Partner, *God of Battles* (1997), p. 95; Lewis, *Islam and the West*, p. 12; Ferro, *Colonization*, p. 3.
37 See the contrast Peter Partner makes between the view of the Christian Franks that their conquests from Rome had been legitimated by prescription and their scarcely consistent denial that the Islamic conquests had been likewise prescriptively legitimated: Partner, op. cit., p. 283.
38 Alfonso VI's envoy to Abd Allah (King of Granada 1074/5–1090): quoted (with source) by O'Callaghan, *A History of Medieval Spain* (1975), p. 204.
39 See p. 61.
40 Who, after two thousand years of successive conquests by Romans, Vandals, Byzantines, Arabs, Ottoman Turks and French, still maintain a strong cultural and ethnic identity in Algeria and Morocco. As to their customary political and legal order, necessarily subordinate during effective rule by successive conquerors, see Brett and Fentress, *The Berbers* (1996), ch. 7.
41 Ferro, *Colonization* (1997), p. 4.
42 Fanon, *The Wretched of the Earth*, n. 22 above, pp. 128–129.
43 See ch. 1, pp. 15–16ff.
44 See Pocock, *The Ancient Constitution and the Feudal Law* (1957; 1987), esp. ch. 2 ('The Common-Law Mind: Custom and the Immemorial').
45 Cf. n. 123, p. 193.
46 *Puritanism and Revolution* (1958), ch. 3 ('The Norman Yoke'); Hill, *Liberty Against The Law* (1996), ch. 6 ('Robin Hood . . . and the Norman Yoke').
47 For a recent discussion see Gillingham, 'The Beginnings of English Imperialism' (1992) 5 *Journal of Historical Sociology* 392, pp. 392–396.
48 See pp. 70ff.
49 See Le Patourel, *The Norman Empire* (1976), pp. 65ff.
50 Ibid., 67; Bartlett, *The Making of Europe* (1993), p. 220.
51 27 Hen VIII, c. 26. See Bartlett, loc. cit.
52 Le Patourel, op. cit., pp. 69ff.
53 See MacMillan, *State, Society and Authority in Ireland* (1993).
54 Op. cit., p. 3.
55 See n. 12, p. 187.
56 MacMillan, op. cit., p. 8.
57 See p. 57.
58 See Gillingham, n. 47 above, pp. 396ff. To a modern eye there seems to have been some justification for the perception, in, e.g., the persistence of slavery and slave hunting in Celtic societies when those things had died out in England: ibid., pp. 401–402.
59 Ibid., p. 405.
60 *Britons: Forging the Nation 1708–1837)* (1992), p. 388 (references omitted).
61 See now article 4 of the Universal Declaration of Human Rights. Slavery was abolished in the nineteenth century successively in the British, French, Dutch and Russian empires and

then in Islamic states, initially under Western (especially British) pressure and encouragement. Slavery in some Islamic states has lasted into well into the 20th century. See Lewis, *Race and Slavery in the Middle East* (1990), ch. 11. Slavery in the British and New Zealand contexts is considered further in ch. 6, pp. 141–143 and 159–161.
62 See in the New Zealand context ch. 6, p. 145ff.
63 As to customary law, see further ch. 1, pp. 17–18; and (in the New Zealand context) ch. 4, pp. 86–90.
64 Hamnett, *Chieftainship and Legitimacy* (1975), p. 22. His emphasis.
65 Cf. ibid., p. 89.
66 See further ch. 4, p. 90. Generally see, e.g., Joseph, *Constitutional and Administrative Law* (1993), ch. 8.
67 See however ch. 4, pp. 93–94.
68 Generally on constitutional conventions, see Joseph, op. cit., ch. 9 and Marshall, *Constitutional Conventions* (1984; 1986).
69 The South African legal system in the apartheid days and (worse) the legal system in Nazi Germany are obvious modern examples.
70 Thompson, *Whigs and Hunters* (1975), p. 259.
71 Ibid., p. 265.
72 Ibid.
73 Ibid., p. 266.
74 Ibid.
75 For discussion in African contexts, see e.g. El-Obaid and Appiagyei-Atua, 'Human Rights in Africa' (1996) 41 *McG LJ* 819 and Mqeke, 'Customary Law and Human Rights' (1996) 113 *SALJ* 364.
76 See ch. 6, pp. 146–148.
77 Collins, *Marxism and Law* (1982), p. 144.
78 Ibid., pp. 145–146.
79 The matter of Marxism and the rule of law has come for renewed consideration in light of the collapse in the East European communists states. See, e.g., Krygier, 'Marxism and the Rule of Law' (1990) 15 *Law and Social Inquiry* 633.
80 *Liberty Against the Law* (1996), p. 338 (emphasis added).
81 Gramsci, *Selections from the Prison Notebooks* (ed. and trans. Hoare and Nowell Smith; 1971), pp. 245–246. 'The conception of law will have to be freed from every residue of transcendentalism and from every absolute . . .': ibid., p. 246.
82 Adamson, *Hegemony and Revolution* (1980), pp. 226–227.
83 Ibid.
84 Ibid., p. 227, See Gramsci, op. cit., p. 229, where, perhaps surprisingly, strikes appear as a form of war of manoeuvre.
85 Gramsci, op. cit., p. 243; Adamson, op. cit., p. 224.
86 Gramsci, op. cit., pp. 106ff.; Adamson, op. cit., p. 186.
87 See ch. 6, pp. 136ff.
88 Honoré, 'The Right to Rebel' (1988) 8 *Oxford Journal of Legal Studies* 34. Honoré discusses the nature of the right and its international recognition in light of, e.g., the United Nations Declaration on the Granting of Independence to Colonial Countries and Peoples (UN General Assembly Resolution 1514 (XV), 14 December 1960. See also GA Res 1541 (XV), 15 December 1960. The Resolutions provided the legal basis for the independence of the overseas colonies of the Western states after the Second World War; but, on the 'blue water thesis', not for indigenous or tribal peoples within the external boundaries of independent states. See for discussion Anaya, *Indigenous Peoples in International Law* (1996), pp. 43, 60

nn. 26–29.
89 Honoré, n. 88 above, pp. 44–45.
90 This is in effect the limited right recognized by the Supreme Court of Canada in *Re Secession of Quebec* (1998) 161 Dominion Law Reports (4th) 385. For discussion of the controversy over secession in international law and references, see: Anaya, op. cit., pp. 84–85, 94–95 (n. 71) and Hannum, *Autonomy, Sovereignty, and Self-Determination* (1990), pp. 471ff.
91 See ch. 2, p. 51 and ch. 7, p. 172.
92 Anaya, op. cit., p. 47.
93 See Anaya, ibid., pp. 77–80, for the varying views of the Covenants (International Covenant on Economic, Social and Cultural Rights, 16 December 1966 (GA Res 2200 (XXI)), art 1(1) and International Covenant on Civil and Political Rights, 16 December 1966 (GA Res 2200 (XXI)), art 1(1).
94 The draft Declaration is an appendix to Anaya, op. cit., pp. 207ff. and to Quentin-Baxter (ed.), *Recognising the Rights of Indigenous Peoples* (1998), pp. 201ff. (See the latter work generally for discussion in the New Zealand context.) The Working Group is an organ of the UN Sub-Commission on Prevention of Discrimination and Protection of Minorities.
95 See Brownlie, *Treaties and Indigenous Peoples* (1992), ch. 3.
96 Sanders, 'Indigenous Peoples at the United Nations' [1996] 2 *CNLR* 20, p. 21 (emphasis added).
97 Hannum, op. cit., p. 75.
98 See UN Doc E/CN 4/Sub 2/1986/7/Add 4, para 379 (1986), quoted by Anaya, op. cit., p. 5.
99 Quoted by Barsh, 'Indigenous Peoples: An Emerging Object of International Law' (1986) 80 *American Journal of International Law* 369, pp. 375–376.
100 See ch. 5, p. 122.
101 See ch. 6, pp. 158ff.
102 See p. 66.
103 See pp. 60–61.
104 *Cultures in Conflict* (1995), pp. 73–74.
105 Ibid., p. 74.

Chapter 4

1 'The Constitutional Status of the Treaty of Waitangi' (1990) 14 *NZULRev* 9.
2 Ibid., p. 10.
3 See ch. 1, p. 16.
4 The interpretation of the British Crown's seizure of power over New Zealand, that began in 1840, as a revolution follows that in some of my earlier writings on the country's constitutional origins. Cf. the conclusion of Paul McHugh in his discussion of the 'constitutional basis of the Crown's sovereignty' in *The Maori Magna Carta* (1991), p. 64.
5 See pp. 97–98.
6 E. T. Durie, *Custom Law* (1994), p. 4. See ch. 1, pp. 17–18 and ch. 3, pp. 70–71.
7 See ch. 1, pp. 17–18.
8 Ballara, *Iwi* (1998), ch. 12; Durie, op. cit., pp. 16, 29.
9 Into which Joseph Banks observed the country to be 'certainly divided' (as quoted by Salmond, *Two Worlds* (1991), p. 144).
10 Ballara, op. cit., ch. 13.
11 Op. cit., Part VI.
12 See Durie, op. cit., p. 88; Ballara, op. cit., pp. 194–195, 283–284. Greater certainty of boundaries comes with land sales in the 19th century: ibid.
13 See further ch. 1, p. 17.

14 Durie, op. cit., p. 4.
15 Ballara, op. cit., p. 182.
16 See Durie, op. cit., pp. 44–45.
17 Kelsen, *Pure Theory of Law* (1960; 2nd edn; trans. Knight 1967), p. 323.
18 A norm 'of special importance': ibid.
19 Jackson, 'Maori Law, Pakeha Law and the Treaty of Waitangi' in *Mana Tiriti* (1991), 14, p. 16.
20 Durie, op. cit., pp. 3–4.
21 Ibid., p. 4.
22 Hart, *Concept of Law* (2nd edn, 1994), pp. 91–94. See discussion by Green (reviewing that edition) in (1996) 94 *Michigan L Rev* 1698.
23 Hart, op. cit., p. 92.
24 Durie, op. cit., p. 4.
25 *Hineiti Rirerire Arani v Public Trustee* NZPCC 1, 6.
26 Hart, op. cit., 94ff.
27 Walker, in Melbourne (ed.), *Maori Sovereignty: The Maori Perspective* (1995), 23, p. 27. See n. 38 below.
28 Ballara, op. cit., p. 204.
29 See ch. 1, pp. 15–27, for the distinction.
30 Ballara, op. cit., p. 193.
31 Ibid., pp. 204–205.
32 E. T. Durie, *Custom Law* (1994), p. 39.
33 'During and shortly after war or oppression, the authority of a single rangatira could be absolute': ibid., p. 35.
34 Ibid., p. 34.
35 Ibid., p. 36.
36 See: (i) Kawharu as quoted in *Finding of the Waitangi Tribunal on the Kaituna Claim*, p. 18; (ii) Jackson, 'The Treaty and the Word', in Oddie and Perrett (eds), *Justice, Ethics, and New Zealand Society* (1992), 1, p. 8. This aspect of the power is strongly emphasized by Bishop Muru Walters in 'A Maori Perspective' in Crawford (ed.), *Church and State: Te Tino Rangatiratanga* (1998), 66.
37 See pp. 103–104.
38 E. T. Durie, op. cit., p. 41. The 'Maori King of New Zealand' of Ranginui Walker's speculation (see at n. 27 above) would have attained kingship by conquests requiring to be so legitimated.
39 See ch. 3, pp. 60–61.
40 Durie, op. cit., p. 65.
41 As to what follows and for recent explanation of the complex position, see Ballara, *Iwi* (1998), ch. 13 ('Hapu in Communities'). On conquest as a source of title (apparently exaggerated in the traditional colonialist view), see (i) E. T. Durie, op. cit., pp. 41, 65 and 84 and also his 'Custom Law' (1994) 24 *VUWLRev* 325, pp. 328–329 and 'Will the Settlers Settle?' (1996) 8 *Otago LRev* 449, pp. 452–453; (ii) Ballara, op. cit., passim; and (iii) D. V. Williams *'Te Kooti tango whenua'* (1999), pp. 187–189. Customary tenure in the early 19th century context is summarized generally in Kawharu, *Maori Land Tenure* (1977), pp. 40ff.
42 See p. 105. (The complication of Ireland whose separate Parliament was abolished in 1801 is not dealt with.)
43 See further ch. 3, p. 71. Generally see, e.g., Joseph, *Constitutional and Administrative Law* (1993), ch. 8.
44 See below, n. 112, pp. 218–219.

Notes

45 Pollard, *The Evolution of Parliament* (1926), p. 262.
46 12 and 13 Wm. III, c. 2. See the Imperial Laws Application Act 1988, s. 3(1).
47 See ch. 1, pp. 15–16 and 28–29.
48 See ch. 1, p. 16.
49 For the applicable conventions and exceptions to them, see Marshall, *Constitutional Conventions* (1984; reprinted with additions, 1986), ch. 2; and, specifically in relation to present-day New Zealand, my 'The Governor-General and the Constitution' in Gold (ed.), *New Zealand Politics in Perspective* (3rd edn; 1992), 77 and Joseph, *Constitutional and Administrative Law* (1993), pp. 246ff. For the development of the conventions in colonial New Zealand, see ch. 5, pp. 119ff.
50 See n. 49 above. The reserve powers generally relate to critical circumstances where the monarch (or the Governor-General) may act independently of advice from ministers responsible to the elected House.
51 Le May, *The Victorian Constitution* (1979), ch. 3.
52 *Ferrer's Case* (1542). See Elton, *The Tudor Constitution* (2nd edn; 1982), pp. 275–277 and (for Elton's comment) p. 14.
53 This doctrine, generally associated with the name of A. V. Dicey, may still be described as orthodox but it has been much controverted in recent legal writing. For discussion and references, see e.g. Joseph, *Constitutional and Administrative Law* (1993), ch. 14. And see Allan, 'Parliamentary Sovereignty: Law, Politics and Revolution' (1997) 113 *Law Quarterly Review* 443 and his 'Fairness, Equality, Rationality' in Forsyth and Hare (eds), *The Golden Metwand and the Crooked Cord* (1998), 15, esp. pp. 19–24.
54 The American War of Independence can be seen as enforcing by revolution the contention of the colonists that the British Parliament had no legal power to impose taxation on the colonies. See McIlwain, *The American Revolution: A Constitutional Interpretation* (1923; 1958).
55 This was the effect of ss. 2 and 3 of the Colonial Laws Validity Act 1865 (UK).
56 This and the plenary nature of the conferred power was made clear in a number of 19th century cases reviewed, with later authorities to the same effect, by the High Court of Australia in *Union Steamship Co of Australia Pty Ltd v King* (1988) 166 CLR 1. See further n. 67 below.
57 Zines, *Constitutional Change in the Commonwealth* (1991), p. 43.
   See n. 53 above.
58 See my 'Parliament, the Treaty and Freedom' in Joseph (ed.), *Essays on the Constitution* (1995), 41, p. 54.
59 *Taylor v New Zealand Poultry Board* [1984] 1 NZLR 394, 398 (CA). See the possible limitations on the supremacy of Parliament tentatively allowed for extreme cases by Gallen J. (obiter) in *Mangawaro Enterprises Ltd v Attorney-General* [1994] 2 NZLR 451, pp. 457–458.
   For references and for discussion, see Brookfield, loc. cit., pp. 54–56. See also Joseph, op. cit., n. 53 above, pp. 189, 444–445, 454–456, and for most recent critical comment, Kirby, 'The Struggle for Simplicity: Lord Cooke and Fundamental Rights', (1998) 24 *Commonwealth Law Bulletin* 496.
60 See Brookfield, n. 58 above, p. 55.
61 See *Brader v Ministry of Transport* [1981] 1 NZLR 73, 78 (CA).
62 *New Zealand Drivers Association v New Zealand Road Carriers* [1982] 1 NZLR 374, 390 (CA).
63 Cooke, *Turning Points of the Common Law* (1997), p. 79.
64 See ch. 3, p. 71.

65 See ch. 7, pp. 173ff.
66 36 SASR 376 (Full SC).
67 The Parliament of South Australia, the parliament of a separate colony originally but since federation that of a state of the Australian Commonwealth, is still empowered by a 'peace, welfare and good government' provision in its constitution.
      See further at n. 56 above.
68 36 SASR, p. 385.
69 See ch. 5, pp. 130–131.
70 See McNab, *Historical Records of New Zealand* (1908), vol i, pp. 316–318, cited by McLintock, *Crown Colony Government in New Zealand* (1958), p. 10. For discussion and references, see Williams, 'The Foundation of Colonial Rule in New Zealand' (1988) 13 *NZULRev* 54 and McLintock, loc. cit..
    This early protective jurisdiction in relation to Maori, thus somewhat tentatively asserted by the Crown, seemed to be given some late effect in *Re Tupuna Maori* (1988; unreported; noted Brookfield [1989] *NZRecLRev* 217), where Greig J. granted Letters of Administration in the estate of a Maori warrior who died in or about 1820.
71 57 Geo. III, c. 53; 4 Geo. IV, c. 96; 9 Geo. IV, c. 83.
72 See Orange, *The Treaty of Waitangi* (1987), p. 8.
73 Ibid., pp. 12–13.
74 Ibid., pp. 19–23. For the Maori and English texts of the Declaration, see *Facsimiles of the Declaration of Independence and the Treaty of Waitangi* (Wellington, 1976), copied as an appendix in Orange, op. cit., pp. 255–256.
75 The protection was to be 'consistent with a due regard to the just rights of others and to the interests of His Majesty's subjects': quoted ibid, p. 21.
76 'Restructuring the Nation' in Fitzpatrick (ed.), *Nationalism, Racism and the Rule of Law* (1995) 177, p. 179. Emphasis added.
77 'New Zealand lacked an indigenous political foundation for such a structure . . .': Orange, op. cit., p. 23. And see Ward, *An Unsettled History* (1999), pp. 11–12.
78 Kelsey, n. 76 above, p. 179.
79 Kelsenian, that is, as distinct from Kelseyian. See ch. 1, pp. 17–18.
80 There was some meeting of chiefly committees summoned by Busby and some evidence that work was done on a more detailed constitution: Orange, op. cit., p. 22.
81 Unreported; noted Brookfield, [1993] *NZLRev* 278.
82 See ch. 1, pp. 19, 23 and 32–33.
83 For the text see Hobson's despatch to the Secretary of State for the Colonies, 25 May 1840, *GBPP* 1841/311, 15, pp. 18–19.
84 See note 123, p.208.
85 See pp. 103–104.
86 3 NZJur R (NS) SC 72.
87 At p. 78.
88 [1941] NZLR 590.
89 'The Treaty of Waitangi in the Courts' (1990) 14 *NZULRev* 37.
90 *The Maori Magna Carta* (1991), pp. 176ff.
91 'The Treaty of Waitangi: some international law aspects' in Kawharu (ed.), *Waitangi: Maori and Pakeha Perspectives of the Treaty of Waitangi* (1989), 121.
92 *Treaties and Indigenous Peoples* (1992).
93 Ibid., p. 8.
94 Ibid., pp. 8–9. The reference is to Lord McNair, *The Law of Treaties* (1961), pp. 52–54.
95 See Joseph, *Constitutional and Administrative Law* (1993), pp. 36–38; Round, *Truth or Treaty?*

(1998), pp. 110ff.
96 Brownlie, op. cit., p. 9.
97 Ibid..
98 See ch. 2, p. 55.
99 See below, ch. 6, pp. 152–153.
100 *New Zealand Maori Council v Attorney-General* (unreported; 3 May 1991). See Brookfield, [1991] *NZRecLRev* 257, p. 258. The unease is shown clearly in the differences of opinion of members of the Waitangi Tribunal in its *Radio Spectrum Management and Development Final Report* (1999; Wai 167), noted only briefly here. The majority (J. M. Anderson and Prof M. P. K. Sorrenson) determined that Maori were entitled to a 'fair and equitable share' of the radio spectrum, under a number of Treaty principles but especially (it seems) as a taonga protected by the rangatiratanga reserved by article 2. The dissenting view of Judge Savage to the effect that the share claimed was not a taonga of Maori, but rather included in the taonga of the human race generally, is likely to be endorsed by the Courts if and when the question comes before them.
101 As quoted in the *Report of the Waitangi Tribunal on the Kaituna River claim* (Wai 4; 1984), p. 14.
102 'Immigration Policy and the Political Economy of New Zealand' in Greif (ed.), *Immigration and National Identity in New Zealand* (1995), 282.
103 *Ka Whawhai Tonu Matou* (1990), p. 93.
104 Ibid.
105 'The Treaty of Waitangi and Maori Independence' (1990) *9th Commonwealth Law Conference Papers* 249.
106 'Restructuring the Nation' in Fitzpatrick (ed.), *Nationalism, Racism and the Rule of Law* (1995) 177, p. 180 (her emphasis).
107 Ibid.
108 In Archie, *Maori Sovereignty: The Pakeha Perspective* (1995), 103, p. 105.
109 'Globalisation and the Demise of the Colonial State' in Trainor (ed.), *Republicanism in New Zealand* (1996), 137, pp. 139 and 151.
110 Ibid., pp. 151–152.
111 Ibid., p. 152.
112 'Maori Law, Pakeha Law and the Treaty of Waitangi' in *Mana Tiriti* (1991), 14, p. 19. See also, e.g., Tunks, '*Mana Tiriti*' in Trainor (ed.), n. 109 above, 113, pp. 114–115.
113 *The Treaty of Waitangi* (1987), p. 46. But the protectorate regime as part of British imperial practice did not develop until later in the century: see McHugh, *The Maori Magna Carta* (1991), pp. 46–47. Protectorates were, at least technically, outside the dominions of the Crown. As to the distinction between colonies and protectorates, see my 'Maori Rights and Two Radical Writers' [1990] *NZLJ* 406, pp. 408–409. As to protectorates generally, see Roberts-Wray, *Commonwealth and Colonial Law* (1966), pp. 47ff.
114 *Te Mana, Te Kawanatanga* (1998), p. 2.
115 Ibid.
116 Ibid., p. 3.
117 Ibid.
118 Appendix to *Waitangi: Maori and Pakeha Perspectives*, n. 91 above, 319, pp. 319, 321.
119 'A Pakeha Perspective' in Crawford (ed.), *Church and State: Te Tino Rangatiratanga* (1998), 1, pp. 3–5.
120 Ibid., p. 3.
121 'Maori Law, Pakeha Law and the Treaty of Waitangi' in *Mana Tiriti* (1991), 14, p. 19.
122 See p. 99.

123 Appendix to *Waitangi: Maori and Pakeha Perspectives*, n. 91 (p. 206) above, 319, p. 320, n. 11. (His emphasis.)
124 'Restructuring the Nation', n. 106 above, p. 180.
125 See my 'The Treaty of Waitangi, the Constitution and the Future' (1995) *British Review of New Zealand Studies* (No. 8), 4, p. 10, citing the late Professor J. D. B. Mitchell in [1956] *PL* 294, p. 295.
126 Wai 414; p. xxv. See Mikaere and Milroy, [1998] *NZLRev* 467, p. 469.
127 Wai 22, p. 187.
128 At pp. 186–187.
129 *Report of the Waitangi Tribunal on the Orakei Claim* (Wai 9; 1987), p. 149.
130 *New Zealand Maori Council v Attorney-General* [1987] 1 NZLR 641 (the *SOE* case), p. 671 (Richardson J.).

Chapter 5
1 See n. 113, p. 207.
2 Opinion of 27 December, 1842. See *GBPP,* 1844/556 (Appendix), 470, p. 471; *CO* 209/16, pp. 487–494.
3 The Minute is at the end of the opinion, in *CO* 209/16. The emphasis is the Under-Secretary's.
4 *GBPP* 1844/556 (Appendix), p. 475.
5 21 NZLR 655, p. 666.
6 See ch. 1, p. 17.
7 See ch. 4, pp. 92–93.
8 *Mabo v Queensland* [No. 2] (1992) 175 CLR 1, p. 38 (Brennan J.)
9 8 Co. Rep. 1a, p. 10b.
10 Opinion of the Attorney-General (30 June 1869) 1869 *AJHR* A 14.
11 Newcastle to Grey, 26 Feb 1863: *AJHR* 1863, E 7, No. 4, p. 6; *GBPP* 1863 (467), 134, p. 141.
12 1861–63 *NZPD* 792.
13 *The New Zealand Wars* (1986), p. 80.
14 The reasons he gave appear to have been insufficient: fear of exasperating the settlers if he made public Te Rauparaha's alleged crimes (Rutherford, *Sir George Grey* (1961), p. 114; Wards, *The Shadow of the Land* (1968), p. 280) and, in the other matters, urgency and alleged practical difficulties of proceeding regularly (Rutherford, op. cit., pp. 115–116). In any case, the state of current war emergency which would have justified proceeding by martial law had ceased by the time the trials took place (Wards, op. cit., p. 296). Also on contemporary doubts as to the legality of Grey's proceedings, see Bohan, *To Be a Hero* (1998), p. 86.
As to martial law, of which court martial proceedings before a military tribunal are an instrument, see ch. 1, p. 20.
15 On this and what follows, see Brookfield, Opinion for the Waitangi Tribunal on Legal Aspects of the Raupatu (1996; Wai 46), paras 19.1–21.8.
16 (1847) NZPCC 387.
17 On this and related matters see Brookfield, n. 15 above, paras 25.1–27.5.
18 I do not attempt to analyse the Government's invasion of the Waikato in these terms. But the ensuing war was in reality, as Belich suggests (see n. 13 above), a war of conquest to impose the new legal order; the Government assuming that the autonomy claimed by the King and the other chiefs was inconsistent with the sovereignty of the Crown. See the preamble to the Waikato Raupatu Claims Settlement Act 1995.
19 Ward, *A Show of Justice* (1974; revised edn 1995), pp. 169–170.
20 Ibid., p. 228.

Notes

21 3 NZJur R (NS) SC 72.
22 See pp. 128-130.
23 See p. 109.
24 *The New Zealand Wars* (1986), p. 306. As recited in the preamble to the Waikato Raupatu Claims Settlement Act 1995, Pootatau Te Wherowhero was 'raised up' as the first King in 1858) 'to unite the iwi, and preserve their rangatiratanga and their economic and cultural integrity . . .'. A number of Waikato chiefs 'formally pledged their land' and 'gave up ultimate authority' over it to him, 'along with ultimate responsibility for the well-being of the people', and thus 'bound their communities to the Kiingitanga, resisting further alienation of their land'.

As to the King Movement, see, e.g., Sorrenson, 'The Maori King Movement, 1858-1885' in Chapman and Sinclair (eds), *Studies of a Small Democracy* (1963), 33.

25 Belich, op. cit., p. 306.
26 Ibid., p. 307.
27 *The Origins of the Maori Wars* (1957), p. 76.
28 *Kinds of Peace* (1991), p. 25.
29 Ibid.
30 Ibid.
31 An early example is the runanga of the chief Wiremu Tamihana, which was providing local government and dispensing justice at Peria in the 1840s: *Dictionary of New Zealand Biography*, vol i (1990), 516 (Stokes).
32 See ch. 4, pp. 87-88.
33 Ward, op. cit., p. 97; citing 1860 *AJHR*, F3 p. 113, where the translated text of the code appears as an enclosure to the despatch from Governor Gore-Brown to the Secretary of State (9 May 1857), ibid., 111.
34 See ch. 2, p. 47.
35 As to the bank, see Park, 'Te Peeke o Aotearoa' (1992) 26 *NZJH* 161.
36 Ibid., p. 176.
37 See p. 118.
38 See ch. 2, p. 50.
39 See ch. 2, pp. 50-51.
40 *R v Knowles* (12 October 1998; CA 146/98; unreported); noted *Maori L Rev*, December 1998 – January 1999, 1.
41 By Letters Patent, 14 Nov., 1857. See *New Zealand Gazette,* 11 Feb. 1858, p. 20.
42 See ch. 4, p. 91.
43 See ch. 2, pp. 49, 51.
44 Memorandum, 12 March 1885, enclosed with despatch, Jervois to the Secretary of State, 28 March 1885, *GBPP* 1884-85 (C4413), referred to by Orange, *The Treaty of Waitangi* (1987), p. 215.
45 Ward, *A Show of Justice* (1974; revised edn 1995), pp. 61-62.
46 Sinclair, *Kinds of Peace* (1991), p. 55.
47 Ibid., p. 57.
48 *A Question of Honour* (1990), p. 218. For the conventions of responsible government, see further ch. 4, p. 91.
49 [1987] 1 NZLR 641.
50 'The Monarchy and the Constitution Today' [1992] *NZLJ* 438, p. 439.
51 Newcastle to Grey, 26 Feb. 1863 (*AJHR* 1863, E No. 7, No 4, p. 7; *GBPP* 1863 (467), 134, p. 142).
52 Somewhat anomalously the negative powers remained until 1983, when the last set of

colonial-type Royal Instructions, those of 1917, were replaced by a set consistent with New Zealand's status as a separate realm (see p. 123). But, well before that, the negative powers must be deemed to have been annulled by the division of the Crown, now to be discussed.

53 32 NZLR 321.
54 At p. 347.
55 See n. 71 below.
56 See ch. 4, p. 205.
57 Passed by the United Kingdom Parliament at New Zealand request; necessary because the Statute of Westminster itself (see s. 8) did not add to the General Assembly's limited power to amend the New Zealand Constitution Act 1852 (UK).

　　The power conferred in 1947 was exercised principally in the passing of (i) the Legislative Council Abolition Act 1950, (ii) the New Zealand Constitution Amendment Act 1973 and (iii) the Constitution Act 1986 (consolidating and completing the changes of 1973).
58 SR 1983/225. See my 'The Reconstituted Office of Governor-General' [1985] *NZLJ* 256.
59 See my 'Kelsen, the Constitution and the Treaty' (1992) 15 *NZULRev* 163. 169–172 and 'Republican New Zealand' [1995] *NZLRev* 310, pp. 314–315. For a different view see Lord Cooke, 'Suggested Revolution against the Crown' in Joseph (ed.), *Essays on the Constitution* (1995), 28, p. 32, n. 13.
60 Theoretically the same problem may arise in other countries of the Commonwealth that have retained Queen as Head of State, if no legislation has actually divided the unitary Imperial Crown into a plurality.
61 See [1976] *NZLJ* 458. My changed view appears in 'The Monarchy and the Constitution Today', n. 50 above.
62 [1982] QB 892.
63 At p. 916.
64 At pp. 919ff.
65 [1983] Ch 77, pp. 89ff.
66 At p. 91.
67 *Re Resolution to Amend the Constitution* [1981] 1 SCR 753 (SCC) (Patriation Reference, Canada).
68 [1982] QB 892 at p. 937.
69 [1983] Ch at p. 94.
70 See n. 65 p. 222.
71 As to these and the later deputations, see Walker, *Ka Whawhai Tonu Matou*, pp. 160–165, 183–184; and his 'The Treaty of Waitangi as the Focus of Maori Protest' in Kawharu (ed.), *Waitangi: Maori and Pakeha Perspectives of the Treaty of Waitangi* (1989), 263, pp. 272–274.
72 See p. 121.
73 [1994] 1 NZLR 513, p. 517. It is ironic that the Privy Council itself, in relation to New Zealand, appears to be an institution of the old imperial Crown rather than of the Crown in right of New Zealand as a separate realm. In relation to New Zealand, however, its authority depends on the separate New Zealand basic norm.
74 See ch. 4, p. 91.
75 'The "Pakeha Constitutional Revolution?" Five Perspectives on Maori Rights and Pakeha Duties' (1993) 1 *Waikato L Rev* 53, p. 60.
76 See ch. 2, p. 51.
77 Originally by the English Laws Act 1858. See now s. 5 of the Imperial Laws Application Act 1988. Whatever element of cession occurred under the Treaty of Waitangi, New Zealand

Notes

has been treated in law as a 'settled' rather than as a ceded colony, with English law automatically received on settlement (see ch. 2, pp. 49–50) and the uncertain date fixed by statute. For discussion of the New Zealand position, see Roberts-Wray, *Commonwealth and Colonial Law* (1966), pp. 101–102, and Joseph, *Constitutional and Administrative Law* (1993), pp. 32–34.

78 [1994] 2 NZLR 20, pp. 23–24. See ch. 2 at n. 85.
79 (1847) NZPCC 387.
80 (1872) NZ 2 CA 41, p. 49.
81 (1877) 3 NZJur R (NS) SC 72.
82 [1986] 1 NZLR 680.
83 See p. 128. That establishing the limits of the doctrine, especially in relation to relevant legislation, may still be difficult in particular circumstances is shown by the decision of the Court of Appeal in *Taranaki Fish and Game Council v McRitchie* [1998] 3 NZLR 611 that the taking of introduced species of trout, always regulated by statute, was not covered by Maori customary fishing rights. The decision does not appear to affect the general principles discussed in the text.
84 *Tamihana Korokai v Solicitor-General* (1912) 32 NZLR 321, p. 341 (Stout C.J.). See ch. 6, p. 141.
85 [1963] NZLR 461, p. 468.
86 *Mabo v Queensland (No 2)* (1992) 175 CLR 1, pp. 63–64 (Brennan J.), 110–111 (Deane and Gaudron JJ.). For the view that legislative authority is necessary, see at p. 196 (Toohey J.).
87 See ch. 2, pp. 53–54.
88 *Faulkner v Tauranga District Council* [1996] 1 NZLR 357 (Blanchard J.). See also *Te Runanganui o Te Ika Whenua Inc Soc v Attorney-General* [1994] 2 NZLR 20, p. 24 (CA), requiring in cases of extinguishment 'strict compliance with the provisions of any relevant statutes'. See further p. 113.

The earliest New Zealand cases appear inconsistent with any prerogative (as distinct from statutory) power of the Crown to extinguish Maori customary title. See *R v Symonds* (1847) NZPCC 387 (esp. the judgment of Chapman J.) and the dictum of the Court of Appeal *In re 'The Lundon and Whitaker Claims Act, 1871'* (1872) NZ 2 CA 41, p. 49, quoted at p. 129.

For further discussion, see McHugh, 'Aboriginal Title in New Zealand Courts' (1984) 2 *Canterbury L Rev* 235, pp. 261–263.
89 Opinion, 14 May 1864. (See *CO 209/186 218*, p. 219b).
90 See latterly ss. 155, 157 and 158 of the Maori Affairs Act 1953. The substance of these provisions has not been carried forward to the present statute, Te Ture Whenua Act 1993. But the Limitation Act 1950 has been amended to ensure that there could not as a result be any bringing of Maori claims against the Crown except where the wrong complained of occurred within the last 12 years (see s. 6(1A) and s. 7A of that Act). Maori customary land is otherwise generally protected against the operation of that Act, by s. 6(1). Cf. n. 113, p. 192.
91 See pp. 122–123.
92 *Maori Land Tenure* (1977), p. 15.
93 See s. 17(1)(a). And see D. V. Williams, *'Te Kooti tango whenua'* (1999), pp. 15–17 ('From Native Land Court to Maori Land Court').
94 See also Gilling, 'Engine of Destruction?' (1994) 24 *VUWLRev* 115, pp. 136–137; and, especially for the period to 1909, D.V. Williams, op.cit., ch. 7, et passim. Essentially agreeing in result with Dr Williams's thesis (see Williams, op.cit., pp. 236–238), I see the Native Land Court as a statutory court with powers over Maori that the legislature could legitimately confer only under the kawanatanga ceded to the Crown by article 1 of the

Treaty of Waitangi. (Cf. the position of statutory authorities discussed in n. 112, pp. 218–219.) In fact the Court's powers, in being destructive of the rangatiratanga properly reserved by article 2, far exceeded what could be so conferred. I agree with Williams that the doctrine of separation of powers (as to which see ch. 3, p. 71 and ch. 4, p. 90) cannot be invoked to excuse the Crown from operations of the Court that were thus in breach of Treaty principles.

95 See Adams, Te Uira and Parsonson, '"Behold a Kite Flies towards You": the Kiingitanga and the "Opening" of the King Country' in (1997) 31 *NZJH* 99 and Binney, 'Te Mana Tuatoru: the Rohe Potae of Tuhoe', ibid., 117.

96 See ss. 9 and 10 (d), extinguishing common law rights as to commercial fishing and, with exceptions, non-commercial fishing, respectively.

97 See s. 129(2)(a) and s. 3 of the Act.

98 [1996] 1 NZLR 357, p. 363. The question of unextinguished Maori customary title to land under water is apparently overlooked by Sir Douglas Graham in *Trick or Treaty?* (1997); see ibid., p. 13. As to the same question in the Waitangi Tribunal, see n. 104 below.

99 175 CLR 1 at p. 64.

100 [1986] 1 NZLR 680, 691.

101 The original provision, declaring the beds of navigable rivers to have always been vested in the Crown (except where the bed had been granted to some person), was s. 14 of the Coalmines Act Amendment Act 1903. The last re-enactment was s. 261 of the Coal Mines Act 1979, repealed by s. 120(1) of the Crown Minerals Act 1991. But the repeal does not affect the Crown's title to the lands affected, which continues by s. 354(1) of the Resource Management Act 1991. For the test of navigability, see latterly s. 261(1) of the Act of 1979; and, for discussion on that and other difficult aspects of the matter and for references, see *Laws NZ*, Water (1997; Brookfield), para 60; Hinde, McMorland and Sim, *Butterworths Land Law in New Zealand* (1997), para 2.232. And see n. 104 below.

102 Sections 4 and 5 of the Foreshore and Seabed Endowment Revesting Act 1991 revested in the Crown certain areas of foreshore and seabed, which it had alienated, as if they had never been alienated. See *Laws NZ*, Water, n. 101 above, paras 18 and 10.

103 Declared by s. 7 of the Territorial Sea, Contiguous Zone, and Exclusive Economic Zone Act 1977 (substantially re-enacting s. 7 of the Territorial Sea and Fishing Zone Act 1965) to be 'deemed to be and always to have been vested in the Crown' (except where granted). See *Laws NZ*, Water, n. 101 above, para 10. And see n. 104 below.

104 See the dictum of the Court of Appeal in *Te Runanganui o Te Ika Whenua Inc Soc v Attorney-General* [1994] 2 NZLR 20, p. 26, that the statutory vesting of the beds of navigable rivers in the Crown 'may not be sufficiently explicit to override or dispose of the concept' of a river as an indivisible entity and taonga under the Treaty of Waitangi. If that is so, it would follow that, generally in respect of river, lake and sea beds, considered separately from the water in accordance with common law conceptions, a general statutory vesting in the Crown is insufficient to extinguish the customary title. That accords with a provisional determination (which is under appeal to the Maori Appellate Court) by Judge Hingston in the Maori Land Court, as to the effect of s. 7 of the Territorial Sea, Contiguous Zone, and Exclusive Economic Zone Act 1977 (see n. 103 above): *In Re Marlborough Sounds* (22A Nelson MB 1, 22 Dec 1997 (noted in the *Maori Law Review* Dec 1997/Jan 1998 4 and by Milroy, [1998] *NZL Rev*, pp. 485–487). The contrary assumption of the Planning Tribunal in *Haddon v Auckland Regional Council* [1994] NZRMA 49 and in *Sea-Tow Ltd v Auckland Regional Council* [1994] NZRMA 204 appears incorrect (see Brookfield, [1994] *NZRecLRev*, pp. 381–382).

For the somewhat differing views of the Waitangi Tribunal, see its *Whanganui River Report* (1999; Wai 167). There it dealt with the matter of title to the bed of the part of the

Notes

river which is an arm of the sea (and thus part of the 'internal waters'), without reference to s. 7 of the 1977 Act. The Tribunal found that the *common law* presumption of the Crown's title (which governed the whole matter before the general *statutory* declaration first made by s. 7 of the Territorial Sea and Fishing Zone Act 1965) had been applied by the Crown in breach of the principles of the Treaty of Waitangi (see pp. 267-269 and 288-290). But, as already indicated, the true position is likely to be that the Crown's title, whether at common law (which generally still applies to the foreshore) or as declared by statute (in respect of the actual sea bed), remains subject to the customary title where it is shown to exist, as in the Whanganui River claim. With regard to the bed of the navigable Whanganui above the reaches of the sea, the matter may be more difficult. Here the Tribunal (see pp. 268-269 and 304 -307 of the *Report*) apparently felt constrained to accept Hay J.'s decision in *R v Morison* [1950] NZLR 247, pp. 267-268, that the general statutory declaration of the Crown's title to the bed of navigable rivers (n. 101 above) was effective to destroy the customary title in the bed. (Hence the Tribunal found a further breach of Treaty principles.) Hay J.'s decision on that point is however directly contrary in its approach to the one described as 'well-settled' by Blanchard J. in *Faulkner v Tauranga District Council* [1996] 1 NZLR 357 (see p. 133 above; not referred to by the Tribunal) and is unlikely to be followed by the High Court today, let alone approved by the Court of Appeal. On the other hand, if Hay J. was correct in finding that the Crown was in 'possession' of the bed under the Wanganui River Trust Act 1891, that would support his view that the Maori customary title had (anyway) been extinguished by s. 115 of the Maori Land Act 1931. (Until repeal in 1993 that section survived in substance as s. 157(2) of the Maori Affairs Act 1953: see n. 90, p. 211 above.)

    For fuller discussion see Brookfield, 'The Waitangi Tribunal and the Whanganui Riverbed' (forthcoming).

105 [1963] NZLR 461 (CA).
106 For the vesting of the respective beds, see (i) s. 27 of the Native Land Amendment and Native Land Claims Adjustment Act 1922 (repealed by s. 118 of the Maori Purposes Act 1931 but without affecting the vesting), dealing with the Arawa lakes; and (ii) s. 14 of the Maori Land Amendment and Maori Land Claims Adjustment Act 1926 (Lake Taupo and the Waikato River, down to the Huka Falls). See *Laws NZ*, Water, n. 101 above, para 68.
107 Those lakes include Lakes Rotorua and Waikaremoana; and also the comparatively small Lake Omapere, as to which see the judgment of Judge Acheson in the Native Land Court (1929), quoted extensively and with approval by the Waitangi Tribunal in *Te Whanganui-a-Orotu Report* 1995 (Wai 55) 9 WTR, para 12.3.4 and in *The Whanganui River Report* 1999 (Wai 167), para 9.2.15. The explanation in these cases (differing from that in the passages quoted by the Tribunal) must be that, as in the case of land not covered by water, the radical or allodial title to the lake beds was vested in the Crown on the assumption of sovereignty. (See *Southern Centre of Theosophy Inc v South Australia* (1979) 21 SASR 399, pp. 411-412 (Zelling J., obiter); reversed on another matter [1982] AC 706). But, again as with land not under water, the vesting was subject to Maori customary rights. See *Laws NZ*, Water, n. 101 above, para 68.
108 *In re the Bed of the Wanganui River* [1962] NZLR 600.
109 [1994] 2 NZLR 20.
110 At p. 26.
111 At p. 27.
112 The New Zealand practice of not including in certificates of title under the Land Transfer Act 1952 the riparian owner's share of the stream bed has been judicially approved; though apparently the practice has not been followed in all cases. For references, discussion and difficulties, see my 'Prescription and Adverse Possession' in Hinde (ed.), *The New Zealand*

· 213 ·

Torrens System Centennial Essays (1971), 162, pp. 197–203.
Where the practice is followed, the provisions of the Land Transfer Act guaranteeing and protecting the registered proprietor's title would of course not have the effect of extinguishing any outstanding customary title in the stream bed.

Chapter 6

1. 'Parliament, the Treaty and Freedom' [1994] *NZLJ* 462. An annotated and slightly revised version appears in Joseph (ed.), *Essays on the Constitution* (1995), 41.
2. *The Dominion*, 1 May 1995; *The Press*, 2 May 1995.
3. *The New Zealand Herald*, 4 May 1995.
4. See ch. 3, pp. 74–75.
5. Melbourne, *Maori Sovereignty* (1995), p. 31.
6. Ibid., p. 32.
7. Kelsey, *New Zealand Experiment* (1995; new edn 1997), p. 342.
8. Ibid., p. 344. See also Kelsey, 'From Flagpoles to Pine Trees' in Spoonley et al. (eds), *Nga Patai* (1996) 177, pp. 177–179.
9. See comments on this in my 'Revolutions, Referendums and the Treaty' [1997] *NZLJ* 328, pp. 329–330.
10. For further discussion see Brookfield, n. 9 above.
11. See ch. 5, pp. 110ff.
12. See ch. 1, p. 30.
13. 1 Dallas 53.
14. See ch. 7, pp. 177ff.
15. *Pace* Moana Jackson, if he means to suggest otherwise: see ch. 3, p. 63 and n. 30, p. 200.
16. See ch. 2, p. 38.
17. 'The New Zealand Constitution' in Kawharu (ed.), *Waitangi: Maori and Pakeha Perspectives* (1989) 1, p. 4.
18. Renwick, *The Treaty Now* (1990), p. 93. As to the conventions of responsible government, see ch. 4, p. 91 and (in New Zealand) ch. 5, pp. 119ff.
19. See ch. 2, p. 38.
20. See ch. 3, pp. 60–61.
21. See ch. 2, pp. 45–46.
22. Samuel Marsden (1815), quoted by Anne Salmond in *Between Worlds* (1997), p. 465.
23. See Davidson, *Christianity in Aotearoa* (1991), p. 7.
24. Walker, *Nga Pepa a Ranginui* (1996), p. 61.
25. 'The Treaty and the Word' in Oddie and Perrett (eds), *Justice, Ethics, and New Zealand Society* (1992), 1.
26. See ch. 3, p. 69.
27. See ch. 3, p. 57.
28. 32 NZLR 321, p. 340. See ch. 5, p. 129.
29. 'Use It or Lose It' (1996) 30 *NZJH* 141, p. 160.
30. Adams, Te Uira and Parsonson, '"Behold a Kite Flies towards You"' (1997) 31 *NZJH* 99.
31. Binney, 'Te Mana Tuatoru' (1997) 31 *NZJH* 117.
32. *Travesty After Travesty* (1996), pp. 39–41. As with so much else in his two books — the other is *The Travesty of Waitangi* (1995) — Scott either arbitrarily dismissed, or was unaware of, much case law and relevant scholarship, legal and historical.
33. Salmond, *Hui* (1975), p. 13.
34. Ballara, *Iwi* (1998), p. 294.
35. E. T. Durie, *Custom Law* (1994), p. 33.

Notes

36 Ngapora to Grey, 19 Feb 1848 (enclosed with despatch to Earl Grey, 3 April 1848). See *GBPP*, 1849 (1120), 18, p. 19 (quoted by Gould, Evidence before the Waitangi Tribunal in Chatham Islands Claims (Wai 64), p. 34. The letter is also referred to by Sinclair, *Kinds of Peace* (1991), p. 49, citing Ward, *A Show of Justice* (1974; revd edn 1995), p. 84.

37 Baker, 'Personal Liberty under the Common Law' in Davis (ed.), *The Origins of Modern Freedom in the West* (1995), 178, pp. 184–191.

38 Lofft 1. For recent discussions of the case, see Shyllon, *Black Slaves in Britain* (1974), ch. 7; and Thomas, *The Slave Trade* (1997), p. 474.

39 20 St Tr 2–7n. (Court of Session).

40 3&4 Wm. IV, c.73.

41 See ch. 4, pp. 100ff.

42 See the discussion of the ending of slavery in Maori society in Gould, Evidence, n. 36 above, pp. 33–40. Dr Gould concludes from available evidence that on the mainland 'slavery was still part of the fabric of Maori society until the end of the 1840s and perhaps later still', though he allows for possible evolution of the institution 'in face of social, political, and economic changes': ibid., p. 33. A gradual (rather than sudden) ending of slavery, to avoid or lessen the competing evil of social disruption, might have been morally justified in the circumstances. See Sandel, 'Judgmental Toleration' in George (ed.), *Natural Law, Liberalism and Morality* (1996) 107, pp. 110–111.

43 47 Geo. III, c.36

44 See 'The Treaty and the Word', n. 25 above.

45 *Between Worlds* (1997), p. 160.

46 Cf. Justice E. T. Durie in 'Justice, Biculturalism and the Politics of Law' in Wilson and Yeatman (eds), *Justice and Identity* (1995), 33: '. . . one culture should not be judged by the standards of another; each must be appreciated on its own terms'. I dissent from this if and so far as it is a denial of the possibility of transcultural standards. See further my 'Parliament, the Treaty and Freedom' in Joseph (ed.), *Essays on the Constitution* (1995), 41, p. 49 (n. 26).

47 See ch. 5, pp. 116ff.

48 Salmond, loc. cit.

49 Ibid., 177–179.

50 See Langbein, *Torture and the Law of Proof* (1976), pp. 134–135. For the present statutory illegality of torture, see s. 9 of the New Zealand Bill of Rights Act 1990 and the Crimes of Torture Act 1989. See further Brookfield, n. 46 above, p. 54.

51 See Brookfield, ibid., p. 55.

52 The common law punishment is fully described in Radzinowicz, *A History of English Criminal Law* (1948), vol. i, pp. 220–221. The mitigation consisted in the executioner's ensuring that the offender died by hanging before being disembowelled. A statute of 1814, 54 Geo III, c. 146, made hanging the method of inflicting death (followed by indignities to the corpse) but with the alternative of beheading allowed at the discretion of the Sovereign, under s. 2. Prompted by the convictions of Maori 'rebels' for treason under the Disturbed Districts Act 1869 (NZ) (see Ward, *A Show of Justice* (1974; revd edn 1995), pp. 228–229), the Punishment of High Treason Act 1870 (NZ) replaced the 1814 Act in New Zealand, making death by hanging the only punishment applicable, without the indignities to the corpse or the alternative of beheading. The common law punishment was never in force in New Zealand.

53 Abolished in 1772 (12 Geo. III c. 20).

54 Baker, n. 37 above, p. 190.

55 *Comm.*, iv, p. 377. Holdsworth (*A History of English Law*, vol. xi (1938), p. 556) notes of Blackstone's list that it 'comes from all ages in the history of English law'.

56 'Criminal Courts and Procedure' in Cockburn (ed.), *Crime in England 1550-1800* (1977), 15, p. 44.
57 Hanging was the penalty under a greatly increased number of statutes in 18th century Britain though, as Salmond noted in *Two Worlds* (1991), p. 90, there were fewer actual executions. On the relaxation of the administration of the capital statutes towards the end of the century, see Radzinowicz, n. 52 above, pp. 151ff.
58 See, e.g., Kelsey, 'Treaty of Waitangi and Maori Independence' (1990) *9th Commonwealth Law Conference Papers*, 249, pp. 254, 256 (and my comments in 'Maori Rights and Two Radical Writers' [1990] *NZLJ* 406, 414-415).
59 Treaty of Waitangi Act 1975, s. 6(1).
60 *Whigs and Hunters* (1975), p. 266.
61 Ibid.
62 Ibid., p. 265.
63 Ibid.
64 *Hui* (1976; 2nd edn), p. 13. Cf. her *Between Worlds* (1997), p. 144 ('If the return was too little, or excessive, the exchanges carried on'). In the latter work Salmond tends to emphasize the ideal nature of utu as the 'principle of balanced return' (p. 509 et passim). As to the propensity of utu to get out of hand, cf. on blood feuds generally Miller, 'Choosing the Avenger' (1983) 1 *Law & History Review* 159, pp. 161-162. Jane Kelsey, in her advocacy of 'Maori ... processes of conflict resolution as ... intrinsically valid', that the Courts will be 'required to recognise', ignored the problem of how utu could be adopted in a modern, fully developed legal system: see her 'Decolonization in the "First World"' (1985) 5 *Windsor Yearbook of Access to Justice* 102, p. 112 (discussing *Police v Dalton* (Magistrate's Court, Auckland; June 1979; unreported) in which utu was apparently rejected as a cultural defence of Maori charged with assaulting engineering students who had parodied the haka).
65 *A Show of Justice* (1974; revd edn 1995), p. 222. Cf. ibid., pp. 170 and 176.
66 *Making Peoples* (1996), pp. 267-268.
67 *The New Zealand Wars and the Victorian Interpretation of Racial Conflict* (1986), p. 308.
68 *Making Peoples* (1996), p. 268. See also my 'Revolutions, Referendums and the Treaty' [1997] *NZLJ* 328, p. 331.
69 Ollivier, Bell, and Fitz-Gerald's New Zealand Reports 76.
70 See now s. 91 of the Crimes Act 1961.
71 Ballara, *Iwi* (1998), p. 198.
72 See ch. 4, pp. 92-93.
73 *A Question of Honour* (1990), pp. 211-212. The long list of oppressive 'settler government laws' cited by Kelsey begins with the New Zealand Settlements Act 1863 and ends by including (extraordinarily) the Maori Language Act 1987.
74 *R v Rua* [1916] GLR 658. The case has been fully dealt with on the historical evidence by Professor Judith Binney in *Mihaia* (1996), pp. 124-128. For comments on legal aspects see my 'Maori Rights and Two Radical Writers' [1990] *NZLJ* 406, pp. 413-414.
Kelsey's other examples are *Goodall v Te Kooti* (1890) 9 NZLR 26 and *Raglan Golf Club v Raglan C.C.* (1980; unreported but noted [1980] *NZRecLaw* 334). For comment, see Brookfield, loc. cit. See also Kelsey's treatment of *Dalton's* case (n. 64 above).
75 Op. cit., p. 15 and p. 273 (n.14).
76 3 NZJur R (NS) SC 72.
77 'Decolonization in the "First World"', n. 64 above, p. 109. (Cf. her treatment of *Dalton's* case: ibid., pp. 111-112 (n. 64 above).) It is necessary to show just how the judges' values and priorities affected the way they dealt with cases if one is to be so sweepingly condemnatory. See further her extravagant 'Legal Imperialism and the Colonization of Aotearoa' in Spoonley

Notes

et al. (eds), *Tauiwi* (1984), 20, somewhat uncritically accepted by Sharp, *Justice and the Maori* (2nd edn; 1997), pp. 3 and 282.
78 *The Maori and the Criminal Justice System*, Part 2 (1988), p. 114.
79 Ibid.
80 See ch. 5, pp. 116ff.
81 See ch. 5, pp. 118–119.
82 Apparently legislation would now be needed, if this were to be done. The Urewera Lands Act 1921–1922 (which repealed the Act of 1896) was amended by s. 83 of the Maori Purposes Act 1931, to enable reserves to be set aside by Governor-General's warrant on Tuhoe land (awarded to the Crown under the 1921–1922 Act), for former owners or other Maori. But the 1931 provision has been repealed by s. 6(1) of the Maori Purposes Act 1956. On the proposals for limited Tuhoe self-government that led up to the Act of 1896 and the government's subsequent undercutting of its own scheme, see Binney, 'Te Mana Tuatoru' (1997) 31 *NZJH* 117. (I am indebted to Professors Binney and Keith Sorrenson for discussion.) See further ch. 7, p. 172.
83 See Cox, *Kotahitanga* (1993), ch. 5. There was also a system of Resident Magistrates (who sat with Maori assessors in cases between Maori), set up first under Part V of the Resident Magistrates' Courts Ordinance of 1846 and abolished by the Magistrates' Courts Act 1893. See Cox, ibid., and Ward, *A Show of Justice* (1974; revd edn 1995) pp. 74–75, 222, 243–244, et passim. See also the Native Circuit Courts Act 1858 repealed (with the Native Districts Regulation Act 1858) by the Repeals Act 1891.
84 Cox, op. cit., p. 108.
85 Treaty of Waitangi Act 1975, s. 6(1) and (2).
86 Treaty of Waitangi Act 1975, s. 6(3) and (4). In respect of private land the Tribunal may not in general recommend its return to Maori or that the Crown acquire it: s. 6(4A). But (with certain exceptions) the Tribunal may make recommendations, binding on the Crown, for the return to Maori of land vested or previously vested in a State enterprise or education institution: see s. 8A(2)(a) of that Act, ss. 27B and 27C of the State-Owned Enterprises Act 1986 and ss. 212 and 213 of the Education Act 1989. The Tribunal may also make binding recommendations for the return to Maori of Crown forest land under forestry licence: see s. 8HB (1) (a) of the 1975 Act and s. 36 of the Crown Forest Assets Act 1989.
The Tribunal's recommendations are not otherwise binding.
As to the limited power to make binding recommendations, see the Tribunal's *Turangi Township Remedies Report* (1998; Wai 84) and (for discussion) D. V. Williams, 'Te Kooti tango whenua' (1999), pp. 9–11.
87 Cf. *Maori Electoral Option Report* (1994) (Wai 413) 7 WTR, 4.
88 See e.g. Annie Mikaere's criticism of the *Maori Electoral Option Report* (n. 87 above) in [1994] *NZRecLRev*, 265, pp. 273–274 and for comment thereon Brookfield, [1994] *NZRecLRev* pp. 376, pp. 383–384. Earlier criticisms of the Tribunal along the above lines by Mrs Mikaere and Jane Kelsey are discussed in my 'Sovereignty: the Treaty, the Courts and the Tribunal' [1989] *NZRecLRev* 292.
89 Report on the Muriwhenua Fishing Claim (1988) (Wai 17), p. xxi, S 6.1.
90 Ibid.
91 See, e.g., Kelsey, *A Question of Honour* (1990), pp. 216–217 et passim.
92 [1994] 1 NZLR 513.
93 At p. 517. For further comment, see Brookfield, [1994] *NZRecLRev* 376.
94 See ch. 2, p. 52 and n. 75, p. 197.
95 Notable critics are K. Minogue, *Waitangi: Morality and Reality* (1998) and D. Round, *Truth or Treaty?* (1998).

96   See ch. 1, p. 19; ch. 4, p. 94.
97   See ch. 4, pp. 93ff.
98   See ch. 4, p. 93.
99   See, e.g., Winiata, 'Revolution by Lawful Means' 1993 *New Zealand Law Conference Papers, The Law and Politics*, vol ii, 13, pp. 16-18.
100 See ch. 1, pp. 13-14.
101 [1941] NZLR 590.
102 [1987] 1 NZLR 641, p. 667.
103 [1993] 2 NZLR 301.
104 At p. 305.
105 [1994] 1 NZLR 513.
106 At p. 516.
107 The formulae include both those in the more demanding terms of s. 9 of the State-Owned Enterprises Act 1986 (nothing in the Act is to permit the Crown to 'act in a manner that is inconsistent with the principles' of the Treaty) and s. 4 of the Conservation Act 1987 (the Act 'shall so be interpreted and administered as to give effect to the principles of the Treaty') and also less demanding provisions such as s. 8 of the Resource Management Act 1991 merely requiring that the principles be 'take[n] into account' (see further n. 112 below).
108 The cases begin with *New Zealand Maori Council v Attorney-General* [1987] 1 NZLR 641 (in which s. 9 of the State-Owned Enterprises Act 1986 (see n. 107 above) was given a degree of force perhaps unexpected by some individual legislators) and, as regards contextual review, with *Huakina Development Trust v Waikato Valley Authority* [1987] 2 NZLR 188. For a recent analysis of the cases, see Joseph, 'Constitutional Review Now' [1998] *NZLRev* 85, pp. 93-108; and the following papers delivered at the Legal Research Foundation's Symposium 'The Struggle for Simplicity' (Auckland, April 1997): J. O. Upton, 'Maori in the New Zealand Court of Appeal under Lord Cooke' and J. Williams, 'The Position of Maori at the End of the Cooke Era'.
109 *Huakina Development Trust v Waikato Valley Authority* [1987] 2 NZLR 188, p. 206. Cf. at p. 210 ('. . . the Treaty is part of the fabric of New Zealand society'.)
110 See p. 152.
111 See nn. 107 above and 112 below. For an important general principle that, in a statute (such as the Resource Management Act 1991) protecting Maori interests or values but with reference to a community standard of reasonableness, the standard is that of society as a whole rather than of the Maori community as such, see *Watercare Services Ltd v Minhinnick* [1998] 1 NZLR 294 (CA).
112 To the contrary, the decision of the Planning Tribunal in *Hanton v Auckland City Council* [1994] NZRMA 289, interpreting s. 8 of the Resource Management Act 1991. That section requires 'all persons exercising functions and powers' under the Act in relation to stipulated matters of resource management, to 'take into account the principles' of the Treaty. The Tribunal held that the City Council, as a consent authority under the Act, in taking into account those principles was, in contrast to a Minister of the Crown as a consent authority, not required to take into account the *obligations* 'under the Treaty or its principles' — in this case the obligation to consult the tangata whenua (at p. 301). But, with respect, the distinction is not tenable: there appears to be nothing in s. 8 or elsewhere in the Act to counter the proposition that, in relation to the Treaty, the constitutional origin of the functions and powers which are referred to in s. 8 is the same, whichever legal entity exercises them. Here it is the Crown (including the Crown in Parliament) as a unity, which exercises kawanatanga through legislative or executive acts (including those in the sphere of local government), that is significant. (Cf. ch. 4, p. 90.)

Notes

113 *A Question of Honour* (1990), pp. 236–237.
114 See ch. 3, pp. 74–75.
115 'Treaty Justice in the 1880s' in Spoonley, Pearson and Macpherson (eds), *Nga Take* (1991), 108, p. 128. And see her *Rolling Back The State* (1993), p. 289.
116 3 NZJur R (NS) SC 72.
117 See ch. 2, pp. 47ff.
118 See ch. 3, pp. 74–75.
119 See ch. 3, pp. 60–61.
120 [1989] 2 Qd R 79. See ch. 2, pp. 38ff.
121 I am especially indebted in what follows to M. King, *Moriori: A People Rediscovered* (1989), D. G. Sutton, 'The Whence of the Moriori' (1985) 19 *NZJH* 3, B. D. Gilling, 'By Whose Custom?' (1993) 23 *VUWLRev* 45, and A. Gould, Evidence to the Waitangi Tribunal in the Moriori Chatham Islands Claims (Wai 64 and 308).
122 Sutton, n. 121 above, p. 6.
123 Sutton, 'Conclusion': in Sutton (ed.) *The Origins of the First New Zealanders* (1994), 243, p. 256. (See also Clark, 'Moriori and Maori: the Linguistic Evidence' in the same work, 123.)
124 *New Zealand Government Gazette*, vol. ii, no. 45 (2 November, 1842).
125 See Gilling, n. 121 above, pp. 51–55.
126 See the quotation in King, *Moriori*, n. 121 above, p. 127, from the Minutes of the Native Land Court, Chatham Islands, 16 June 1870. See also Gilling, n. 121 above, p. 54. Professor R. Walker gives the number of Moriori killed by the invaders as 226, out of a surviving population estimated at 1663: *Ka Whawhai Tonu Matou* (1990), p. 41. (Introduced European diseases had already reduced the population by a fifth: ibid.)
127 See ch. 3, pp. 60–61.
128 See ch. 2, p. 45f.
129 See King, op. cit., pp. 115, 118–119 (manumission declared in 1863). But see also Gould's differing views in his Evidence to the Waitangi Tribunal, n. 121 above, summarized at pp. 99–100 (no formal manumission in 1863 and, apparently, slavery largely at an end by 1858). I do not attempt to summarize the disagreements between the historians.
130 See pp. 141–142.
131 See the account of the proceedings in Gilling, n. 121 above.
132 See King, op. cit., pp. 132–133; Gilling, n. 121 above, pp. 55–56.
133 The rule (originally laid down in Compensation Court hearings in 1866) that Maori in actual possession of land at the time of the establishment of the Crown's government of New Zealand in 1840 were to be taken as owners of it, in Native Land Court proceedings. See Gilling, n. 121 above, pp. 48–51; and his '"The Queen's Sovereignty Must Be Vindicated": The 1840 Rule in the Maori Land Court' (1994) 16 *NZULRev* 136.
134 Wai 64 and 308.
135 Wai 65.
136 See ch. 2, pp. 40ff.

Chapter 7

1 See ch. 6, pp. 136–139.
2 See ch. 3, p. 66.
3 *Waitangi: Morality and Reality* (1998), p. 22.
4 Ibid.
5 *Truth or Treaty?* (1998), p. 135. Quite eccentrically he cites *Wi Parata v Bishop of Wellington* (1877) 3 NZJur R (NS) SC 72 in support of the doctrine. See as to this case ch. 5, pp. 129–130.

Round's somewhat strident criticism of the 'activism' of the courts in developing a jurisprudence of the 'principles' of the Treaty seems to me much vitiated by his acknowledgment that the Court of Appeal, in initiating the development in *New Zealand Maori Council v Attorney-General* [1987] 1 NZLR 641, was free as a matter of interpretation to give force to s. 9 of the State-Owned Enterprises Act 1986, instead of in effect accepting it as (in Round's view of the section, at p. 122) 'little more than a pious and reasonably [sic] meaningless piece of lip-service [to the Treaty]'. The Court, that is, properly did justice according to law. Once that is allowed, the courts' role in developing Treaty principles is a proper one, however Round and the (Business) Roundtable (both in agreement on this point) may dislike the politics of it and find cause to criticize in particular cases.

The views of the Business Roundtable on the matter are indicated by R. Kerr, [1997] *NZLJ* 361, p. 364.

6 *The Travesty of Waitangi* (1995) and *Travesty After Travesty* (1996).
7 Minogue, op. cit., pp. 90–91; Round, op. cit. p. 200.
8 Minogue, op, cit., p. 88.
9 Ibid. His emphasis.
10 Ibid.
11 Ibid. Cf. ibid., p. 13.
12 See ch. 3, pp. 75ff.
13 Minogue, op. cit., p. 22.
14 'The "Pakeha Constitutional Revolution"?' (1993) 1 *Waikato L Rev* 53.
15 'Slaying the Leviathan' (1998) 28 *VUWLRev* 683.
16 'Maori Rights and Two Radical Writers' [1990] *NZLJ* 406, pp. 411 ff.
17 Upston-Hooper, n. 15 above, p. 696.
18 See ch. 3, pp. 74–75.
19 To adopt Mark Lilla's description of American academic post-modernism in 'The Politics of Jacques Derrida', *New York Review of Books,* 25 June 1998, 36.
20 See, e.g., *Kohu v Police* (1989) 5 CRNZ 194, *Kaihau v Inland Revenue Department* [1990] 3 NZLR 344 and *Berkett v Tauranga District Court* [1992] 3 NZLR 206.
21 See n. 20 above.
22 At p. 214.
23 [1992] *NZRecLRev* 156. Her emphasis.
24 [1991] *NZRecLRev* 150, commenting on *R v Kohu* (1990; CA, unreported) and *Harawira v Police* (1990; HC; unreported). As to these cases see also Brookfield, [1990] *NZRecLRev* 213 (Kohu) and [1991] *NZRecLRev* 253 (Harawira).
25 See ch. 1, pp. 19–20 and 32–34.
26 See pp. 177ff.
27 [1989] 2 Qd R 79. See ch. 2, pp. 38ff.
28 The point was made in Tom Scott's cartoon of the Maori protester declaring non-acceptance of Pakeha law and then invoking that law to complain about the police (*New Zealand Listener*, 29 April 1995).
29 See ch. 1, pp. 20–22.
30 Quoted by Kelsey, *The New Zealand Experiment* (1995; new edn 1997), p. 342.
31 See ch. 2, p. 38.
32 '"Rogernomics" and the Treaty of Waitangi' (1989) 7 *Law in Context* 66, p. 90.
33 Ibid.
34 Ibid.
35 Ibid., p. 91.
36 'Aotearoa/New Zealand' in Sharp (ed.), *Leap Into the Dark* (1994) 178, pp. 202–203.

37 'The Treaty of Waitangi and Maori Independence' (1990) *9th Commonwealth Law Conference Papers* 249, p. 255.
38 See ch. 3, pp. 74–75.
39 See ch. 1, p. 15.
40 See ch. 3, pp. 75ff.
41 See his 'Law, History and the Treaty of Waitangi' (1997) 31 *NZJH* 38.
42 Ibid., p. 57.
43 McHugh, 'Constitutional Voices' (1996) 26 *VUWLRev* 499. See also his 'Aboriginal Identity and Relations' in Coates and McHugh, *Living Relationships* (1998) 107.
44 [1987] 1 NZLR 641 (as to which see ch. 6, pp. 154–155).
45 'Constitutional Voices', n. 43 above, p. 524.
46 'Aboriginal Identity and Relations', n. 43 above, p. 178.
47 'Constitutional Voices', n. 43 above, p. 524.
48 See pp. 174ff and nn. 61–63 below.
49 For the Crown's attitude, see Sir Douglas Graham (Minister in charge of Treaty of Waitangi Negotiations), 'The New Zealand Government's Policy' in Quentin-Baxter (ed), *Recognising the Rights of Indigenous Peoples* (1998), 3, pp. 8–9 and cf. his *Trick or Treaty?* (1997), pp. 17–19. See also Mason Durie's account in *Te Mana, Te Kawanatanga* (1998), p. 232.
50 See ch. 5, p. 116.
51 See ch. 6, p. 150.
52 See Binney, 'Te Mana Tuatoru' (1997) 31 *NZJH* 117.
53 J. Williams, 'The Position of Maori in New Zealand Law at the End of the Cooke Era' (paper delivered at the Legal Research Foundation's Symposium 'The Struggle for Simplicity', Auckland, April 1997, p. 12.)
54 See Jackson, *The Maori and the Criminal Justice System*, Part II (1988) and Harris, 'Equal Access to Justice' [1995] *NZLRev* 282, pp. 294–297.
55 Ibid., p. 296.
56 See also McHugh's views in 'Aboriginal Identity and Relations', n. 43 above, p. 172–173.
57 I am indebted to Professor M. Durie's discussion of 'Mana Motuhake: Autonomy, Governance, and Nationhood' in *Te Mana, Te Kawanatanga* (1998), ch. 8.
58 See ch. 6, pp. 150–151.
59 M. Durie, op. cit., p. 220.
60 As to which see ch. 2, p. 55. Cf. the protection for the Treaty proposed in clause 4 of the original draft New Zealand Bill of Rights: see *A Bill of Rights for New Zealand* (Government White Paper, 1985).
61 Treaty rights, and principles, to the extent that they are now cognizable in law, would in any event survive the transition to a republic even without new constitutional arrangements providing for them. This has been the case with George III's proclamation of 1763 recognizing and protecting the rights of the North American First Nations, which survived the American Revolution and has been applied in American as well as Canadian courts: see, e.g., *Johnson v M'Intosh* 8 Wheat 543 (1823). But the proclamation is constitutionally protected in Canada only, under s. 35(1) of the Constitution Act 1982. It is recognition and protection of that sort that is necessary in New Zealand.
   In my view the New Zealand Bill of Rights, at present enacted in an ordinary statute (the 1990 Act of that name), should become part of the new Constitution and be protected by entrenchment. But that matter does not need to be considered here. See my 'Parliament, the Treaty, and Freedom' in Joseph (ed.), *Essays on the Constitution* (1995) 41, pp. 57–59.
62 See my 'Republican New Zealand' [1995] *NZLRev* 310.
63 See my 'Revolutions, Referendums and the Treaty' [1997] NZLJ 328, pp. 331–332. For the

argument that Parliament (which consists of the Sovereign as well as the House of Representatives) has no legal power to abolish the monarchy (so that abolition must necessarily be revolutionary), because it cannot annul itself by abolishing one of its constituent parts or because, the Crown being party to the Treaty, the monarchy is a 'fundamental postulate' of the New Zealand Constitution, see ibid. and cf. my 'Republican New Zealand', n. 62 above, pp. 314–317. See also on the need for 'reasonably substantial Maori concurrence' for the change to a republic, Lord Cooke, 'The Suggested Revolution Against the Crown' in Joseph (ed.), *Essays on the Constitution*, n. 61 above, 28, p. 38.
For an opposing view (discussed [1997] *NZLJ*, p. 332), see Stockley, 'Becoming a Republic?' in Trainor (ed.), *Republicanism in New Zealand* (1996) 81, pp. 98–102 and 'Parliament, Crown and Treaty' (1996) 17 *NZULRev* 193.

64 See ch. 1, p. 15.
65 The phrase is used to include all the considerations extraneous to the present rules of law making (and hence technically revolutionary in their effect on the law) which are relied on to establish the change and prompt the courts to recognize it. Cf. Sir William Wade's use of the phrase in *Constitutional Fundamentals* (1989; revd edn), p. 37 (though apparently he would not see constitutional facts of this nature as being technically revolutionary).
See also my 'Kelsen, the Constitution and the Treaty' (1992) 15 *NZULRev* 163, pp. 173–175; and, for my earlier and rather different views on making this kind of basic constitutional change, 'Parliamentary Sovereignty and Constitutional Entrenchment' (1984) 5 *Otago L Rev* 603.
66 See n. 12, p. 187.
67 See ch. 1, pp. 26–28, 32; and my 'Revolutions, Referendums and the Treaty', n. 63 above, p. 332.
68 'The Fragility of Pakeha Support', commentary in *Living Relationships*, n. 43 above, 222, pp. 229–231.
69 'Representing *Justice and the Maori*', *Political Theory Newsletter* (1992), 4, p. 27. (I am grateful to Professor Sharp for the reference.)
70 Ibid., p. 38.
71 Ibid., pp. 37–38.
72 Ibid., p. 38.
73 *Waitangi: Morality and Reality* (1998), p. 34. Minogue points out (ibid., p. 38) that 'the entire Waitangi process... depends upon a transcultural recognition of a universal idea of what is just.' And, discussing the 'moral dogmatism' of activists in the Waitangi context (ibid., p. 34), he writes of 'many of the educated young' that (his emphasis) they 'have managed to convince themselves *both* that moral judgments are purely a function of culture, *and* that there are absolute standards of right and justice which ought to regulate relations between peoples.' But of course one may avoid the criticized inconsistency by holding (as I do) the view that moral judgments are not purely cultural. The transcultural standard that 'ought to regulate relations between peoples' is offended at the outset by the 'immense intrusion into other people's business' (see ch. 3, pp. 60–61) or 'fair thievish purchase' (see ch. 2, p. 45) that generally characterizes a conquest or similar seizure of a people's territory. But the standard still applies in the future dealings between the peoples concerned in any given case (as in the doing of justice in the Waitangi process), albeit modified in its application by whatever legitimation of the legal and political order imposed by the conquest has taken place.
74 McHugh, 'Aboriginal Identity and Relations', n. 43 above, p. 178.
75 Durie, n. 49 above, p. 232.
76 Ibid.

Notes

77 See ch. 3, pp. 74–75.
78 *The New Zealand Experiment* (1995; new edn 1997), p. 343. Compare Kelsey's earlier statement of the third claim, of what was necessary to satisfy the Maori claim to tino rangatiratanga:

> ... political, legal and economic reform which recognises the independent sovereignty of the *tangata whenua* — not through a dependent or interdependent [sic] nationhood subordinate to the Pakeha state but as co-existing constitutional entities [sic] within one nation.

('The Treaty of Waitangi and Maori Independence' (1990) *9th Commonwealth Law Conference Papers* 249, p. 255. Italics as in the original.)
79 *Rolling Back the State* (1993), p. 291.
80 'The Struggle for Sovereignty', *New Zealand Political Review*, April–May 1995, 16.
81 Ibid., p. 22.
82 Ibid., pp. 23, 25–27.
83 Ibid., p. 22.
84 1 Dallas 53. See ch. 1, pp. 30–31.
85 See ch. 1, pp. 20–22.
86 See ch. 3, p. 71 and ch. 4, p. 90.
87 See ch. 3, pp. 74–75.
88 See ch. 3, p. 72.
89 See ch. 6, pp. 150–151.
90 See ch. 6, pp. 141 and 145–148.
91 See p. 176.
92 Usefully detailed proposals for constitutional reform, based on the Treaty of Waitangi as a foundation, are under discussion in the Anglican church (see the Report of the Commission on Constitutional Arrangements (1998), made to the General Synod). See also S. Reeves, *To Honour the Treaty: The Argument for Equal Seats* (2nd edn; 1996). Such proposals, so far as they imply or seek to give effect to an equality between the Crown and Maori in constitutional matters, seem to me to take insufficient account of the facts of power and the moral consequences that over time attach to those facts — an important part of the process of legitimation that has occupied us in this book.
93 See ch. 2, p. 43.
94 See ch. 3, pp. 81–82.
95 'Law, Sovereignty and History in a Divided Culture' (1998) 43 *McG LJ* 481, p. 506.
96 See, e.g., her *The New Zealand Experiment* (1995; new edn 1997). She appears sceptical that the power of the present New Zealand nation-state can be adequately retained or reasserted in the relevant economic and other areas and looks rather to a 'reconstructed and reconceptualised state' (ibid., p. 393) that would result (one infers) from the emergence of 'political strategies premised on popular sovereignty' (ibid., p. 370) and from the satisfying of radical Maori demands within the range she has put forward (ibid., p. 343; and see n. 78 above).

SELECT BIBLIOGRAPHY

Adams, Tui; Te Uira, Ngahinaturae; and Parsonson, Ann. '"Behold a Kite Flies towards You": The Kiingitanga and the "Opening" of the King Country' (1997) 31 *NZJH* (Essays in Honour of M. P. K. Sorrenson) 99–116.

Adamson, Walter L. *Hegemony and Revolution: A Study of Antonio Gramsci's Political and Cultural Theory.* Berkeley, Los Angeles and London: University of California Press, 1980.

Allan, T. R. S. 'Fairness, Equality, Rationality: Constitutional Theory and Judicial Review' in C. Forsyth and I. Hare (eds), *The Golden Metwand and the Crooked Cord: Essays on Public Law in Honour of Sir William Wade QC.* (Oxford: Clarendon Press, 1998), 15–37.

—— 'Parliamentary Sovereignty: Law, Politics and Revolution' (1997) 113 *Law Quarterly Review* 443–452.

Allott, Antony. *Essays in African Law.* London: Butterworths, 1960.

Anaya, S. James. *Indigenous Peoples in International Law.* New York and Oxford: Oxford University Press, 1996.

Anderson, J. N. D. 'Customary Law and Islamic Law in British African Territories' in *The Future of Customary Law in Africa.* Leiden: Universitaire Pers Leiden, 1956.

Archie, Carol. *Maori Sovereignty: The Pakeha Perspective.* Auckland: Hodder Moa Beckett, 1995.

Ascham, Anthony. *On the Confusions and Revolutions of Governments.* London: 1649 (Scholars' Facsimiles and Reprints, Delmar, New York, 1975).

Augustine, of Hippo. *De Civitate Dei,* Book IV (trans. W. M. Green, *The City of God against the Pagans,* Loeb Classical Library, vol ii: London, William Heinemann and Cambridge (Mass.), Harvard University Press; 1963).

Bakari, Adam H. 'Africa's Paradoxes of Legal Pluralism in Personal Laws: A Comparative Case Study of Tanzania and Kenya'. (1991) 3 *RADIC (African Journal of International and Comparative Law)* 545–557.

Baker, J. H. 'Criminal Courts and Procedure at Common Law 1550–1800', in J. S. Cockburn (ed.), *Crime in England 1550–1800* (Princeton: Princeton University Press, 1977), 15–48.

—— 'Personal Liberty under the Common Law of England, 1200–1600' in R. W. Davis (ed.), *The Origins of Modern Freedom in the West* (Stanford: Stanford University Press, 1995), 178–202.

Ballara, Angela. *Iwi: The Dynamics of Maori Tribal Organisation from c. 1769 to c. 1945.* Wellington: Victoria University Press, 1998.

Barsh, R. L. 'Indigenous Peoples: An Emerging Object of International Law' (1986) 80 *American Journal of International Law* 369–385.

Bartlett, Robert. *The Making of Europe: Conquest, Colonization and Cultural Change 950–*

Select Bibliography

1350. London: Allen Lane, 1993 and Penguin, 1994.

Beetham, David. *The Legitimation of Power*. Atlantic Highlands, N.J.: Humanities Press, 1991.

Belich, James. *Making Peoples: A History of the New Zealanders from Polynesian Settlement to the End of the Nineteenth Century*. Auckland: Penguin, 1996.

—— *The New Zealand Wars and the Victorian Interpretation of Racial Conflict*. Auckland: Auckland University Press, 1986; and Penguin, 1988.

Berman, Harold J. *Law and Revolution: The Formation of the Western Legal Tradition*. Cambridge, Mass. and London: Harvard University Press, 1983.

Binney, Judith. 'Te Mana Tuatoru: The Rohe Potae of Tuhoe' (1997) 31 *NZJH* (Essays in Honour of M. P. K. Sorrenson) 117–131.

—— *Mihaia: The Prophet Rua Kenana and His Community at Maungapohatu*. Wellington: Oxford University Press, 1979; new edn, Auckland: Auckland University Press and Bridget Williams Books, 1996.

Blackstone, William. *Commentaries on the Laws of England*, Book IV, 9th edn (1783). New York and London: facsimile Garland Publishing, 1978.

Boast, Richard. '*In re Ninety Mile Beach* Revisited: The Native Land Court and the Foreshore in New Zealand Legal History' (1993) 23 *VUWLRev* 145–170.

Bohan, Edmund. *To Be a Hero: A Biography of Sir George Grey 1812–1898*. Auckland: HarperCollins, 1998.

Boivin, Richard. 'The *Coté* Decision: Laying to Rest the Royal Proclamation'. [1995] 1 *CNLR* 1–22.

Booth, Revd Ken. 'A Pakeha Perspective on Te Tino Rangatiratanga' in Crawford (ed.), *Church and State* (1998), 1–36.

Brett, Michael, and Fentress, Elizabeth. *The Berbers*. Oxford and Cambridge (Mass.): Blackwell, 1996.

Brookfield, F. M. 'The Courts, Kelsen, and the Rhodesian Revolution' (1969) 19 *UTLJ* 326–352.

—— 'The Fiji Revolutions of 1987' [1988] *NZLJ* 250–256.

—— 'The Governor-General and the Constitution' in H. Gold (ed.), *New Zealand Politics in Perspective* (Auckland: Longman Paul, 1992 (3rd edn)), 77–85.

—— 'Kelsen, the Constitution and the Treaty' (1992) 15 *NZULRev* 163–177.

—— 'Maori Rights and Two Radical Writers: Review and Response' [1990] *NZLJ* 406–420.

—— 'The Monarchy and the Constitution Today: A New Zealand Perspective' [1992] *NZLJ* 438–444

—— 'The MP and the De Facto Doctrine' [1983] *NZLJ* 86–88.

—— 'The New Zealand Constitution: The Search for Legitimacy' in Kawharu (ed.), *Waitangi* (1989), 1–24.

—— Opinion for the Waitangi Tribunal on Legal Aspects of the Raupatu (particularly in Taranaki and the Bay of Plenty (Wai 46 #2.169, 26 January 1996).

—— 'Parliament, the Treaty, and Freedom — Millennial Hopes and Speculations' in Joseph (ed.), *Essays on the Constitution* (1995), 41–60.

—— 'Parliamentary Supremacy and Constitutional Entrenchment: A Jurisprudential Approach' (1984) 5 *Otago L Rev* 603–634.

—— 'Prescription and Adverse Possession' in G.W. Hinde (ed.), *The New Zealand Torrens System Centennial Essays* (Wellington: Butterworths, 1971), 162–209.
—— 'Protest and Possession at Bastion Point: Intrusion on Crown land' [1978] *NZLJ* 383–392.
—— 'Republican New Zealand: Legal Aspects and Consequences' [1995] *NZLRev* 310–327
—— 'Revolutions, Referendums and the Treaty' [1997] *NZLJ* 328–332.
—— 'Sovereignty: The Treaty, the Courts and the Tribunal' [1989] *NZRecLRev* 292–298.
—— 'The Treaty of Waitangi, the Constitution and the Future' (1995) *British Review of New Zealand Studies*, No. 8, 4–20.
—— 'The Treaty, the 1840 Revolution and Responsible Government' (1992) 5 *Canterbury L Rev* 59.
—— Water, in *The Laws of New Zealand*. Wellington: Butterworths, 1997.
Brooking, Tom. 'Use it or Lose it: Unravelling the Land Debate in Late Nineteenth- Century New Zealand' (1996) 30 *NZJH* 141–162.
Brownlie, Ian. *Treaties and Indigenous Peoples: The Robb Lectures 1991* (ed. F. M. Brookfield) Oxford: Clarendon Press, 1992.
Bryce, James. *Studies in History and Jurisprudence*, vol ii. Oxford: Clarendon Press, 1901.
Burnell, P. 'The Problem of Service to Unjust Regimes in Augustine's *City of God*' in D. F. Donnelly (ed.), *The City of God: A Collection of Critical Essays* (New York: Peter Lang Publishers, 1995), 37–49.
Canuel, Edward T. 'Nationalism, Self-Determination, and Nationalist Movements: Exploring the Palestinian Drives for Independence' (1997) 20 *BostCICL Rev* 85–122.
Clark, Ross. 'Moriori and Maori: The Linguistic Evidence' in Sutton (ed.), *Origins* (1994), 123–125.
Coates, Ken S. and McHugh, P. G. (with commentaries). *Living Relationships: Kokiri Ngatahi: The Treaty of Waitangi in the New Millennium*. Wellington: Victoria University Press, 1998.
Coke, Sir Edward. *Institutes of the Laws of England* Third Part. London: printed for W. Clarke and Sons, 1817.
Colley, Linda. *Britons: Forging the Nation 1707–1837* London: Yale University Press, 1992 and Vintage, 1996.
Collins, Hugh. *Marxism and Law*. Oxford and New York: Oxford University Press, 1982.
Cooke, R.B. (Lord Cooke of Thorndon). 'Suggested Revolution Against the Crown' in Joseph (ed.), *Essays on the Constitution* (1995), 28–40.
—— *Turning Points of the Common Law* (Hamlyn Lectures, 1996) London: Sweet and Maxwell, 1997.
Cox, Lindsay. *Kotahitanga: The Search for Maori Political Unity*. Auckland: Oxford University Press, 1993.
Crawford, J. (ed.) *Church and State: Te Tino Rangatiratanga* (Selwyn Lectures 1996) Auckland: College of St John the Evangelist, 1998.
Dahrendorf, Ralph. *After 1989: Morals, Revolution and Civil Society*. Basingstoke: Macmillan in association with St Antony's College, Oxford, 1997.
Davidson, Allan. *Christianity in Aotearoa: A History of Church and Society in New Zealand*. Wellington: New Zealand Education for the Ministry Board, 1991.

De Smith, Stanley and Brazier Rodney. *Constitutional and Administrative Law*. London: Penguin, 1994 (7th edn).
Deane, H. A. *The Political and Social Ideas of St Augustine*. New York and London: Columbia University Press, 1963.
Delany, V. T. H. 'The Constitution of Ireland' (1957–58) 12 *UTLJ* 1–26.
Dias, R.W.M. 'Legal Politics: Norms behind the *Grundnorm*' [1968] *CLJ* 233–259.
Dickinson, H. T. *Liberty and Property: Political Ideology in Eighteenth-Century Britain*. London: Methuen, 1977.
Durie, E. T. 'Custom Law' (1994) 24 *VUWLRev* 325–331.
—— *Custom Law: A Discussion Paper*. [Wellington]: Waitangi Tribunal, 1994.
—— 'Justice, Biculturalism and the Politics of Law' in Wilson and Yeatman (eds), *Justice and Identity* (1995), 33–44.
—— 'Will the Settlers Settle? Cultural Conciliation and Law' (1996) 8 *Otago L Rev* 449–465.
Durie, M. H. *Te Mana, Te Kawanatanga: The Politics of Maori Self-Determination*. Auckland: Oxford University Press, 1998.
Eagleton, Terry. *Ideology: An Introduction*. London and New York: Verso, 1991.
Eekelaar, J. M. 'Principles of Revolutionary Legality' in Simpson (ed.), *Oxford Essays* (1973), 22–43.
El-Obaid, E. A. and Appiagyei-Atua, K. 'Human Rights in Africa: A New Perspective on Linking the Past to the Present' (1996) 41 *McGill LJ* 819–854.
Elton, G. R. *The Tudor Constitution: Documents and Commentary*. Cambridge: Cambridge University Press, 1982 (2nd edn).
Fanon, Frantz. *The Wretched of the Earth*. (*Damnés de la Terre,* trans C. Farrington) Harmondsworth: Penguin, 1967.
Fenton, James. 'Goodbye to All That?' *New York Review of Books,* 20 June 1996, 59–64.
Ferro, Marc. *Colonization: A Global History*. London and New York: Routledge, 1997. (Original French edition *Histoire des Colonisations* (1994); trans K. D. Prithipaul).
Finnis, John M. 'Revolutions and Continuity of Law' in Simpson (ed.), *Oxford Essays* (1973), 44–76.
—— *Natural Law and Natural Rights*. Oxford: Clarendon Press, 1980.
Fletcher, Anthony and MacCullough, Diarmaid. *Tudor Rebellions*. Harlow, Essex: Addison, Wesley Longman, 1997 (4th edn).
Ghai, Yash. 'Constitutions and Governance in Africa: A Prolegomenon' in S. Adelman and A. Paliwala (eds), *Law and Crisis in the Third World* (London: Hans Zell Publishers (for the Centre of Modern African Studies, University of Warwick), 1993), 51–75.
Gilling, Bryan D. 'By Whose Custom? The Operation of the Native Land Court in the Chatham Islands' (1993) 23 *VUWLRev* 45–58.
—— 'Engine of Destruction? An Introduction to the History of the Maori Land Court' (1994) 24 *VUWLRev* 115–139.
—— '"The Queen's Sovereignty must be Vindicated": The 1840 Rule in the Maori Land Court' (1994) 16 *NZULRev* 136–174.
Gillingham, John. 'The Beginnings of English Imperialism' (1992) 5 *Journal of Historical Sociology* 392–409.
Gould, Ashley. Evidence before the Waitangi Tribunal in the Moriori Chatham Islands Claim

(Wai 64 and 308).
Graham, Sir Douglas. 'The New Zealand Government's Policy' in Quentin-Baxter (ed.), *Recognising the Rights of Indigenous Peoples* (1998), 3–21
—— *Trick or Treaty?* Wellington: Institute of Policy Studies, 1997.
Gramsci, Antonio. *Selections from the Prison Notebooks,* ed. and trans. Q. Hoare and G. Nowell Smith. London: Lawrence and Wishart; New York, International Publishers, 1971.
Green, Judith. *The Aristocracy of Norman England.* Cambridge: Cambridge University Press, 1997.
Green, Leslie. 'The Concept of Law Revisited' (1996) 94 *Michigan L Rev* 1687–1717.
Grotius, Hugo. *De Jure Belli ac Pacis* (The Law of War and Peace; English edn; 1738).
Hamnett, Ian. *Chieftainship and Legitimacy: An Anthropological Study of Executive Law in Lesotho.* London and Boston: Routledge and Keegan Paul, 1975.
Hannum, Hurst. *Autonomy, Sovereignty, and Self-Determination: The Accommodation of Conflicting Rights.* Philadelphia: University of Pennsylvania Press, 1990.
Harris, B. V. 'Equal Access to Justice: A Constitutional Principle in Need of a Higher Profile' [1995] *NZLRev* 282–309.
Harris, J. W. 'When and Why Does the Grundnorm Change?' [1971] *CLJ* 103–133.
Harris's Criminal Law. London: Sweet and Maxwell, 1973 (22nd edn; Ian McLean and Peter Morrish).
Hart, H. L. A. *The Concept of Law.* Oxford: Clarendon Press, 1994 (2nd edn; with postscript by Penelope A. Bulloch and Joseph Raz).
Havemann, Paul. '"The Pakeha Constitutional Revolution?" Five Perspectives on Maori Rights and Pakeha Duties' (1993) 1 *Waikato L Rev* 53–77.
—— (ed.) *Indigenous Peoples' Rights in Australia, Canada, & New Zealand.* Auckland: Oxford University Press, 1999.
Hawkins, William. *A Treatise of the Pleas of the Crown,* vol i. London: printed by E. Nutt for J. Walthoe, 1716; facsimile London and New York, Garland Publishing Inc., 1978.
Hill, Christopher. *Liberty Against The Law: Some Seventeenth-Century Controversies.* London: Allen Lane The Penguin Press, 1996.
—— *Puritanism and Revolution: Studies in Interpretation of the English Revolution of the 17th Century.* London: Martin Secker and Warburg, 1958.
Hinde, McMorland and Sim (G. W. Hinde and D. W. McMorland, with N. R. Campbell and D. P. Grinlinton). *Butterworths Land Law in New Zealand.* Wellington: Butterworths, 1997.
Hogg, Peter. *Canadian Constitutional Law.* Scarborough, Ontario: Carswell, 1992 (3rd edn).
Holdsworth, W. S. *A History of English Law,* vol. xi. London: Methuen & Co, 1938.
Honoré, Tony (A. M.). 'Allegiance and the Usurper' [1967] *CLJ* 214–223.
—— 'Reflections on Revolutions' (1967) 2 *Irish Jurist* (New Series) 268.
—— 'The Right to Rebel' (1988) 8 *Oxford Journal of Legal Studies* 34–54.
Hume, David. *A Treatise of Human Nature,* Book III (Everymans edn, vol ii).
Jackson, Moana. *The Maori and the Criminal Justice System — a New Perspective: He Whaipaanga Hou* (Part 2). Wellington: Dept of Justice, 1988.
—— 'Maori Law, Pakeha Law and the Treaty of Waitangi' in *Mana Tiriti: The Art of Protest and Partnership* (Haeata Project Waitangi; City Art Gallery, Wellington City Council).

Select Bibliography

(Wellington: Daphne Brasell Associates Press, 1991), 14–21.

—— 'The Treaty and the Word: The Colonization of Maori Philosophy' in G. Oddie and R. W. Perrett (eds), *Justice, Ethics, and New Zealand Society* (Auckland: Oxford University Press, 1992), 1–10.

Johnson, J. T. *Ideology, Reason and the Limitation of War: Religious and Secular Concepts 1200–1740.* Princeton: Princeton University Press, 1975.

Joseph, Philip A. *Constitutional and Administrative Law in New Zealand.* Sydney: The Law Book Co., 1993.

—— 'Constitutional Review Now' [1998] *NZLRev* 85–128.

—— (ed.) *Essays on the Constitution.* Wellington: Brookers, 1995.

Kawharu, I. H. (Sir Hugh). *Maori Land Tenure* (Oxford: Clarendon Press, 1977).

—— (ed.) *Waitangi: Maori and Pakeha Perspectives of the Treaty of Waitangi.* Auckland: Oxford University Press, 1989.

Keith, Sir Kenneth. 'The Treaty of Waitangi in the Courts' (1990) 14 *NZULRev* 37–61.

Kelsen, Hans. *General Theory of Law and State* (Wedberg's translation). Cambridge, Mass.: Harvard University Press, 1945; reprinted Union, N.J.: Law Book Exchange, 1999.

—— *General Theory of Norms* (translated by M. Hartney) Oxford: Clarendon Press, 1991.

—— *Pure Theory of Law* (Max Knight's translation of *Reine Rechtslehre*, 2nd edn., 1960). Berkeley and Los Angeles: University of California Press, 1967.

Kelsey, Jane. 'Aotearoa-New Zealand: The Anatomy of a State in Crisis' in Sharp (ed.), *Leap into the Dark* (1994), 178–205.

—— 'Decolonization in the "First World" — Indigenous Minorities Struggle for Justice and Self-Determination' (1985) 5 *Windsor Yearbook of Access to Justice* 102–141.

—— 'From Flagpoles to Pine Trees: Tino Rangatiratanga and Treaty Policy Today' in P. Spoonley, C. Macpherson and D. Pearson (eds), *Nga Patai: Racism and Ethnic Relations in Aotearoa-New Zealand* (Palmerston North: Dunmore Press, 1996), 177–201, 285–286.

—— 'Globalisation and the Demise of the Colonial State: Options for Decolonisation in Aotearoa-New Zealand' in Trainor (ed.), *Republicanism* (1996), 37–159, 178–180.

—— 'Globalisation, State and Law' in C. Arup and L. A. Marks (eds), *Cross Currents: Internationalism, National Identity and Law* (special issue from (1996) 14 *Law in Context*, no 1), 31–51.

—— 'Legal Imperialism and the Colonization of Aotearoa-New Zealand' in P. Spoonley, C. Macpherson, D. Pearson and C. Sedgwick (eds), *Tauiwi: Racism and Ethnicity in New Zealand* (Palmerston North: Dunmore Press, 1984), 20–43.

—— *The New Zealand Experiment: A World Model for Structural Adjustment.* Auckland: Auckland University Press with Bridget Williams Books, 1995 (new edn, 1997).

—— *A Question of Honour? Labour and the Treaty 1984–1989.* Wellington: Allen and Unwin, 1990.

—— *Reclaiming the Future: New Zealand and the Global Economy.* Wellington: Bridget Williams Books, 1999.

—— 'Restructuring the Nation: The Decline of the Colonial Nation-State and Competing Nationalisms in Aotearoa/New Zealand', in P. Fitzpatrick (ed.), *Nationalism, Racism and the Rule of Law* (Aldershot (Hants) and Brookfield (Vermont): Dartmouth Publishing Co, 1995), 177–194.

—— '"Rogernomics" and the Treaty of Waitangi: An Irresolvable Contradiction?' (1989) 7 *Law in Context* 66–92.

—— *Rolling Back the State: Privatisation of Power in Aotearoa-New Zealand.* Wellington: Bridget Williams Books, 1993.

—— 'Treaty Justice in the 1980s' in P. Spoonley, D. Pearson and C. Macpherson (eds), *Nga Take: Ethnic Relations and Racism in Aotearoa-New Zealand* (Palmerston North: Dunmore Press, 1991), 108–130.

—— 'The Treaty of Waitangi and Maori Independence — Future Directions' (1990) *9th Commonwealth Law Conference Papers* 249–256.

King, Michael. *Moriori: A People Rediscovered.* Auckland: Viking (Penguin), 1989.

Kingsbury, Benedict. 'The Treaty of Waitangi: Some International Law Aspects' in Kawharu (ed.), *Waitangi* (1989), 121 157.

Kirby, M. D. 'The Struggle for Simplicity: Lord Cooke and Fundamental Rights' (1998) 24 *Commonwealth Law Bulletin* 496–516.

Korman, Sharon. *The Right of Conquest: The Acquisition of Territory by Force in International Law and Practice.* Oxford: Clarendon Press, 1996.

Krygier, Martin. 'Marxism and the Rule of Law: Reflections After the Collapse of Communism' (1990) 15 *Law and Social Inquiry* 633–663.

Kunkel, Wolfgang. *An Introduction to Roman Legal and Constitutional History* (based on *Romische Rechtsgeschichte*, 6th edn; trans J. M. Kelly) Oxford: Clarendon Press, 1973 (2nd edn.).

Langbein, John H. *Torture and the Law of Proof: Europe and England in the Ancien Régime.* Chicago and London: University of Chicago Press, 1976.

Las Casas, Bartolomé de. *The Devastation of the Indies: A Brief Account* (1552). Trans. H. Briffault and intro. Bill M. Donovan. Baltimore and London: John Hopkins University Press, 1992.

—— *In Defense of the Indians* (ca 1552). Trans. and ed. Stafford Poole. DeKalb: Northern Illinois University Press, 1992.

Law Commission. *Final Report on Emergencies* (Report No 22; Wellington, 1991).

Le May, G. H. L. *The Victorian Constitution: Conventions, Usages and Contingencies.* London: Duckworth, 1979.

Le Patourel, John. *The Norman Empire.* Oxford: Clarendon Press, 1976.

Lewis, Bernard. *Cultures in Conflict: Christians, Muslims, and Jews in the Age of Discovery.* New York and Oxford: Oxford University Press, 1995.

—— *Islam and the West.* New York and Oxford: Oxford University Press, 1993.

—— *Race and Slavery in the Middle East: An Historical Enquiry.* New York and Oxford: Oxford University Press, 1990.

Locke, John. *Two Treatises of Government* (1698); ed. P. Laslett. Cambridge: Cambridge University Press, 1988 (student edn).

Luttwak, Edward. *Coup d'Etat — A Practical Handbook.* Harmondsworth, Middlesex: Penguin Press, 1968; Penguin Books, 1969.

McHugh, P. G. 'Aboriginal Identity and Relations in North America and Australasia' in Coates and McHugh, *Living Relationships: Kokiri Ngatahi* (1998), 107–186.

—— 'Aboriginal Title in New Zealand Courts' (1984) 2 *Canterbury L Rev* 235–265

—— 'Constitutional Voices' (1996) 26 *VUWLRev* 499–529.

Select Bibliography

—— 'Law, History and the Treaty of Waitangi' (1997) 31 *NZJH* (Essays in Honour of M. P. K. Sorrenson) 38–57.
—— *The Maori Magna Carta: New Zealand Law and the Treaty of Waitangi* Auckland: Oxford University Press, 1991.
McIlwain, Charles Howard. *The American Revolution: A Constitutional Interpretation.* 1923; reissued Ithaca, New York: Cornell University Press, 1958.
Mackenthun, Gesa. *Metaphors of Dispossession: American Beginnings and the Translation of Empire, 1492–1637.* Norman and London: University of Oklahoma Press, 1997.
McLintock, A. H. *Crown Colony Government in New Zealand.* Wellington: Government Printer, 1958.
MacMillan, Gretchen M. *State, Society and Authority in Ireland: The Foundations of the Modern Irish State.* Dublin: Gill and Macmillan, 1993.
McNab, Robert. *Historical Records of New Zealand,* vol i. Wellington: Government Printer, 1908.
McNeil, Kent. 'Aboriginal Title and Aboriginal Rights: What's the Connection?' (1997) 36 *Alberta L Rev* 117–148.
—— 'Co-existence of Indigenous Rights and Other Interests in Land in Australia and Canada' [1997] 3 *CNLR* 1–18.
—— *Common Law Aboriginal Title.* Oxford: Clarendon Press, 1989.
—— 'Envisaging Constitutional Space for Aboriginal Governments' (1993) 19 *QLJ* 95–136.
Marshall, Geoffrey. *Constitutional Conventions: The Rules and Forms of Political Accountability.* Oxford: Clarendon Press, 1984 (reprinted with additions 1986).
Mason, Roger A. 'The Scottish Reformation and the origins of Anglo-British imperialism' in *Scots and Britons: Scottish Political Thought and the Union of 1603* (Cambridge and New York: Cambridge University Press, 1994), 161–186.
Melbourne, Hineani. *Maori Sovereignty: The Maori Perspective.* Auckland: Hodder Moa Beckett, 1995.
Miller, William Ian. 'Choosing the Avenger: Some Aspects of the Bloodfeud in Medieval Iceland and England' (1983) 1 *Law and History Review* 159–203.
Minogue, Kenneth. *Waitangi: Morality and Reality.* Wellington: New Zealand Business Roundtable, 1998.
Mitchell, J. D. B. [1956] *Public Law* 294–297 (book review).
Morse, Bradford W. 'Permafrost Rights: Aboriginal Self-government and the Supreme Court in *R v Pamajewon*' (1997) 42 *McGLJ* 1011–1042.
Mqeke, R. B. 'Customary Law and Human Rights' (1996) 113 *SALJ* 364–369.
Muldoon, James. *The Americas in the Spanish World Order: The Justification for Conquest in the Seventeenth Century.* Philadelphia: University of Pennsylvania Press, 1994.
—— *Popes, Lawyers, and Infidels.* Liverpool: Liverpool University Press, 1979.
Newton, N. J. 'Federal Power over Indians: Its Sources, Scope, and Limitations' (1984) 132 *University of Pennsylvania L Rev* 195–288.
O'Callaghan, Joseph F. *A History of Medieval Spain.* Ithaca and London: Cornell University Press, 1975.
O'Connell, Daniel P. 'Monarchy or Republic?' in G. Dutton (ed.), *Republican Australia?* (Melbourne: Sun Books, 1977), 23–43.

Oliver, W. H., 'The Fragility of Pakeha Support', commentary in Coates and McHugh, *Living Relationships: Kokiri Ngatahi* (1998), 222–231.
Orange, Claudia. *The Treaty of Waitangi.* Wellington: Allen and Unwin and Port Nicholson Press, 1987.
Park, Stuart. 'Te Peeke o Aotearoa: The Bank of King Tawhiao' (1992) 26 *NZJH* 161–183.
Partner, Peter. *God of Battles: Holy Wars of Christianity and Islam.* London: HarperCollins, 1997.
Passerin d'Entrèves, A. *The Notion of the State: An Introduction to Political Theory.* Oxford: Clarendon Press, 1967.
Paulson, Stanley L. 'Kelsen's Legal Theory: The Final Round' (1992) 12 *Oxford Journal of Legal Studies* 265–274.
Pocock, J. G. A. *The Ancient Constitution and the Feudal Law: English Historical Thought in the Seventeenth Century.* Cambridge: Cambridge University Press, 1957; reissued with retrospect, 1987.
—— 'Law, Sovereignty and History in a Divided Culture: The Case of New Zealand and the Treaty of Waitangi' (1998) 43 *McGLJ* 181–506.
Pollard, A. F. *The Evolution of Parliament.* London: Longman, Green, 1926.
Prawer, Joshua. *The Latin Kingdom of Jerusalem: European Colonialism in the Middle Ages.* London: Weidenfeld and Nicolson, 1972.
Pugh, Robert D. J. 'Are Northern Lands Reserved for the Indians?' (1982) 60 *CBRev* 36–80.
Quentin-Baxter, Alison (ed.) *Recognising the Rights of Indigenous Peoples.* Wellington: Institute of Policy Studies, 1998.
Radzinowicz, Leon. *A History of English Criminal Law and Its Administration from 1750*, vol i. London: Steven and Sons, 1948.
Reeves, Simon. *To Honour the Treaty: The Argument for Equal Seats.* Auckland: Earth Restoration Ltd, 1996 (2nd edn).
Renwick, William (ed.) *Sovereignty and Indigenous Rights: The Treaty of Waitangi in International Contexts.* Wellington: Victoria University Press, 1991.
—— *The Treaty Now.* Wellington: GP Publications, 1990.
Reynolds, Susan. *Fiefs and Vassals: The Medieval Evidence Reinterpreted.* Oxford; New York: Oxford University Press, 1994.
Ring, Jim. *Erskine Childers.* London: J. Murray, 1996.
Roberts-Wray, Sir Kenneth. *Commonwealth and Colonial Law.* London: Stevens and Sons, 1966.
Robinson, William M. *Justice in Grey: A History of the Judicial System of the Confederate States of America.* New York: Russell and Russell, 1941 (1968).
Round, David. *Truth or Treaty? Commonsense Questions about the Treaty of Waitangi.* Christchurch: Canterbury University Press, 1998.
Russell on Crime (12th edn; J. W. C. Turner) (London: Steven and Sons, 1964), vol. i.
Rutherford, James. *Sir George Grey: A Study in Colonial Government.* London: Cassell, 1961.
Salmond, Dame Anne. *Between Worlds: Early Exchanges Between Maori and Europeans 1773–1815.* Auckland: Viking (Penguin), 1997.
—— *Hui: A Study of Maori Ceremonial Gatherings.* Auckland: Reed Methuen, 1976 (2nd edn).
—— *Two Worlds: First Meetings Between Maori and Europeans 1642–1772.* Auckland and

London: Penguin, 1991.
Sandel, Michael J. 'Judgemental Toleration', in Robert P. George (ed.), *Natural Law, Liberalism, and Morality* (Oxford: Clarendon Press; New York: Oxford University Press, 1996), 107–112.
Sanders, Douglas. 'Indigenous Peoples at the United Nations: An Overview' [1996] 2 *CNLR* 20–24.
Sanneh, Lamin. *The Crown and The Turban: Muslims and West African Pluralism*. Boulder (Colorado) and Oxford: Westview Press, 1997.
Scott, Stuart C. *Travesty After Travesty*. Christchurch: Certes Press, 1996.
—— *The Travesty of Waitangi: Towards Anarchy*. Dunedin: Campbell Press, 1995.
Seed, Patricia. 'Taking Possession and Reading Texts: Establishing the Authority of Overseas Empires' (1992) 49 *William and Mary Quarterly* 183–209.
Sharp, Andrew. *Justice and the Maori: Maori Claims in New Zealand Political Argument in the 1980s*. Auckland: Oxford University Press, 1997 (2nd edn).
—— (ed.) *Leap into the Dark: The Changing Role of the State in New Zealand Since 1984*. Auckland: Auckland University Press, 1994.
—— *Political Ideas of the English Civil Wars 1641–1649* (a collection of representative texts with commentary). London and New York: Longmans, 1983.
—— 'Pride, Resentment and Change in the State and the Economy' in Sharp (ed.), *Leap into the Dark* (1994), 225–249.
—— 'Representing *Justice and the Maori*: on why it ought not to be construed as a postmodernist text' *Political Theory Newsletter*, (1992), 4, 27–38.
—— 'Why Be Bicultural?' in Wilson and Yeatman (eds), *Justice and Identity* (1995), 116–133.
Shyllon, F. O. *Black Slaves in Britain*. London; New York: Oxford University Press (for Institute of Race Relations), 1974.
Simpson, A. W. B. (ed.) *Oxford Essays in Jurisprudence* (2nd series) Oxford: Clarendon Press, 1973.
Sinclair, Sir Keith. *A History of New Zealand*. Auckland and London: Pelican and Allen Lane, 1991 (4th edn).
—— *Kinds of Peace: Maori People After the Wars 1870–85*. Auckland: Auckland University Press, 1991.
—— *The Origins of the Maori Wars*. Wellington: New Zealand University Press, 1957.
Slattery, Brian. *Ancestral Lands, Alien Laws: Judicial Perspectives on Aboriginal Title* (Saskatoon: University of Saskatchewan Native Law Centre, 1983).
—— 'Understanding Aboriginal Rights' (1987) 66 *CBRev* 727–783.
Smith, T. B. 'The Union of 1707 as Fundamental Law' [1957] *Public Law* 99–121.
Sorrenson, M. P. K. 'The Maori King Movement, 1858–1885' in R. Chapman and K. Sinclair (eds), *Studies of a Small Democracy: Essays in Honour of Willis Airey*. Hamilton: Paul's Book Arcade (for University of Auckland), 1963.
—— 'Treaties in British Colonial Policy: Precedents for Waitangi' in Renwick (ed.), *Sovereignty and Indigenous Rights* (1991), 15–29.
Stephen, Sir James Fitzjames. *A History of the Criminal Law of England* vol i. London: Macmillan and Co, 1883; reprinted S. Hein and Co. Inc., Buffalo, NY [1980?].
Stockley, Andrew P. 'Becoming a Republic? Issues of Law' in Trainor (ed.), *Republicanism*

(1996), 81–111.
—— 'Parliament, Crown and Treaty: Inextricably Linked?' (1996) 17 *NZULRev* 193–220.
Stokes, Evelyn. 'Te Waharoa, Wiremu Tamihana Tarapipi' in *The Dictionary of New Zealand Biography*, vol i, 1769–1869 (Wellington: Allen and Unwin and Department of Internal Affairs, 1990).
Sutton, Douglas G. 'Conclusion: Origins' in Sutton (ed.), *Origins* (1994), 243–258.
—— (ed.) *The Origins of the First New Zealanders*. Auckland: Auckland University Press, 1994.
—— 'The Whence of the Moriori' (1985) 19 *NZJH* 3–13.
Thomas, Hugh. *The Slave Trade: The History of the Atlantic Slave Trade 1440–1870.* London: Picador; New York: Simon and Schuster, 1997.
Thompson, E. P. *Whigs and Hunters*. Harmondsworth: Allen Lane, 1975; Peregrine Books, 1977.
Tilly, Charles. *European Revolutions 1492–1992*. Oxford: Blackwell, 1993.
Trainor, Luke (ed.) *Republicanism in New Zealand*. Palmerston North: Dunmore Press, 1996.
Trotter, Chris. 'The Struggle for Sovereignty' *New Zealand Political Review*, April–May 1995, 16–28.
Tunks, Andrea. '*Mana Tiriti*' in Trainor (ed.), *Republicanism* (1996), 113–132, 173–178.
Upston-Hooper, K. 'Slaying the Leviathan: Critical Jurisprudence and the Treaty of Waitangi' (1998) 28 *VUWLRev* 683–717.
Upton, John O. 'Maori in the Court of Appeal under Lord Cooke' in papers delivered at the Legal Research Foundation's Symposium 'The Struggle for Simplicity' (Auckland: April 1997).
Vitoria, Francisco de. *De Indis,* translated in Anthony Pagden and Jeremy Lawrance (eds), *Vitoria: Political Writings*, ch. 6, 'On the American Indians'. Cambridge, New York and Melbourne: Cambridge University Press, 1991.
Wade, Sir William (H. W. R.). 'The Basis of Legal Sovereignty' [1955] *CLJ* 172–197.
—— *Constitutional Fundamentals* (The Hamlyn Lectures 1980) London: Stevens and Sons, 1989 (revd edn).
Walker, Ranginui. 'Immigration Policy and the Political Economy of New Zealand' in S. W. Greif (ed.), *Immigration and National Identity in New Zealand: One People — Two Peoples — Many Peoples?* (Palmerston North: Dunmore Press, 1995), 282–302.
—— 'Maori Sovereignty, Colonial and Post-Colonial Discourses' in Havemann (ed.), *Indigenous Peoples' Rights* (1999), 108–122.
—— *Nga Pepa a Ranginui: The Walker Papers*. Auckland: Penguin, 1996.
—— *Ka Whawhai Tonu Matou: Strife Without End*. Auckland: Penguin, 1990.
Walters, Mark. 'British Imperial Constitutional Law and Aboriginal Rights: a comment on *Delgamuukw v British Columbia*' (1992) 17 *QLJ* 350–413.
Walters, Rt Revd Bishop Muru. 'A Maori Perspective on Te Tino Rangatiratanga' in Crawford (ed.), *Church and State* (1998), 66–75.
Ward, Alan. *A Show of Justice: Racial 'Amalgamation' in Nineteenth Century New Zealand*. Auckland: Auckland University Press, 1995 (revd edn).
—— *An Unsettled History: Treaty Claims in New Zealand Today*. Wellington: Bridget Williams Books, 1999.

Select Bibliography

Wards, Ian. *The Shadow of the Land: A Study of British Policy and Racial Conflict in New Zealand 1832–1852.* Wellington: Department of Internal Affairs, 1968.

Watson, Alan. *The Trial of Jesus.* Athens, Georgia; and London: University of Georgia Press, 1995.

Weiner, Justus R. 'The Palestinian Refugees' "Right to Return" and the Peace Process' (1997) 20 *BostCICLRev* 1–53.

Wheare, K.C. *The Constitutional Structure of the Commonwealth.* Oxford: Clarendon Press, 1960.

Williams, David V. 'The Constitutional Status of the Treaty of Waitangi' (1990) 14 *NZULRev* 9–36.

—— 'The Foundation of Colonial Rule in New Zealand' (1988) 13 *NZULRev* 54–67.

—— *'Te Kooti tango whenua': The Native Land Court 1864–1909.* Wellington: Huia Publishers, 1999.

—— *'The Queen v Symonds* Reconsidered' (1989) 19 *VUWLRev* 385–402.

Williams, Joe. 'The Position of Maori at the End of the Cooke Era' in papers delivered at the Legal Research Foundation's Symposium 'The Struggle for Simplicity' (Auckland: April 1997).

Wilson, Margaret. 'The Reconfiguration of New Zealand's Constitutional Institutions: The Transformation of Tino Rangatiratanga into Political Reality' (1997) 5 *Waikato L Rev* 17–34.

Wilson, Margaret and Yeatman, Anna (eds) *Justice and Identity: Antipodean Practices.* Wellington: Bridget Williams Books, 1995.

Winiata, Whatarangi. 'Revolution by Lawful Means' in 1993 *New Zealand Law Conference Papers, The Law and Politics* vol ii, 13–21.

Winter, Paul. *On the Trial of Jesus.* Berlin: Walter de Gruyter, 1961.

Zines, Leslie. *Constitutional Change in the Commonwealth.* Cambridge: Cambridge University Press, 1991.

Zion, James W. and Yazzie, Robert. 'Indigenous Law in North America in the Wake of Conquest' (1997) 20 *BostCICLRev* 55–84.

TABLE OF CASES

Adams v Adams [1971] P (Probate, Divorce and Admiralty Divn; England) 188 16n19
Aldridge, Re (1893) 15 NZLR 361(CA) 16n19 21n45
Amodu Tijani v Secretary, Southern Rhodesia [1921] 2 AC 399 (PC) 50n54 52n79
Ararimu Farms Ltd v Sotter (1992) [1993] *NZRecLRev* 286. 21n45

Baldy v Hunter 171 US 388 (1898) 21
Berkett v Tauranga District Court [1992] 3 NZLR 206(HC) 166
Bhutto v Chief of Army Staff PLD 1977 SC (Pakistan) 657 21n50 25n64 27-28 42
Blankard v Galdy (1693) 2 Salkeld (KB) 411 49n49
Brader v Ministry of Transport [1981] 1 NZLR 73 (CA) 94n61
Buckinghamshire County Council v Moran [1990] Ch 623 35n112

Calder v Attorney-General of British Columbia [1973] SCR 313 52nn75 & 78
Calvin's Case (1608) 8 Coke's Repts 1a 111
Campbell v Hall (1774) 1 Cowper 204 49n52 53n83
(Canada) Re Resolution to Amend the Constitution (Patriation Reference) [1981] 1 SCR 753 125n67
Captain Streater's Case (1653) 5 St Tr 365 30n93
Cherokee Nation v State of Georgia 5 Peters 1 (1831) USSC 50n57
Coe v Commonwealth (1979) 24 Australian Law Repts 118 (HCA) 51n61 53n83
Coe v Commonwealth (1993) 118 Australian Law Repts 193 (HCA) 51n61
Connolly v Woolrich (1867) 1 CNLC 70 (Quebec SC) 50n59

Delgamuukw v British Columbia [1997] 3 SCR 1010 50-51n60 52n78

Faulkner v Tauranga District Council [1996] 1 NZLR 357 (HC) 130n88 133
Ferrer's Case (1542) 92n52
Fletcher v Peck 6 Cranch 87 (1810) USSC 52n76

Goodall v Te Kooti (1890) 9 NZLR 26 (CA) 216n74
Grace Bible Church v Reedman (1984) 36 SASR 376 (Full SC) 95
Guerin v The Queen [1984] 2 SCR 335 52n78

Haddon v Auckland Regional Council [1994] NZRMA 49 (Planning Tribunal) 212n104
Hanton v Auckland City Council [1994] NZRMA 289 (Planning Tribunal) 218n112

Table of Cases

Harawira v Police (1990; unreported; HC) [1991] *NZRecLRev* 150, 253   220n24
Hineiti Rirerire Arani v Public Trustee for New Zealand (1919) NZPCC 1   53n82   87-88n25
Hlophe v Mahlalela 1998 (1) SALR 449 (Transvaal Provincial Divn)   18n34
Hohepa Wi Neera v Bishop of Wellington (1902) 21 NZLR 655   109
Huakina Development Trust v Waikato Valley Authority [1987] 2 NZLR 188(HC) 218nn108&109

Jilani v Government of Punjab PLD 1972 SC (Pakistan) 139   21n50   25n64   25n71   32n101
Johnson and Graham's Lessee v M'Intosh 8 Wheaton 543 (1823) USSC   52n76   221n61
Johnstone v Connolly (1869) 1 CNLC 151 (Quebec Queen's Bench)   50n59
Jones v Meehan 175 US 1 (1899)   55n99

Kaihau v Inland Revenue Department [1990] 3 NZLR 344 (HC)   220n20
Knight v Wedderburn (1778) 20 St Tr 2-7n. (Court of Session; Scotland)   142
Kohu v Police (1989) 5 Criminal Repts of New Zealand 194   220n20
Kokoliades v Kennedy (1911) 18 Canadian Criminal Cases 495   29

Lord Protector v Mordant (1658) 5 St Tr 907   30n93
'The Lundon and Whitaker Claims Act 1871', Re   (1872) NZ 2 CA 41   52n77   129   130n88
Luther v Borden 7 Howard 1 (1849) USSC   23

Mabo v Queensland (No 2) (1992) 175 CLR 1 (HCA) 52n80   53nn85&87   111n8   130   133   196n50
Madzimbamuto v Larder-Burke N.O. 1968 (2) SA 284 (High Court of Southn Rhodesia: Appellate Divn)   21   23   25n68   35
Madzimbamuto v Larder-Burke [1969] 1 AC 645 (PC)   23   24-25   26   29
Makenete v Lekhanya [1993] 3 LRC 13 (Lesotho CA)   27-28
Mangope v Van der Walt 1994 (3) SA 850 (Bophuthatswana General Divn)   25n67   26nn73&76
Mangawaro Enterprises Ltd v Attorney-General [1994] 2 NZLR 451(HC)   93n59
Manukau, Re (1993; unreported; HC) [1993] *NZRecLRev* 278   97
Marlborough Sounds, Re (22 Dec 1997; unreported; Maori Land Court, Rotorua; 22A Nelson Minute Book 1)   134n104
Matanzima v President of Transkei 1989 (4) SA 989 (Transkei General Divn)   26n73
Minnesota v Mille Lacs Band of Chippewa Indians 526 US — (1999); 143 L Ed 2d 270   199nn93&99
Mitchell v DPP (Director of Public Prosecutions) [1986] LRC (Const) 35   21n51   25n65   27-28

Mitchell v US 9 Peters 711 (1835) USSC 52n76
Mokotso v HM King Moshoeshoe II [1989] LRC (Const) 24 (Lesotho; HC) 25nn66 &68 26nn73&75 26-27n77

New Windsor Corpn v Mellor [1975] Ch 380 53n82
New Zealand Drivers Association v New Zealand Road Carriers [1982] 1 NZLR 374 (CA) 94n62
New Zealand Maori Council v Attorney-General [1987] 1 NZLR 641 (CA) (*SOE* case) 106-10n130 119 154-155 218n108 220n5
New Zealand Maori Council v Attorney-General (1991; unreported; HC) [1991] *NZRecLRev* 257 100n100
New Zealand Maori Council v Attorney-General [1994] 1 NZLR 513 (PC) 126 152 155 156
Ninety Mile Beach, In re [1993] NZLR 461 (CA) 129 130 134
Nireaha Tamaki v Baker (1901) NZPCC 371 52n79
Noltcho v Attorney-General [1983] Ch 77 125
Nowegijick v Canada [1983] 1 SCR 29 55n99

Oneida, County of, v Oneida Indian Nation of New York State 470 US 226 (1985) 197n76
Oyekan v Adele [1957] 2 All England Reports 785 (PC) 52n79

Police v Dalton (June, 1979; unreported; Magistrate's Court, Auckland) 216nn64&77

Quebec, Reference re Secession of (1998) 161 DLR (4th) 385 (SCC) 76n90

Raglan Golf Club v Raglan County Council (1980; unreported; HC) [1980] *New Zealand Recent Law* 334 216n74
Respublica v Chapman 1 Dallas 53 (1781); 1 L Ed 33 (Pennsylvania) 30-31 41n15 138 179
R (Childers) v Adjutant-General of the Provisional Forces [1923] 1 Irish Reports 5 19 33
R v Badger [1996] 1 SCR 771 54n88 55n99
R v Cook (1660) 5 St Tr 1077 29n87
R v Cote [1996] 3 SCR 139 2 51n84
R v Jones and Pamajewon [1993] 3 CNLR 209 (Ontario Provincial Divn) 29
R v Kohu (1990; unreported; CA) [1990] *NZRecLRev* 213; [1991] *NZRecLRev* 150 220n24
R v Knowles (12 Oct 1998; unreported; CA 146/98) *Maori L Rev*, December 1998–January 1999, 1 116-117n40
R v Morison [1950] NZLR 247 213n104
R v Ndhlovu 1968 (4) SA 515 (High Court of Southn Rhodesia: Appellate Divn) 22n53

Table of Cases

R v Niramoana (1880) Ollivier, Bell and Fitzgerald 76 (CA; NZ)   148
R v Pamejewon [1996] 2 SCR 821   30n92   50-51n60
R v Rua [1916] 18 Gazette Law Repts 658(SC)   149
R v Secretary of State for Foreign and Commonwealth Affairs, ex parte Indian Association of Alberta [1982] QB 892 (CA)   53n82   124-125
R v Sparrow [1990] 1 SCR 1075   52n78   55n98
R v Symonds (1847) NZPCC 387 (SC)   52n77   53n85   128-129   130n88
R v Van der Peet [1996] 2 SCR 507   52n78   55n97
R v Vane (1662) 6 St Tr 119   29n87
R v Walker [1989] 2 Qd R 79   28n83   33n109   38-40   42-43   158   167

Sea-Tow Ltd v Auckland Regional Council [1994] NZRMA 204 (Planning Tribunal)   212n104
Simon v The Queen [1985] 2 SCR 387   54n90   55n99
Sirdar Bhagwan Singh v Secretary of State for India (1874) LR 2 Indian Appeals 38 (PC)   53n83
Somerset v Stewart (1772) Lofft 1   142
Southern Centre of Theosophy Inc v South Australia (1979) 21 SASR 399 (Full SC)   213n107
Southern Rhodesia, In re [1919] AC 211 (PC)   50n54
St Catherine's [Catharines] Milling and Lumber Co v The Queen (1885) 10 Ontario Reports 196 (Ontario Chancery)   52nn74&78; (1887) 13 SCR 577 (SCC)   50n59   52nn73&78; (1888) 14 App Cas 46 (PC)   52n79
State v Dosso [1958] 2 Pakistan Supreme Court Repts 180   25nn64&68
State v Eight Rotuman Chiefs (1988) Law Report, *Fiji Times*, 10 June 1988   30n94
Sze v Kung [1997] 1 Weekly Law Repts 1232 (PC)   35n112

Tamihana Korokai v Solicitor-General (1912) 32 NZLR 321 (CA)   121   125   129n84   141
Taranaki Fish and Game Council v McRitchie [1998] 3 NZLR 611   211n83
Taylor v New Zealand Poultry Board [1984] 1 NZLR 394 (CA)   93n59
Tee-Hit-Ton Indians v United States 348 US 272 (1955)   197n76
Te Heuheu Tukino v Aotea District Maori Land Board [1941] NZLR 590 (PC)   99   154-155
Te Runanganui o Te Ika Whenua Inc Soc v Attorney-General [1994] 2 NZLR 20 (CA)   53n85   128   129   134n104   135
Te Runanga o Wharekauri Rekohu Inc v Attorney-General [1993] 2 NZLR 301 (CA)   155
Te Weehi v Regional Fisheries Officer [1986] 1 NZLR 680 (HC)   129   133
Texas v White 7 Wallace 700 (1869) USSC   21
Tupuna Maori, Re (1988; unreported; HC) [1989] *NZRecLRev* 217   206n70

Uganda v Commissioner of Prisons, ex parte Matovu [1966] EA (East Africa) 514 25nn63&68
Union Steamship Co of Australia Pty Ltd v King (1988) 166 CLR 1 (HCA) 92-93n56
United States v Wheeler 435 US 313 (1978) 54n92

Vajesingji Joravarsingji v Secretary of State for India (1924) LR 51 Indian Appeals 357 (PC) 50n53
Veale v Brown (1868) 1 NZCA 152 53n85

Walker v New South Wales (1994) 182 CLR 45 50n55
Wallis v Solicitor-General (1903) NZPCC 23 52n79
Wanganui River, In re the Bed of [1962] NZLR 600 (CA) 135n108
Watercare Services Ltd v Minhinnick [1998] 1 NZLR 294 (CA) 218n111
Western Australia v The Commonwealth (1995) 183 CLR 373 52n80 53n87
Wi Parata v Bishop of Wellington (1877) 3 NZJurist Repts (New Series) (SC) 72 99 113-114 129-130 149 157 220n5
Wik Peoples v Queensland (1996) 187 CLR 1 52n80
Worcester v Georgia 6 Peters 515 (1832) USSC 50n57 52n76 54n93

TABLE OF LEGISLATION AND CONSTITUTIONAL INSTRUMENTS

New Zealand Legislation

Coal-mines Act Amendment Act 1903
s.14 134n101

Coal Mines Act 1979 134n101
s.261 134n101
s.261(1) 212n101

Conservation Act 1987
s.4 218n107

Constitution Act 1986 23 122 123 210n57
s.2(1) 123
s.5 23
s.5(1) 23n56

Crimes Act 1961 166
s.64 29
s.91 148n70

Crimes of Torture Act 1989 94 215n50

Criminal Code Act 1893
s.72 29

Crown Forest Assets Act 1989
s.36 217n86

Crown Minerals Act 1991
s.120(1) 212n101

Disturbed Districts Act 1869 215n52

Education Act 1989
ss.212 and 213 217n86

English Laws Act 1858 128n77

Foreshore and Seabed Endowment Revesting Act 1991
ss. 4 and 5 134n102

Imperial Laws Application Act 1988
s.3(1)
s.5 128n77

Judicature Act 1908 18 153

Justices of the Peace Act 1882 148

Land Transfer Act 1952 213n112
s.64 192n114

Land Transfer Amendment Act 1963
Part I 192n114
s.3 192n113

Legislative Council Abolition Act 1950 210n57

Limitation Act 1950
s.6(1) 192n113
s.6(1A) 192n113 211n90
s.7 192n113
s. 7A 192n113 211n90
s.18 192n113

Local Government Act 1974 156

Magistrates' Courts Act 1893 217n83

Maori Affairs Act 1953 131
ss. 155, 157 and 158 131n90
s.157(2) 213n104

Maori Community Development Act 1962 150

Maori Councils Act 1900 150

Maori Land Amendment and Maori Land Claims Adjustment Act 1926
s.14 213n106

Maori Land Act 1931
s.115 213n104

Maori Land Act 1993. *See* Te Ture Whenua Maori Act 1993

Maori Language Act 1987 216n73

Maori Purposes Act 1931
s.83 217n82

Maori Purposes Act 1956
s6(1) 217n82

Native Circuit Courts Act 1858 217n83

Native Districts Regulation Act 1858 217n83

Native Land Amendment and Native Land Claims Adjustment Act 1922
s.27 213n106

Native Land Court Act 1880 118

Native Rights Act 1865 111

New Zealand Bill of Rights Act 1990 172
s. 9 93 215n50 221n61

New Zealand Constitution Amendment Act 1973 210n57

New Zealand Settlements Act 1863 95 115 131 146 216n73

Punishment of High Treason Act 1870 215n52

Repeals Act 1891 217n83

Resident Magistrates' Courts Ordinance 1846
Part V 217n83

Resource Management Act 1991 156
s.8 218nn107 &112
s354(1) 212n101

Royal Titles Act 1974 123

State-Owned Enterprises Act 1986 155 156 169
s.9 218n107 220n5
s.27B 217n86
s. 27C 217n86

Suppression of Rebellion Act 1863 131

Te Ture Whenua Maori Act 1993 (Maori Land Act 1993) 132 133 211n90 158
s. 3 133n97
s. 17(1)(a) 132n93
s.129(2)(a) 133n97

Territorial Sea and Fishing Zone Act 1965
s.7 212n103 213n104

Territorial Sea, Contiguous Zone, and Exclusive Economic Zone Act 1977
s.7 134n103 212n104

Treaty of Waitangi Act 1975 11n2 151 152
s.6(1) & (2) 151n85
s.6(3)&(4) 151n86
s.6(4A) 217n 86
s.8A(2(a) 217n86
s.8HB(1)(a) 217n86

Treaty of Waitangi Amendment Act 1985 11n2 151

Treaty of Waitangi (Fisheries Claims) Settlement Act 1992 132 134
s.9 132n96
s. 10(d) 132n96

Urewera District Native Reserve Act 1896 150 172

Urewera Lands Act 1921-1922 217n82

Waikato Raupatu Claims Settlement Act 1995 208n18 209n24

Wanganui River Trust Act 1891 213n104

Imperial Statutes (Parliaments of England, Great Britain and the United Kingdom) (in chronological order)

Magna Carta 1297 (25 Edw I, c. 29) 152
Statutes of Forcible Entry: 1381 (5 Ric.II Stat.1, c. 7); 1391 (15 Ric. II , c. 2); 1429 (8 Hen. VI, c.9) 148n70
1 Edw. IV, c.1 (Confirmation of usurpers' acts) 1460 188n19
11 Hen. VII, c. 1 (Treason) 1495 28ff 90
27 Hen. VIII, c. 26 (Law of Wales) 1535-36 67n51
12 Car. II, c. 2 (Confirmation of judicial proceedings) 1660 188n19
Bill of Rights, 1688 (1 Wm. and Mary Sess.2, c. 2) 145
Act of Settlement, 1700 (12 and 13 Wm. III, c. 2) 90 190n56
Union with Scotland Act, 1706 (6 Anne, c. 11) 189n33
12 Geo. III, c. 20 (Abolition of peine forte et dure) 1772 145n53
Union with Ireland Act, 1800 (39 & 40 Geo. III, c. 67) 68
47 Geo III, c. 36 (Abolition of slave trade) 1807 143n43
54 Geo III, c. 146 (Treason) 1814 145n52
57 Geo. III, c. 53 (Criminal jurisdiction in respect of New Zealand) 1817 96n71
4 Geo. IV, c. 96 (Criminal jurisdiction in respect of New Zealand) 1823 96n71
9 Geo. IV, c.83 53 (Criminal jurisdiction in respect of New Zealand) 1828 96n71
Slavery Abolition Act 1833 (3 &4 Wm. IV, c. 73) 142n40

Table of Legislation and Constitutional Instruments

New Zealand Constitution Act 1852 (15 &16 Vict. c.72) 108 110 122
s.53 110 130
s.56 110
s.57 110
s.58 110
s.71 110 116ff 144 150 171
s.72 118
s.73 118 119
s.79 117

New Zealand Constitution (Amendment)Act 1857 110

Colonial Laws Validity Act 1865 122
s.2 92n55 130
s.3 92n55 130

Statute Law Revision Act 1892 117

Irish Free State (Agreement) Act 1922 33

Statute of Westminster 1931 122

New Zealand Constitution (Amendment Act) 1947 122

Government of Wales Act 1998 67

Scotland Act 1998 68

Other Jurisdictions

Canada
Constitution Act, 1982
s.35(1) 54 196n60 197n75 198n78 221n61

Criminal Code (Chap C - 46) s.15 29

Eire
(1937 Constitution) 187n12 175n66

Scotland
Protestant Religion and Presbyterian Church Act, 1707 189n33

Union with England Act, 1706 189n33

United States of America
Bill of Rights 152

Constitution, Article VI 54

Index

Aboriginal title (customary title and other rights)
    Australia 52
    British colonial practice and common law 52
    burden on Crown's radical (allodial) title to land 53-54
    Canada 52
    'continuity' doctrine 196 n53
    how extinguished 53-54
    prerogative power to extinguish (is there one?) 54 130
    'recognition' doctrine 196 n53
    Vitoria and 52
    vulnerability of, to acts of state preceding sovereignty 53
    See also Maori customary title
Aboriginal treaty rights
    Canada 54-55
    New Zealand. *See* Treaty of Waitangi
    United States 54
Act of state 53
    in relation to Aotearoa New Zealand 112
    in relation to Australia 198 n83
Adverse possession (of land). *See* Prescription
Alexander the Great and the pirate 45
Algerian war of independence 65-66 81
Allegiance
    shifting of, to revolutionary government 28-31
    when owed to Crown by Maori. *See* Maori
American War of Independence 30-31
Anaya, S.J. 77
'Ancient constitution' (English), myth of 66-67
Anglican Church, proposals for New Zealand constitutional reform 223 n92
Arabs. *See* Islamic conquests and legitimation; Israeli–Palestinian conflict; Ottoman Turks
Ascham, Anthony 39-40
Augustine, St (of Hippo) 40 45 140 (quoted passim)
Aztecs 61-62

Baker J.H. 145
Ballara, Angela 86 148
Banks, Joseph 203 n9
Bartlett, Robert 47-48 55
Basic norm (*grundnorm*)
    New Zealand. *See* Basic norm in New Zealand
    revolutionary change in 17 25ff
    United Kingdom 17
    See also Kelsen
Basic norm in New Zealand 17 123 127
    Declaration of Confederation and Independence (1835), and 97
    Maori customary law 17-18 86
Beetham, David 194 n15 41 44
Belich, James 112 114 147
Berbers 66 81
Bercé, Y.-M. 43
Binney, Judith 216 n74 217 n82
Blackstone, Sir William 145
Booth, Revd Ken 102-103
Bophuthatswana 25
British subjects, Maori as. *See* Maori
Brookfield, F.M. (quoted) 93 119
Brooking, Tom 141
Browne, Thomas Gore (Governor) 117
Brownlie, Ian 99
Bryce, James 35
Burnell, P. 194 n33
Busby, James 96
Business Round Table 220 n5

Canada, constitutional protection of aboriginal rights in 55 173-174
Chatham Islands
    incorporation of, in New Zealand (1842) 159
    Native Land Court on 161-162
    revolutionary seizures of 58 81 158-162 167
    See also Moriori
Childers, Erskine 19-20 33 167

Index

Christendom and Islam 64-66
Civil War (American), constitutional cases arising from 21
Civil War (English) and Interregnum 16
Coke, Sir Edward 191 n86
Colley, Linda 69 140-141
Collins, Hugh 73 nn77 & 78
Colonial legislatures, powers of 92-93. *See also* New Zealand General Assembly (1852), powers of; Parliamentary sovereignty or supremacy
Colonies (British), classification of 49-50
Colonization (Western), ideological motivation of ('Christianize and civilize' etc.) 59-60
    in New Zealand 140-141
Confederation and Independence, Declaration of (New Zealand). *See* Declaration of Confederation and Independence
Confiscation of Maori land. *See* Raupatu
Conquest
    abolition of traditional right of, in international law 36-37 62
    legitimated by custom 79 89
    source of title to land 36. *See also* Prescription
        claimed on Chatham Islands 159
        in Maori custom 89
    species of revolution 14. *See also* Revolutionary conquest
Constitution
    New Zealand
        (1852) 110
        (1857) 110
        (1865) 122
        (1947) 122
        (1983–86) 122-123
        present position 123ff
        See also New Zealand General Assembly (1852)
    United Kingdom 90ff
Conventions, constitutional 71 91 110 117 119ff
Cook, James 144
Cooke, Robin (Lord Cooke of Thorndon) 93-94 153 222 n63
Coup d'état
    definition of 187n7
    Maori tribal organization 88
    non-revolutionary 15-17
Courts

New Zealand, establishment and constitutional position of 18-19 153-154
    recognition of usurpers by 22ff
    revolutionary challenge to 19-20 166-167
    supra-constitutional jurisdiction claimed by 23ff 175 179
    upholders of constitution 18-20 33-34 154 157
    See also Judges; Separation of Powers
Crown (English; British)
    demise of 22-23
    divisibility of. *See* revolutionary division *below*
    original imperial unity of 32 119ff
    revolutionary division 12 32 119ff
    and separate New Zealand Crown 12 119ff
    revolutionary seizure of Aotearoa New Zealand by 15 85 104-105
    See also Crown's radical (allodial) title to land; Monarchy; Separation of powers
Crown's radical (allodial) title to land
    doctrine of 193 n123 53
    doubts as to historical basis of 193 n123
    in relation to land under water. *See* Maori customary title, land under water
Crusades 64-65
Customary law
    communal rights under, in England 53
    definitions of 189 n34
    partial recognition of indigenous rights under common law, in British colonies and former colonies 49ff
    See also Aboriginal title; Maori customary law

Dahrendorf, Ralph 28
Davidson, Allan 140 n23
Declaration of Confederation and Independence (New Zealand; 1835) 88 96-98 103
D'Entreves, A. Passerin 38 n2
De facto authority, doctrine of 20-22 167 179
De facto English monarchs 16
    allegiance due to 28
Dias, R.W.M. 39

• 247 •

Dickinson, H.T. 40
'Domestic dependent nations', concept of 50-51
　　implication for New Zealand 118-119
Donovan, Bill M. 61
Durability (of legal order). *See* Prescription
Durie, Justice E.T. 87 88 89 nn38 and 40
Durie, Mason 101-102 104 173 177

East Timor 36
Elton, Sir Geoffrey 92
England
　　Norman conquest of 66-67
　　republican Interregnum 16 67
　　union with Scotland. *See* Scotland
Enlightenment, influence of, on English criminal law 145
Entrenchment, constitutional 173ff

Fanon, Frantz 60 65-66
Fenton, James 60-61 140 (quoted passim)
Fiji, revolutions in (1987) 18 30 138
Finnis, J.M. 188 n26 191 n70
Fletcher, A. and McCullough, D. 43
Forcible entry, statutes against, used in Maori land dispute 148
Foreshore, Maori customary title to. *See* Maori customary title, land under water
France
　　French revolution 14
　　revolutionary conquest in North Africa 163

Gentili, Alberto 59
Ghai, Yash 188n25
Gilling, B.D. 219 n121
Gillingham, John 201 n58
'Globalization' as imperialism. *See* Imperialism (Western)
'Glorious Revolution' 16 85 90
Goa 193 n129
Gould, Ashley 215 n42 219 n129
Governor-General, letters patent constituting office of (1983) 123
Governors, colonial, Royal instructions to 120
Graham, Rt Hon Sir Douglas 136 137 212 n98
Gramsci, Antonio 74-75
　　his conception of law 74 180
　　on separation of powers 74
　　'war of manoeuvre' 74

　　in New Zealand 168
　　'war of position' 74
　　in New Zealand 165-166 168
　　See also Revolution, 'passive' (Gramscian)
Gray, Robert 52 n74
'Great New Zealand myth' 158-159
Green, Judith 193 n122
Grenada 25 27-28
Grey, Sir George
　　as Governor 112 120 142
　　as Premier 118
　　martial law, use of, by 112
Grotius, Hugo 21 59
Grundnorm. *See* Basic norm

Hamnett, I. 189 n34
Hannum, Hurst 78
Hapu, as independent political units 86
Harris, Bruce 172
Hart, H.L.A. 87-88 114-115 127
Havemann, Paul 127
Hawkins, William 191 n86
Hill, Christopher 67 73-74
Henry IV, King 16
Henry V and Henry VI, Kings 188 n19
Henry VII, King 16
Henry VIII, King 92 95
Hobson, Governor William 97-98. *See also* Proclamations (1840)
Hogg, Peter 54 n90
Holy War, concept of 64-65
Honoré, A.M. (Tony) 75-76 191 n86
Human Rights, Universal Declaration of 72-73 77
Hume, David 40

Ideology
　　Christian versus Islamic 64-66
　　defined 199-200 n1
　　of Western imperialism ('Christianize and civilize') 59-60 69ff
　　in New Zealand 140ff
Imperialism (Western) 57ff 79-82
　　'globalization' as 200 n23
　　See also Colonization (Western)
Indigenous peoples
　　concept of 75
　　and Chatham Islands 160
　　Declaration on the Rights of (draft) 77

Index

international instruments applicable to 77
Indonesia (East Timor) 36
Iraia, Kuao (Chief) 147-148
Ireland
    Anglo-Norman invasion and colonization of 68
    Constitution of Saorstat Eireann (1937) 68 187 n12
    method of establishing, as model for New Zealand 'quiet revolution' 175
    Irish Free State 19-20 68
    Northern 68
    opposition to England and Great Britain 164-165
    union with Great Britain (1800) 68
Islamic conquests and legitimation 64ff 68-69. *See also* Ottoman Turks; Spain (Iberian peninsula)
Israeli-Palestinian conflict 200 n32
Ius gentium 58
Ius naturale 58
Iwi, position in Maori tribal organization 86

Jackson, Moana 89 101 103 104 127 140 143 150 166
Jervois, Governor 118
Jesus Christ, trial of 47 115
Jihad. *See* Holy war, concept of
Johnson, J.T. 199 n1
Joseph, Philip A. 99 n95
Judges
    exercising judicial power of Monarch 16 90 92
    in New Zealand 154
    See also Courts
Just War concept
    application of, to imperialist expansion 58-60
    Maori tribal society 89
    theories of 58
    Vitoria and 58-59

Kauhanganui (de facto Maori Parliament) 151
Kawanatanga 100ff 120 145-146 150 173 180 et passim 193 n125
    did it extend to Maori? 103ff
    exercised by statutory bodies 156
    Native Land Court and 211 n94
    subordinate power? 101 102-103
    See also Treaty of Waitangi, article 1
Kawharu, Sir Hugh 89 100 103-104 131-132
Keith, Sir Kenneth 99
Kelsen, Hans 17-18 21-22 25ff 45 97 109
    See also Basic norm
Kelsey, Jane 96-97 104 119 136ff 143 146 148-150 157 163 165 168 175 178 180 183
Kendall, Thomas 96
Kerr, Roger 220 n5
King Country 114-115 127 132 141
King, Michael 219
Kingsbury, Benedict 99
Korman, Sharon 59 193 n125
Kotahitanga (de facto Maori Parliament) 151

Lake beds. *See* Maori customary title, land under water
Las Casas, Bartolome de 58-59 61
Lawrance, Jeremy 59
Legality, distinguished from legitimacy 34 38 168
Legitimacy
    distinguished from legality. *See above*
    durability of revolutionary legal order as basis for 38ff
    justice in revolutionary legal order and 42ff
    minimal legitimacy of working legal order 38 139 168
    See also Legitimation of revolutionary conquest; Prescription
Legitimation of revolutionary conquest
    of Chatham Islands 158ff
    and ideology 57ff
    New Zealand (of legal order based on 1840 revolution) 136ff 163ff 181
    and prescription (durability). *See* Prescription (durability)
Lesotho 25 27-28
Lewis, Bernard 61 64 81-82 182
Lilla, Mark 165 n19
Locke, John 57 141
Luttwak, Edward 187 n7

Mackenthun, G. 197 n74
MacMillan, Gretchen M. 68 nn54, 56
Macquarie, Governor (NSW) 96
Magrath, Judge 24

· 249 ·

Maori
    allegiance of, claimed by Crown 110ff 138
    analogous to Jews, seen as 115
    British subjects, as 110ff
    deputations to British Monarch 121 125-127
    personal relationship with Monarch 91 126-127
Maori autonomy
    areas of (19th century) 114-115 118 127
    expectation of, under Treaty of Waitangi 106-107
    provision for districts in 1852 Constitution Act 116ff
Maori Congress, National 151
Maori Council, New Zealand 150-151
Maori customary law 86-90 127 163-164. See also Aboriginal title; Maori customary title; Maori legal orders (systems)
Maori customary title 52-53 128ff 157-158 163-164 169
    all of New Zealand originally subject to 141
    land under water 133-135 164
    prerogative power to extinguish (is there one?) 130
    See also Aboriginal title; Maori customary land
Maori customary land
    defined 133
    settlers' 'use or lose' view of 141. See also Locke, John
Maori King, raising up of 209 n24
Maori Land Court 132. See also Native Land Court
    present protective functions of 132
Maori legal orders (systems) 86-90
    development in 114-115
Maori Parliaments, de facto (Kauhanganui, Kotahitanga) 151
Marshall, Chief Justice John 196 n57
Martial law 20
    use of, in New Zealand wars 112-113
Martin, Sir William 141
Marxism and the rule of law 73. See also Gramsci, Antonio
McHugh, Paul 99 169-170 177
McNeil, Kent 199 nn88, 98
Mikaere, A. L. 127 152 n88 166-167

Minogue, Kenneth 153 n95 163-165 176-177
Mitchell, J.D.B. 208 n125
Monarchy
    abolition of, as revolutionary 222
    constitutional position of 90f
    personal relationship of Monarch with Maori 91 120 126-127 174-175
    See also Crown; Republic, New Zealand
Moriori 58 158f 163. See Chatham Islands
Muldoon, James 197 n72
Muru (ritualized plunder) 87

Native Land Court 118
    on Chatham Islands 161-162
    'engine of destruction' of customary title 131-132
    instrument of revolution, as 131-132
    See also Maori Land Court
Natural law 52
Navigable rivers, title to beds of 134
Necessity principle in constitutional law 20
New Zealand as 'settled colony' 210-211 n77
New Zealand General Assembly, powers of under 1852 Constitution Act 110
    to suppress 'rebellion' and confiscate Maori land 130-131
    over Treaty of Waitangi 153-154
    See also Colonial legislatures, powers of; Parliamentary sovereignty or supremacy
Newcastle, Duke of (Secretary of State) 111 120
Ngapora, Tamati 142
Ngapuhi, feuds of 147-148
Ngati Kurapoto 148
Ngati Mutunga 159
Ngati Tama 159
Ngati Whiti 148
Ngatimahuta, 'Sanhedrin' of 115
Norman conquest of England 66-67
'Norman Yoke', (English) myth of 67

O'Connell, D.P. 192 n102
Oliver, W.H. 176 177
Orange, Claudia 101 206 n77
Ottoman Turks, conquest of Arabs by 66 163

Pagden, Anthony 59
Pakistan 25 27
Parihaka 109 114
Park, Stuart 115 n35

Index

Parliamentary Sovereignty or Supremacy 91ff
    New Zealand 93 171-172
    Treaty of Waitangi, and 104-105 151-152
Partner, Peter 201 n37
'Passive revolution'. *See* Gramsci, Antonio;
    Revolution, passive
Paul, St. proceedings against 47 115
'Peace, order and good government'. *See*
    Colonial legislatures, powers of
Pocock, J.G.A. 183 201 n44
Prawer, Joshua 65 n35
Prendergast, Sir James
    as Attorney-General 111
    as Chief Justice 103
Prescription
    legitimating revolutionary seizure of
        power 34-35. *See also* Prescription
        (durability)
    private law principle validating title to
        land obtained by seizure and
        'adverse possession' 35
Prescription (durability)
    countered by ideological opposition 63ff
    principle legitimating legal order based
        on revolutionary seizure of power, as
        34-35 43 62 79 167
    on Chatham Islands 160
    in New Zealand 138-139 158
    revolutionary conquests of Western
        imperialism, and 62ff
    See also Legitimacy; Legitimation
Privy Council, Judicial Committee of
    present position of, in New Zealand
        legal order 210 n73
Proclamation (1763; George III; Canada) 52
    124 152 198 n79 200 n16
    recognized in United States 221 n61
Proclamation (1813; NSW, in respect of New
    Zealand) 96
Proclamations (1840), of British Sovereignty
    over New Zealand (Hobson) 85 97-98 110-
    111
Protectorates, British
    Maori expectation 101
    system of 207 n113

Radzinowicz, L. 215 n52
Rakatau (Chief) 6 126
Rangatiratanga (tino rangatiratanga; highest
    chieftainship or authority) 15 88-89 101-
102 127 150-151 166 171 173 180
    on Chatham Islands 160
    partial legal recognition of 150ff
    See also Treaty of Waitangi, article 2
Raupatu (confiscation of Maori land) 95 130-
    132
Rebel, right to 75-76
Reeves, Simon 223 n92
Renwick, William 139
Republic, English 16 67
Republic, New Zealand 170
    Treaty of Waitangi and 174-175 221 n61
    See also Monarchy
Responsible government
    in New Zealand 119-120 122
    in Maori matters 120 122
    See also Royal instructions
Revolution
    definitions of 13-15
    expectations of losers in 44ff
    durability of, and legitimacy 38ff *See
        also* Prescription (durability)
    Fiji. *See* Fiji
    French 14
    'Glorious' *See* 'Glorious Revolution'
    'passive' (Gramscian) 15 75
    in New Zealand 157-158 163 168 169
        177 178
    'quiet' (as means of basic constitutional
        change) 15 170 175
    Russian 14
    See also Revolutionary conquest
Revolutionary conquest 14 57 et passim
    Chatham Islands. *See* Chatham Islands
    effect on laws of conquered or colonized
        territory, of 48-49
    ideological motivation of 57. *See also*
        Colonization (Western)
    law as instrument of, in New Zealand
        85 145ff 150. *See also* Rule of law
    legitimation of. *See* Legitimation of
        revolutionary conquest
    partial recognition of losers' rights after
        under Rome, Islam and Spain 47-48
        under Western imperialism 48ff
        See also Customary law, partial
            recognition of indigenous rights
            under common law
Revolutionary governments, recognition of. *See*
    Courts, recognition of usurpers by;

Legitimacy; Legitimation of revolutionary
conquest
Reynolds, Susan 193 n123
Richard III, King 16
Richmond, J.C. 111
River, Maori concept of as a taonga 212 n104
River and stream beds
 Maori customary title to. *See* Maori
  customary title, land under water
  middle line rule and registered title 135
Roberts-Wray, Sir K. 51
Ross, Alf 191 n70
Rotuma (and Fiji revolution) 30
Round, David 153n95 164-165
Royal instructions to New Zealand Governors
 120-121
Rua 149
Rule of law
 legacy of Western imperialism, as 70ff
 Maori customary law, and 146-148
 Marxism, and 73-74
 New Zealand 145-150

Salmond, Dame Anne 141-142 n33 143-45
 147
Sandel, Michael 215 n42
Sanders, D. 78
Sanneh, Lamin 59-60 nn18 & 19
Scotland
 'Normanization' of 67-68
 partial autonomy of (1998) 68
 union of with England 17 68; and
  revolution 17 105 187 n13
Scott, Stuart 141 164
Scott, Tom 220 n28
Sea bed, Maori customary title to. *See* Maori
 customary title, land under water
Secession, right to (in international law) 76
Sedition 137
Seed, Patricia 200 n17
Self-determination, right to 75-77
 international instruments, and 76-77
Selwyn, Bishop George Augustus 141
Separation of powers, doctrine of
 Gramsci, and 74
 New Zealand, and Native Land Court
  211 n94
 United Kingdom 90
Sepulveda, Juan Gines de 58
Sharp, Andrew 35 39 176 181

Shortland, Edward 88
Shortland, Acting-Governor Willoughby 108
Sinclair, Sir Keith 114-116
Slattery, Brian 51 52 n73 128
Slavery
 abolition of, as legacy of Western
  imperialism 70
 in Aotearoa New Zealand 141-143
 in British Empire 142-143
 in Chatham Islands 160-161
 English law and 142
 Maori society, in 141-142
 Scots law and 142
Smith, Mike 137
Sorrenson, M. P. K. 217 n82
South African Truth and Reconciliation
 Commission 60
Southern Rhodesia (now Zimbabwe),
 Unilateral Declaration of Independence 21
 Court judgments in respect of 23ff 35
  36
Sovereignty of Parliament, doctrine of. *See*
 Parliamentary Sovereignty or Supremacy
Spain (Iberian Peninsula)
 Christian Reconquest of, and
  legitimation 48 65 68-69 164
Spanish colonization
 attempts to protect Indians in 59
 brutality of 61-62
Stephen, Sir James Fitzjames 108-109
Stockley, A.P. 222 n63
Stokes, Evelyn 209 n31
Stout, Sir Robert 118
Sutton, Douglas G. 159 219 n121
Swainson, William 108-109
Sykes, Annette 137 167-168

Tamihana, Wiremu 209 n31
Tawhiao, King 115 118 150
 his bank 115
Thompson, E.P. 72-74 146-147 180
Tikanga Maori (Maori customary law) 87 133
Te Heuheu 98
Te Rauparaha 112
Te Wherowhero 98
Te Whiti 114
Thierry, Baron de 96
Tilly, Charles 13-15 154
Tohu (prophet) 114
Torture 144-145

Index

Treason
    monarch for time being, and 28-29
    punishment for 145
    See also Allegiance
Treaty of Waitangi 15 98ff 119-120 et passim
    article 1 98 104 173 180. *See also*
        Kawanatanga
    article 2 98ff 115 117 127 132 150
        157 158 166 172 173 180 et passim.
        See also Rangatiratanga (tino rangatiratanga)
    article 3 98 104 110
    constitutional position of 153ff
    'constitutionalizing' of 155ff
    'principles' of 151ff 173
        statutory formulae, as to 155n107
    'revisionist' views of 99 164
    'simple nullity', viewed as 99
    statutory authorities, and 156
    transition to a republic, and 221 n61
Trotter, Chris 178ff 183
Tuhoe 132 141 150 172
    colonial government's scheme for local self-government of 150
Tunks, Andrea 175

Universal Declaration of Human Rights 73 77
Uganda 25
Upston-Hooper, K. 165
Upton, Hon. Simon 136-137
Urewera country. *See* Tuhoe
'Use it or lose it' 141 *See also* Locke, John
Usurpers
    obedience to 28-31
    recognition of, by courts. *See* Courts
Utu 87 (defined) 147 216 n64

Victoria, Queen 90-91
    Maori deputations to 118 121 126-127
Violent societies, British and Maori 144-145
Vitoria, Francisco de 52 58-59

Wade, Sir William (H.W.R.) 39 222n65

Waikato, invasion of 208 n18
Wairarapa, 'pacification' of 112
Waitangi, Treaty of. *See* Treaty of Waitangi
Waitangi Tribunal 11 100 106-107 151-152 et passim
    land under water, and 212-213 n104
    recommendations of, nature 217 n86
    Reports of :
        Kaituna 100
        Maori Election Option 152 n87 217 n88
        Muriwhenua Fishing Claim 11 n1 106
        Orakei 106-107
        Radio Spectrum Management 207 n100
        Te Whanau o Waipareira 105-106
        Te Whanganui-a-Orotu 213 n107
        Whanganui River 212-213 n104 213 n107
Waitara purchase 112
Wales
    conquest of 67
    limited autonomy of (1998) 67
Walters, Rt Revd Bishop Muru 204 n36
Walker, Ranginui 88 100 102 136ff 163 175 219 n126
'War of position'. *See* Gramsci, Antonio
'War of manoeuvre'. *See* Gramsci, Antonio
Ward, Alan 115 118 147
Weiner, Justus R. 200 n32
William and Mary 16
William of Normandy (the Conqueror) 66. *See also* Norman conquest
William III (William of Orange) 16 90
William IV 96
Williams, David V. 85 211 n94
Williams, Chief Judge Joe 172 n53
Winiata, Whatarangi 154 n99

Yazzie, Judge Robert 47 n35

Zion, James 47 n35
Zines, Leslie 93